– 30 –

The Collapse of the Great American Newspaper

– 30 –

THE COLLAPSE OF THE
GREAT AMERICAN NEWSPAPER

Edited with an Introduction by
CHARLES M. MADIGAN

Ivan R. Dee
CHICAGO 2007

– 30 – : THE COLLAPSE OF THE GREAT AMERICAN NEWSPAPER. Copyright © 2007 by Charles M. Madigan. All rights reserved, including the right to reproduce this book or portions thereof in any form. For information, address: Ivan R. Dee, Publisher, 1332 North Halsted Street, Chicago 60622. Manufactured in the United States of America and printed on acid-free paper.

www.ivanrdee.com

Permissions appear on page 233 and are part of this copyright page.

Library of Congress Cataloging-in-Publication Data:
Madigan, Charles M.
    30 : the collapse of the great American newspaper / edited with an introduction by / Charles M. Madigan.
        p. cm.
    Includes index.
    ISBN-13: 978-1-56663-742-8 (cloth : alk. paper)
    ISBN-10: 1-56663-742-2 (cloth : alk. paper)
    1. American newspapers—Ownership. 2. Journalism—Economic aspects—United States. I. Title. II. Title: Thirty. PN4888.O85M33 2007
    071'.3—dc22

                                                                2007008316

Contents

– 30 –

The Collapse of the Great American Newspaper

Introduction:
The Way It Was. The Way It Is.

It's difficult for me to believe that it's been almost forty years since the day I walked into the *Altoona Mirror* to tell the editor that my college career was over and that I really needed a job. He knew my writing because I had worked for another paper owned by the same family. He knew my family too. My mother called him hours before I arrived to tell him I was a good young man, honest and hardworking. Somehow, that added a vintage glaze to the whole experience, as though Anthony Trollope were telling my life story. The editor had picked up a reputation, undeserved, for being hard. It might have been his voice, the product of a Swisher Sweets cigar habit that had lasted for decades. It might have been his politics too. To his way of thinking, nothing had gone well since Franklin D. Roosevelt took office. Communists were the problem. Communists and organized labor and socialism. These attitudes were characteristic in small-town Pennsylvania, and in many of its newspapers, in the 1960s.

He hired me and told me journalism had been a great career for him because it always applied a very simple measure to the performance of its workers: Did you get the story right and deliver it on time? Drunks, drug addicts, fools—he had seen them all, he said. But no matter how they behaved, they always had jobs if they could get the story right and deliver it on time. He told me to keep my opinions to myself, not to drink at the office, and try to avoid the siren call of Altoona's dark side, which lured many a railroad worker to the rocky shores of bad behavior. Be careful about spelling of

3

names in obituaries. Mistakes there were unforgivable. That being said, he recommended I take his ninety-dollar-a-week job for no more than a year, two at the most, and then go up the street to the Bell Telephone Company of Pennsylvania and get a job in public relations. "That's where the future is," he said. "There's no future in this."

He was wrong.

Journalism has been my delight, my salvation, my friend, and my benefactor for most of my life, longer than I have been married, longer than I have been a father. It has tossed me into the clouds and landed me on different continents. It has put me beside presidents and premiers. It has bought lunch with movie stars. It has brought me into close contact with the best and the worst people I have ever met. It has given me a platform for performance, allowing me, in time, even the glories of opinion writing. It has allowed me to do good. It has put me in a position where I can honestly say I am loved and hated by people who will never meet me. It has given me colleagues I would die for, and colleagues I would certainly like to throttle. It has demanded that I confront my greatest fears—of failure, of disappointment, of depression—and press on with the assignment. From the *Altoona Mirror* to the *Harrisburg Patriot* to United Press International and on to the *Chicago Tribune*, it has been a magnificent, delightful, and challenging career.

Now, it seems, it's just about over for me, for many of us.

As 2007 arrived, along with the deadline for this book, some of my best friends were cleaning out their desks and wondering how they would spend the rest of their lives after giving so much of themselves to their newspapers. In Philadelphia a collection of them pondered giving up their jobs at the *Philadelphia Inquirer* to save positions for young people just starting out. A friend in Dallas said farewell to a newspaper she loved and headed off to the Midwest after watching hundreds of her colleagues head out the door. In Chicago, my own paper, the *Tribune*, seemed to be teetering on the edge of a cliff as its parent company tried to salvage what was left of a strategy that clearly had not worked.

Its sister papers, the *Los Angeles Times*, the *Baltimore Sun*, Long Island *Newsday*, and so many others were looking into that same void. Men and women I have worked with for decades found their careers in jeopardy. The paternalism that the Tribune Company had constructed over more than a century of private ownership, a sense that stretched back to Colonel Robert McCormick's era, was gone, along with stock prices that had given the paper's staff a sense that there might be gold in a pot at the end of a *Tribune* career.

The *Washington Post*, a stalwart and model, along with the *New York Times*, for generations of American newspapers, put encouraging amounts of money on the table and lured many of its veteran reporters and writers into early retirement. A generation of experience in the ways of Washington, politics, and the federal government disappeared over a matter of months.

The newspapers that had once been the backbone of the Knight Ridder chain, legendary in journalism only a few decades ago for its quality, its determination, and its pride, found themselves sold off by the McClatchy Company, their new owners, as McClatchy searched for the money it needed to pay off the debt it absorbed when it bought them. For anyone with a sense of journalism history, it seemed as though McClatchy was cutting off body parts and selling an institution one member at a time, a leg here, a hand there.

Even the *New York Times*, long assumed to be immune from the ways of the market, found itself offering buyouts, trimming jobs and cutting costs.

How could this be happening to what was once the most vibrant journalism the world had ever seen, an institution that had in the past amassed fortunes for its private owners and in the modern era impressive value for shareholders?

How could a business that was so close to the American experience that it seemed to have a historical guarantee be shifting toward collapse?

What is killing the big-city newspaper?

That is the question at the heart of this book.

One of the ironies of decline in this industry is that there are many people only too eager to measure it, assess it, write about it, grieve it, celebrate it, or treat it as a big, hot story. These are the people to whom we have turned for our assessments, the people most affected by this transition, the journalists. Some of them are famous names. Some of them deserve to be, are not, and, sadly, probably never will be. But all of them are united in a determined quest to explain what is happening to a business they have loved, some of them for many years.

Their stories create the milestones of a journey through the modern era, starting with an academic and highly revealing look at the impact of technology and tax laws right up to the speculation that what big-city journalism really needs is a new generation of the Hearsts and McCormicks and Pulitzers and Chandlers, the sort of big-money people who built it in the first place, people with egos as big as their pockets are deep. Along the course there are those who bemoan the loss and those who are eager to see the last big papers shut down their presses and get out of the way.

How can this be happening?

The simplistic answer to the question is that the Internet, with its immediacy and its zero-dollar cost of entry, swept in to make newspapers seem every bit the nineteenth-century institutions they are. That has played a role, of course, but maybe not the central role. Great newspapers have been disappearing for years. They are the rags of legend, the *Chicago Daily News*, the *New York Herald Tribune*, the *Philadelphia Bulletin* among them. They were powerhouses in their day, and their disappearance was an augury people may have missed. It wasn't a collapse in quality that killed them. Beyond well written, the *Daily News* frequently delivered literature on its pages. The *Herald Tribune* and the *Bulletin* each had undeniable, clear voices and strengths that bonded them to their readers.

There have been cultural changes, of course.

In an America that seems stripped of leisure time, where young women pound their laptops even as they sip their lattes at Starbucks, and where a vast collection of gizmos has evolved to help everyone multi-task, there may be no time left for a quiet hour during the day for reading a very low-tech account of what happened yesterday. Newspapers evolved in an era in which the definition of news was something like this: "What happened today that didn't happen yesterday, dressed up and delivered tomorrow." Today news is something that happened an instant ago. A collection of media developments that began in the mid-twentieth century with the arrival of television network news also cut into the market for newspapers. Radio—all news and all the time—had its impact.

Of late, media philosophy seems to have changed too.

The thought that there is an authoritative source for anything has fallen under a wave of unchecked, unreported, and unprofessional babbling on the Internet, where no one reviews credentials or facts and the wacky and the wise march hand-in-hand right into the laptops, handheld devices, and living rooms (and basements too) of America. One part of this new culture defines itself in opposition to what it calls the MSM (Main Stream Media) and delights in its own hyperbole—passionate, factless in many cases, and in some bile fueled.

With its own bad behaviors, media has played directly into these criticisms. Fabrication, conflict of interest, dubious ethical behaviors, and an eagerness to trade the solitary challenges of reporting for the delights and rewards of bloviating on television have undoubtedly helped undercut journalism's reputation in the eyes of its reading public. Loud argument has replaced thoughtful presentation. Pandering—to readership, market surveys, and focus groups—has helped strip the modern newspaper of its own voice, its own values, and the thought that it has a clear, well-defined place in modern discourse, even if one disagrees with its positions. The passions that drove the Chandlers, the McCormicks, the Medills, the Sulzbergers, the Knights, the Hearsts, for better or worse seemed to have been thoroughly squeezed out of the industry.

After a brief, bright period of reform in the 1970s and 1980s, what swept in was a withering focus on costs and profits, a process supercharged by public ownership of media companies along with a general media dive toward the lowest common denominator (and the biggest audiences). It's as though the values of local TV programming in the 1970s became viral and infected executive offices everywhere.

It may also be that one culprit in the decline of newspapers had shown up before on the American industrial landscape, as recently as a few decades ago, when two behemoths of American business, the Pennsylvania and the New York Central railroads, merged, collapsed, and then disappeared. The problem, the critics said, was that they never realized they weren't just in the railroad business, they were in the transportation business. It could be that the people who held control over much of the newspaper industry (there were a few visionaries) in this period of sweeping change committed their own version of the same fatal sin.

They were in the information business, not the newspaper business.

Add to that the ambient conditions surrounding the industry — its tendency toward centralization because of technological change and tax law, its eager rush into the market to collect capital by becoming publicly held, its tendency to stick with what worked (at least from a revenue perspective) and avoid change for as long as possible, its embrace of elitism that separated it from many of its readers. All these factors help make the decline more understandable.

Even more than understandable, perhaps inevitable.

So what is to become of us, the journalists?

Amid the gloom, there is light.

In most cases, reporters (as opposed to media personalities, and there is a vast difference) are unusual characters motivated by a passion for truth and deep commitment to public service. People reported and wrote long before there were big-city newspapers to help pay the rent. The business, after all, evolved. Because a more recent generation of managers decided most of the emphasis should be on doing well does not mean reporters can't still be motivated by doing good.

The description "journalist" continues to evolve too, just as it has since the days of that premier journalist, fabricator, inventor, and author, Ben Franklin.

The remaining great city papers will not disappear overnight. They may be diminished. They may figure out how to tap the promise of the Internet. They may revert to an ownership that looks a lot more like the era of the media barons in the late nineteenth century than the shareholders era of the late twentieth. No matter what direction they turn, they still create millions upon millions of dollars in profits every day.

As for the uncertainty, the sense that one might not have a job tomorrow, next week, next month, for people seeking quiet lives the newspaper business has never been the place to settle. It has only been in recent times that a job on a paper has resembled a job at an insurance company. In the words of another of my editors later in my career over a farewell drink (beer for me, very good scotch for him), "Good luck on your new job. Remember, I see people on the way up and I see them on the way down too."

Amid the delight of advancement, it was an unsettling comment but very true and best never forgotten.

The business sits, after all, at the intersection where truth and trouble collide, and that is a risky place. It searches every day for the doom and the delight that define life. It tells sad, happy, pointless, profound stories. It is inconceivable that it would disappear, but not inconceivable that to save itself it will change so much you may not recognize it.

So, this is a story in pieces about a loss even as it plays out, told over time by people at the heart of it.

C. M. M.

Chicago
April 2007

ELIZABETH M. NEIVA

Money, Technology,
Tax Law, and Trouble

*How did an industry that was so robust only a few years
ago—certainly not more than a few decades ago—end
up so close to the rocks? The newspaper business made
a series of choices about ownership, taxes, and technology that inadvertently provided fuel for today's troubles. Elizabeth M. Neiva's prescient investigation, first
published in* Business and Economic History *in 1995,
exposed the roots of those problems.*

Before 1955, small, family-owned dailies dominated the American
newspaper industry. Publishers saw themselves as guardians of age-
old editorial traditions and viewed their papers as local institutions,
not as commercial enterprises. But by 1980, large, publicly traded
media conglomerates dominated the industry, and chief executives
replaced family patriarchs as the arbiters of newspapers' content and
editorial focus. What happened during this twenty-five-year period
to cause such a fundamental shift in ownership structure, and why
did the change happen when it did?

Scholars, including business historians, have tended to overlook the industry. In their view newspapers are idiosyncratic. The industry defies broad generalization and, therefore, does not contribute to our larger understanding of either organizational development or the rise of managerial capitalism. Instead, they have focused on weightier manufacturing industries—such as steel and automobiles—which represent, they believe, the bedrock of our economy.

Because many scholars consider the newspaper industry atypical, few have examined its evolution, particularly during the postwar period. This is a mistake. For nearly three centuries newspapers have provided a vital public service, interpreting, synthesizing, and packaging affordable information. But the industry's consolidation has attenuated newspapers' important role, leaving readers and employees increasingly vulnerable to the vicissitudes of absentee ownership.

Thus, the central question remains, how and why did this immense change take place in such a short period of time?

The consolidation of the American newspaper industry occurred in three stages, each marked by a different external change. Analysis of these three changes represents the core of my argument.

They are: the introduction of electronic typesetting; the application of new labor negotiating techniques; and a shift in the Internal Revenue Service's estate tax appraisal practices.

To underscore the central role that enterprising individuals played in the industry's development, each stage also profiles the career of a representative entrepreneur who capitalized on one of the three external changes. The individuals are: Prescott Low of the *Quincy Patriot Ledger*, Lloyd Schermer of Lee Enterprises, Inc., and Paul Miller of Gannett Company, Inc.

What follows is an examination of the interrelationship between the enterprising individual and the larger competitive environment within which he or she operates. It is arranged in three parts: technology, labor, and chain building.

TECHNOLOGY

The origins of the newspaper industry's rapid transformation can be traced to 1945. Before that time, the industry had enjoyed nearly seventy years of relative stability. There were no significant technological innovations, few new competitive threats, and only minor cost increases. In the words of one publisher, "The whole industry simply coasted through the first half of the twentieth century."

But, in 1945, after the government had lifted wartime wage freezes, production workers began demanding substantial salary increases. Production costs—made worse by postwar inflation—soared. But most publishers were ill-equipped to cope with these sudden cost increases. According to a 1953 Harvard Business School study, publishers of the period had little knowledge of, and considerable contempt for, the skills normally associated with running a business.

But that study also maintained that all publishers were not alike. The authors described "a progressive paper in Quincy, Massachusetts," the 30,000-circulation, *Patriot Ledger*, whose owner, Prescott Low, differed markedly from his colleagues. Low had stumbled upon and had begun promoting a new production technology that he believed would revolutionize the newspaper industry. This new technology was photocomposition.

Prior to the invention of photocomposition nearly all newspaper type was set on a massive, noisy mechanical contraption called a Linotype machine. The Linotype was invented in 1886 by a German watchmaker, who had designed his device with precision, not simplicity, in mind. The machine, which set type in molten lead, had over 10,000 moving parts and took more than four years to learn how to operate.

In 1944, a French inventor and amateur photographer witnessed a Linotype in use. Instantly, he decided there had to be a faster, more efficient way to compose type. With a partner, he designed a machine that would set characters on film, not in lead. But, in war-torn France, the inventors could not get the financing they needed to complete their prototype. They therefore sailed to America where they sought investment partners.

Among those they approached was Vannevar Bush, one of the key scientists behind the development of the atomic bomb. With a handful of other investors, Bush organized a non-profit foundation to fund the promotion of the new French typesetter. After finishing their machine, which they called the Photon, the Frenchmen moved to Boston and arranged a series of demonstrations for local publishers. It was at one of these gatherings that Prescott Low first saw the Photon in operation.

He was astonished. The machine set type at a pace six times faster than the Linotype, and it did so neatly and quietly. Low submitted an immediate order, and the first commercial Photon was installed in Quincy in 1953. For two years Low and his staff worked on integrating photocomposition into the newspaper's production process, and, after resolving countless complications, production costs at the *Patriot Ledger* plummeted.

Low no longer needed a large team of skilled $4.00-an-hour printers; instead, he found he could hire a handful of inexpensive, off-the-street clerical workers to compose the same amount of type. Low channeled the resulting savings into the paper's editorial department, and, before long, the *Patriot Ledger* had established itself as one of New England's most widely respected newspapers.

UNIONS

Due largely to Low's endorsement, other publishers began making the conversion from mechanical Linotypes to electronic Photon machines. According to one study, some papers were realizing immense savings, as much as $250,000 a year. Yet, in spite of the widespread publicity and the considerable savings available, the number of publishers who actually invested in photocomposition remained small. Many feared that, if they installed new Photon machines, the International Typographical Union (ITU) would strike, and without skilled printers, dailies were paralyzed. For example, during the famous citywide strike in 1963, production unions forced every Manhattan newspaper to shut down for over four months.

But strong unions were not publishers' only concern in the early 1960s. Television and magazines had begun penetrating markets that newspapers long had monopolized. Between 1955 and 1965, advertising lineage at the *New York Herald,* for example, fell by nearly 2 million lines. Sandwiched between rising production costs and falling revenues, a handful of frustrated publishers sought ways to sidestep the powerful union printers.

Among those publishers was Lloyd Schermer of the *Missoula* (Montana) *Missoulian.* In the early 1960s, the *Missoulian* was on the brink of bankruptcy, and Schermer realized that the paper would never regain its financial footing unless it converted to photocomposition. But Schermer was aware that leaders from the ITU's national headquarters had instructed every local union to strike if a publisher tried to install Photon machines. Unsure how to proceed, Schermer turned to a labor lawyer who specialized in helping publishers negotiate more effectively with production unions.

In 1966, the two developed a complex plan for peacefully converting the *Missoulian* to photocomposition. Although their strategy involved an intricate series of negotiations with each of the paper's six unions, the cornerstone of their plan was a simple deal with the ITU. If the printers would agree to give up their union affiliation and would allow Schermer to install Photon machines, he promised to give them a generous pension and benefits package in exchange. Just a few years earlier, such an offer would have been unthinkable. No right-minded union member ever would have considered decertification. But as photocomposition became increasingly prevalent, and as the demand for skilled printers fell, fewer new members joined the ITU. As their numbers declined, so too did their pension funds, and members of all ages began worrying about their financial futures.

The union ultimately decided that Schermer's attractive offer far surpassed the haphazard benefits their representatives had negotiated for them. In 1974, local ITU leaders accepted Schermer's offer and renounced their national affiliation. Within ten years, executives at nearly every major newspaper were relying on lawyers to assist them during bargaining sessions, and by 1982, the ITU—the nation's oldest union—ceased to exist as an independent organization.

THE INTERNAL REVENUE SERVICE

As the ITU's power dissipated, and as more papers converted to photocomposition, newspaper profits skyrocketed. But these rapid revenue increases did not go unnoticed. In the 1960s, appraisers from the Internal Revenue Service began studying all family-owned businesses, including newspapers. As the IRS learned more about photocomposition and newspapers' windfall profits, it began appraising papers according to their market values (or what a potential buyer might pay), not according to their book values (or the sum total of their assets).

After the IRS began changing its appraisal practices, the heirs of deceased publishers found it increasingly difficult to meet their estate tax obligations. Since many papers simply did not generate enough cash to pay the government what it demanded, families had no choice but to sell. Between 1960 and 1980, 57 different newspaper owners all sold their properties to the same person: Paul Miller of Gannett.

Throughout his 50-year career Paul Miller was a newspapering legend. As a bureau chief with the Associated Press through the 1930s and '40s, Miller earned a reputation as both an exceptional feature writer and a skilled manager. His talents were so well known that the owner of the nation's largest regional chain, Frank Gannett, chose Miller to succeed him as president of the Gannett Newspaper Group. Once promoted, Miller began transforming the sleepy chain of 25 upstate New York papers into a nationwide publishing empire. Nothing would assist him more in his efforts than the IRS's new appraisal practices.

Beginning in the early 1960s Miller began crisscrossing the country, courting publishers who owned monopoly papers in growing markets. To finance his frequent purchases, Miller became one of the very first newspaper executives to take his company public. He then traded the public shares of Gannett for the privately held stock of the papers he purchased. In 1971, Miller acquired one newspaper every three weeks, and by the time he retired in 1979, the Gannett chain had expanded to 79 papers.

The firm's competitors were soon aware of Gannett's rapid growth and immense profits, and many began imitating Miller's strategy. Between 1969 and 1973, 10 newspaper companies also went public, among them the New York Times, the Washington Post, and Times Mirror.

But, once public, Wall Street's security analysts began exerting considerable pressure on these companies to grow. Executives at these firms therefore spawned what would become an all-out acquisitions frenzy. By 1977, the nation's 170 newspaper groups owned two-thirds of the nation's 1,700 dailies. But by the end of the 1970s, the pool of available independent newspapers had all but dried up. This posed an immense problem for the nation's publicly traded papers. Because of security analysts' incessant demand for growth, these companies needed to continue expanding, but there was nothing to buy. Many therefore began exploring other news-related ventures.

Gannett unveiled the first national newspaper, *USA Today*, in 1982, and other firms diversified into cable television. As many chains began to channel ever-increasing portions of their profit into these new businesses, the quality of their newspaper properties declined. By coddling readers with homogenized, technicolor journalism, chain papers slowly carved the souls out of the local papers that long had bound communities together.

So, what are the larger implications of the newspaper industry's consolidation, and what does it contribute to our larger understanding of the process of organizational development? From this research it is evident that the forces that triggered the rapid transformation of the American newspaper industry were not self-serving publishing moguls or a cluster of irresponsible media executives but the invention and popularization of a relatively simple new technology, photocomposition. This machine prompted a sequence of cumulative changes, each of which was recognized and exploited by one or more savvy entrepreneurs. Yet while it is useful to understand how and why the newspaper industry consolidated, the real contribution of this research is much broader. The experience of twentieth-century newspapers offers a systematic model of industrial development, demonstrating not only that change occurs in cumulative and sequential stages, but also that individuals do matter in the process of industrial change.

DAVID CARR

What Happened to the Readers?

Reading the newspaper was an agenda item for American families for generations, a dedicated behavior that came just after dawn for some and just after work for many others. New York Times *columnist David Carr took a revealing look at the habit as he considered the discounted sale of the* Minneapolis Star Tribune, *a milestone moment in the decline of the industry.*

In the house where I grew up, everybody ate breakfast at the same time. The younger ones would sit at the table elbowing one another for toast while my dad stood, drinking coffee and reading the *Minneapolis Star Tribune*.

He would mumble and curse at the headlines, check the sports, and then tell us it was time to go. When my brother John became a teenager, he left the table and would eat his toast, leaning against the washing machine and reading the paper as well.

This, I thought, is what it means to be a grown-up. You eat your food standing up, and you read the newspaper. So I did the same thing when I turned 13. I still do.

Last Wednesday morning at my house, one of my daughters back from college was staying at a friend's house in the city, no doubt getting alerts on her cellphone for new postings to her Facebook page.

Her sister got up, skipped breakfast, and checked the mail for her NetFlix movies. My wife left early before the papers even arrived to commute to her job in the city while listening to the iPod she got for Christmas.

True enough, my 10-year-old gave me five minutes over a bowl of Cheerios, but then she went into the dining room and opened the laptop to surf the Disney Channel on broadband, leaving me standing in the kitchen with my four newspapers. A few of those included news about the sale of the *Star Tribune*, a newspaper that found itself in reduced circumstances and sold at a reduced price to a private equity group.

I looked around me and realized I didn't really need to read the papers to know why.

Sure, the consolidation of department stores and the flight of classified ads to the Web hurt big metropolitan dailies like the *Star Tribune*. This summer's downturn in overall newspaper advertising landed hard on the paper, with ads off 6.1 percent in the last year from the year before.

The McClatchy Company, which bought the paper's parent company with a great deal of fanfare in 1998 for $1.2 billion, looked at those numbers—and the fact that it had lost 26,000 or so daily readers since it bought the paper—and decided to sell the paper for $530 million. The chain was equally bullish when it bought Knight Ridder for $4.5 billion last summer and then turned around and sold 12 of the papers, including another newspaper in the Twin Cities, the *Pioneer Press* in St. Paul.

But the sale of the *Star Tribune* came completely out of the blue, in part because, as the chain's biggest paper, it was viewed as a marquee property. The parties were able to keep it quiet in part because they all knew each other. The principals for the buyers, Avista Capital Partners, were once a part of a private equity arm of Credit Suisse, which represented McClatchy in the sale.

McClatchy's chief executive, Gary B. Pruitt, said that tax advantages of $160 million made it a good time to sell, partly to offset capital gains from the sale of the Knight Ridder papers. When the stealth auction for the paper ended and word of the sale came out the day after Christmas, Mr. Pruitt said, "I don't feel good about the paper being sold."

Me either. The paper, around in one version or another since 1867, may not have knocked down a lot of Pulitzers, but with its vigorous political reporting and thoughtful cultural coverage, it has served as a center for civic life in Minneapolis and beyond. The *Star Tribune* was not a great paper, but then my first car, a very used '64 Ford Falcon, wasn't great either. I still have a great deal of affection for both.

There are two ways to look at the sale: the second-biggest newspaper operator in the country, with its stock dropping in the wake of the Knight Ridder deal, dumped a paper with near 20 percent profit margins in what looked like a fire sale because big papers are doomed. Or, more brightly, a private equity firm saw an opportunity for a savvy investor who could operate the property without the quarter-to-quarter franticness that comes with making Wall Street happy.

It is a cliché of the media business that the assets go up and down the elevator every day. In Minneapolis, many of those assets are pals from my days of working as a reporter and editor at a weekly there, so I wondered: Who would be controlling their professional destinies, bottom feeders or benefactors?

Private equity owners are often viewed with suspicion, in part because they have limited investment horizons and tend to milk properties for cash flow, clean up the balance sheet, and then flip the property to what is technically known as a "greater fool." The sale of the *Philadelphia Inquirer and Daily News* by McClatchy to a local group of investors has resulted, after a sharp downturn this summer, in a great deal of strife and talks of significant layoffs.

I talked to OhSang Kwon, one of the partners in Avista Capital Partners. "We don't want to rule out anything, but the idea that we bought this paper with a quick exit in mind or that we were going to cut our way to profitability is not correct," he said. "I don't have the hubris to say that we have the answers—we are new to the newspaper business—but the old way was not working. Maybe it is time for a different approach."

Maybe it is. Tomorrow, the *Wall Street Journal*, which is owned by Dow Jones & Company, will hit my doorstep in a smaller size and with a different approach, pushing much of the so-called commoditized news—the daily reports and incremental articles that everyone has—to the Web and filling the physical paper with more analysis and deeper reporting. Google, which has been dining to some degree on ads diverted from newspapers, announced last week that it is expanding a program to sell newspaper advertising using its own auction approach.

As I sat at the kitchen table, I marveled at the low price of a newspaper that had once preoccupied the conversation around my dinner table. Then I looked at the four papers on the table and the empty chairs that surrounded them. Before my second cup of coffee, the rest of my household had already started the day in a way that had nothing to do with the paper artifacts in front of me. Maybe I was the greater fool.

RACHEL SMOLKIN

Everybody Watches
the *New York Times*

The New York Times *has been the model for much of the modern history of journalism. But the greatest paper of them all, too, is wrestling with the question of what it should be. In the* American Journalism Review, *Rachel Smolkin measured the* Times *against the challenge it faces.*

In a small back room adjoining his office on the fourteenth floor of 229 West 43rd Street, Arthur Sulzberger, Jr., lays out his vision for a New York Times Company of the future.

In it, the *New York Times* newspaper and its siblings—the *International Herald Tribune*, the *Boston Globe*, and 15 other dailies—have transcended their old ink-on-paper platforms, appearing as well in text and video via the Web, mobile phones, BlackBerries, and other digital devices. A cluster of Internet sites have cropped up around them, some far removed from newsgathering but offering readers accessible information about topics as varied as weight-loss tools and iPods.

Yet journalism remains the company's unshakable core, defined, especially for the flagship *Times* newspaper, by its continued international reach and ambitions. Sulzberger's great-grandfather, Adolph S. Ochs, bought the struggling New York broadsheet in 1896; through four generations, during some splendid highs and despite some mortifying lows, the paper has set the standard for journalism worldwide.

Sulzberger cannot foresee "always," he tells me with some exasperation as I continue to press him with that word on all manner of topics—unfairly, of course, because who knows what the media landscape will look like next month, much less in the distant future? Will the Times keep the *Globe*? Will Sulzberger and his family take the company private, away from Wall Street's punishing judgment of its worth? Will he hold on to both his titles, chairman of the company and publisher of the *New York Times* newspaper, or accede to the demands of a major shareholder and surrender one? Will a family member always fill both those positions or, in an era fraught with change for the industry, will an outside "professional" assume one?

"There are things that are impossible to know. So I can't deal with 'always.' Let me just deal with now and where the family is in its head now, OK?" he says in response to the last question. "And the answer is yes. The family has made it clear, to me and to others, that the two positions that they feel should be held by family members are publisher of the *New York Times* newspaper and chairman of the New York Times Company."

His father, Arthur Ochs Sulzberger, had three titles, including CEO; when the younger Sulzberger, now 55, assumed control of the company in 1997 (he's been publisher of the *Times* newspaper since 1992), the CEO position went to an outsider for the first time. Janet L. Robinson, 56, who sits next to Sulzberger at the shining oval table during our interview, is the company's president and its second non-family chief executive. "For the foreseeable future, as long as I can see into the future, this family seems united, is united, around its commitment to this company and its commitment to this newspaper," Sulzberger says.

They are able to maintain control of both through a two-tier stock structure. The family dominates the powerful Class B shares, which represent less than 1 percent of the company's equity but shape its destiny: these shareholders elect nine of 13 board members. Only a decision by at least six of eight family trustees can alter that structure, something Sulzberger says they have no interest in doing.

"Why change it?" he asks. "It was built for times like this. It gives us the flexibility to be in the public market, to have access to the capital markets when you need them for, say, acquisitions, but it gives you the protection so critical to ensure that our journalism is kept really at the forefront of all that we do. So this is why we have this system. Now is when you need to use it, not to think about changing it."

But are you looking at taking the company private? I persist, citing recent media reports that claim he's doing just that. "No."

No interest in it, whatsoever? "That would be no."

Other media companies in a similar financial situation but lacking the two-tier protection would be—and have been, and are—facing dissolution. In January, the Times Company stock was trading at $23, down more than 50 percent from its 2002 peak.

For the six-month period ending September 2006, the *Times* newspaper's circulation had dropped 3.5 percent during the week and on Sunday from the same period a year earlier, bringing its Sunday total to 1,623,697 and its weekday average to 1,086,798. At the *Globe*, sales had fallen 6.7 percent during the week, to 386,415, and 9.9 percent on Sunday, to 587,292.

Dragged down by the *Globe's* lackluster performance in an unkind New England economy, the operating profit margin for the Times' newspaper division fell to 3.5 percent in the third quarter of 2006, the lowest of the publicly held newspaper companies, according to calculations by newspaper analyst and *AJR* columnist John

Morton. (The Times does not break out its newspaper earnings separately from its News Media Group.) By contrast, the Washington Post's profit margin for its newspaper division that quarter was 7.8 percent; the embattled Tribune Company's was 14.8 percent.

In late December, Standard & Poor's cut the company's credit rating from A— to BBB+, a development that is not particularly significant from Wall Street's perspective but would cost the Times Company more if it needed to borrow money in the near future, says Edward Atorino, a media analyst at the New York–based brokerage firm Benchmark Company.

"This has been a tough year," Robinson told two groups of financial analysts at annual media conferences in New York on December 6. "A tough few years actually, as we—like many other companies in our sector—have been dealing with a transformation unlike any we have seen in our lifetimes."

Dissatisfied with the results, Morgan Stanley Investment Management, which owns 7.5 percent of the Class A shares, has launched a public assault on the Times' stock structure and management. At last year's annual meeting, investors holding more than 30 percent of the Class A shares, including Morgan Stanley's London-based management fund, withheld their votes for directors to demonstrate their displeasure.

Led by Managing Director Hassan Elmasry, the fund commissioned a November 1 report by the consulting firm Davis Global Advisors that criticized the *Times'* financial showing compared with that of the *Washington Post*, another top-flight, family-owned newspaper buttressed by a dual-class stock structure. The report notes that over the past five years, the *Post* has "significantly outperformed" the *Times* on measures including revenue growth and stock performance.

It also skewers the Times' "governance" and its compensation packages for executives, citing average pay for *Post* CEO Donald E. Graham of $642,770, compared with Robinson's roughly $2.7 million. (In September, Sulzberger and his cousin Michael Golden, company vice chairman and publisher of the *IHT*, asked the board to lower their compensation last year and this year by not awarding them stock options; that money will be used instead for an employee bonus pool.)

Sulzberger's leadership has come under fire, not only through Morgan Stanley's attack but also in high-profile articles disparaging both his news and business acumen. A December 2005 piece by the *New Yorker*'s Ken Auletta posited a "crisis of identity" at the paper and asserted that "Within the newsroom, there is a sense of rudderlessness and a fear that a series of business misjudgments may so weaken the company's finances that the brilliance of the *Times* and, ultimately, the historic mission of the company will be at serious risk."

On November 8, Elmasry submitted a resolution that he hoped the Times Company would put to a vote at its next annual shareholder meeting in April. Among his proposals were eliminating the company's two-tiered stock structure; separating the titles of publisher and chairman; and requiring that the chairman be independent of the company. But the Times Company does not intend to include the resolution in its annual proxy statement to shareholders, which will be mailed in March, says company spokeswoman Catherine Mathis.

The day after Elmasry submitted his resolution, Morgan Stanley publishing analyst Lisa Monaco downgraded the rating of the Times' stock from "equal weight" to "underweight," effectively telling stockholders to ditch their shares.

Morton is underwhelmed by Elmasry's campaign. "My observation is that a snowball won't melt in hell before there's any change in that dual stock structure," he says, although he wishes the Times Company would go private to quiet all the "brouhaha" about its financial performance. "Even though the family controls the shares, once you get into public ownership, you become to some extent a part of the culture," he says. "You have to listen to idiots like this guy at Morgan Stanley." (Elmasry declined to comment for this article.)

"You can imagine what happens to the *New York Times* newspaper if it was governed by people who were primarily concerned about the bottom line," Morton adds. "There's a reason that the *Times* has one of the lowest operating margins in the industry: because they spend more money on journalism."

In an era of dwindling newspaper ambitions, of paring back and turning inward, "local news" has become an unsettling mantra in a global world. While it often is touted as a way to add unique value unmatched by a cacophony of competitors, it also is invoked to provide protective cover when companies shutter costly far-flung bureaus to save money.

At the *Philadelphia Inquirer*, Publisher Brian P. Tierney, whose local group of investors bought the former Knight Ridder paper in June, told *Washington Post* media writer Howard Kurtz five months later: "I don't see us sending 25 people to do me-too coverage of Katrina" and "I can get what's going on in Iraq online. What I can't get is what's happening in this region." This philosophy, from an owner whose paper is now privately held, is a stark reminder that refuge from Wall Street is no tonic for financial pressures and fading aspirations. In January, Tierney slashed 68 newsroom positions, 17 percent of the editorial staff.

At the *Los Angeles Times*, parent Tribune Company installed David Hiller as publisher in October after his predecessor publicly backed then-Editor Dean Baquet in refusing to enact further newsroom cuts. In a November memo to his new staff, Hiller wrote that the *L.A. Times* needed to "Focus relentlessly on growing local audience. . . . In a related vein, a number of you have raised whether we are too focused on being like the *New York Times*. The *New York Times* has chosen a national audience strategy, and in so doing has seen significant drops in circulation and readership in their own metro market. That is not the path we want to go down."

New York Times executives are thinking far more expansively. When I refer to the *Times* as a national paper, Sulzberger, a primary architect of the national sales strategy, immediately interrupts: "No.

It's an international paper now. I mean, important. Important. Between the *New York Times* and the *International Herald Tribune*, which carries *New York Times* journalism—right?—in print and on the Web, we are an international paper."

In interviews, Sulzberger, Golden, and *Times* Executive Editor Bill Keller all point with pride to the *Times'* record in Iraq. When the U.S. Army rolled into Baghdad, there were 1,000 journalists in the country. By last year, the number had dwindled to 75, according to a *Los Angeles Times* story. The *Times'* leaders cite that figure, and add one of their own: the *New York Times* has seven correspondents assigned to Iraq.

It is fitting, then, that during its present difficulties with Wall Street's quarterly obsession, the New York Times Company has hired a futurist. Michael Rogers' planned career in the semiconductor industry was short-circuited when he was offered a job as a writer at *Rolling Stone*. He later became vice president of the Washington Post Company's new-media division and editor and general manager of Newsweek.com. In 2004, he founded a consulting firm called Practical Futurist and, in September, he was appointed to a one-year position as futurist-in-residence at the *Times*.

Rogers, who emphasizes that he's the type of futurist who tries to figure out what will actually work in three to five years, not the sort who plays with flying cars, spends his days reading engineering journals ("I understand maybe every fourth word," he says), scanning obscure blogs (one, by a Microsoft employee, ponders the future of identity), and attending conferences in Europe and Asia, which are about two years ahead of the United States in their use of mobile technology.

He is one of a team of six who report to Michael Zimbalist, the Times Company's vice president of research and development. Robinson created the R&D team last year because she felt the company needed a capacity to "look around corners," as Zimbalist puts it, to study "what the trends are going to become in consumer behavior, in technology, and how those are going to intersect with our core mission of providing high-quality news, information and entertainment."

The R&D team—a commonplace unit across Fortune 500 businesses but unprecedented within media organizations, Zimbalist says, when Robinson launched his—is tasked with leading the long-term innovation strategy. Its role is to bring "new ideas and new views of the future into the company," which includes the formidable task of transforming the organization's thinking by imbuing it with a desire to experiment, to launch a digital innovation, and then smooth out the kinks rather than wasting years in the planning stages.

In September, the group helped the *Times* newspaper staff debut a "beta," or test, launch of *Times Reader*, the product of a partnership with Microsoft that attempts to create a paginated, newspaper-like experience on the computer. Ideally suited for portable computers, it offers the look and experience of the printed page and an opportunity for readers to take notes on or search through those pages.

The experimental beginning last year afforded users a chance to share problems downloading and using the application and to offer feedback about what they liked or didn't. It also gave *Times* executives time to think about pricing and business models before the formal launch in February. In its initial form, pricing for *Times Reader* mirrored that of NYTimes.com—free for general use but paid for columns and other premium content.

In early December, the Times Company unveiled a new search function for Boston.com, the *Globe*'s Web site, reflecting a growing conviction that papers should provide myriad services to readers within a particular region. A search for local churches, for example, turns up *Globe* news stories as well as Yellow Pages listings and coverage by other news outlets, including the Christian New England News Network. Similar search options are planned this year for NYTimes.com and the regional sites.

"It's as much of a marketing challenge as it is a technical one," says Zimbalist's boss, Martin A. Nisenholtz, the company's senior vice president for digital operations, about the difficulty of educating consumers about the sites' wealth of information. On NYTimes .com, visitors not only can read movie reviews but also can buy tickets or scan show times. "We really have two tasks," Nisenholtz says. "One is we need to create a differentiated search experience, and we think we can do that. But the other task is getting people simply to understand that they can do it."

Zimbalist's team also develops mobile technology initiatives. While there's no inherent connection between consumers reading a newspaper story and then scurrying off to their laptops to seek more in-depth coverage online, Zimbalist and Rogers think mobile devices may complement print better because both can be viewed on the move. In 2006, the Times Company launched Web sites for these devices for the *Times*, the *Globe*, and the *Gainesville Sun*. "I think that print's role in the mix may change," Zimbalist says. "Print may be kind of a guidebook to more and deeper experiences in a digital world."

The team sees video on the Web as another area with major growth potential. It's searching for easier ways to share video across the company's business units as the newsrooms increase their video output. Vivian Schiller, general manager of NYTimes.com, says that will be a major focus over the next year as the *Times* newspaper steps up its training of print journalists in the use of video cameras. Currently, the paper offers upwards of 25 new video packages each week on NYTimes.com; viewer traffic is highest when the videos are embedded within a story.

User-generated video opportunities are expanding as well. NYTimes.com will unveil user-produced options around Valentine's Day for couples featured in the paper's Weddings & Celebrations section. Its leaders aren't sure what form these will take but expect more riveting videos than, say, couples divvying up their wedding cake. Times' readers are "very creative, very smart, so what we anticipate is we're going to get a really interesting diversity of video," Schiller says. "I would be shocked if they were all, like, cutting the cake."

A large part of the mission of the digital operations team and the R&D unit is attempting to anticipate where the rapid pace of transformation will take the industry. As he calls up *Times Reader* on his sleek notebook computer to show off its cool features, Nisenholtz notes, "We don't expect this version of the *Reader* to have a material impact on our business, but we hope that we will be really well-positioned if one of these things starts to really go, like the iPod did. I mean, the iPod took the music industry by storm. They didn't even know what hit them. And we don't want to be in that position."

Central to the success of all this creative thinking is how many users the new technologies will attract, and how much revenue they ultimately will generate.

Times executives are pleased with their foray into the perilous world of paid content on the Web. Schiller says *TimesSelect*, the paid portion of NYTimes.com that debuted in September 2005 (home subscribers get it free; others pay $49.95 annually), had netted 206,000 paying subscribers in December, exceeding the company's expectations.

NYTimes.com is the largest newspaper Web site, with 13.2 million unique visitors in the United States in December, according to Nielsen/NetRatings. The Times Company represents the ninth largest Internet presence, with 44.2 million unique visitors to all of the company's Web properties that month.

At the investor conferences in December, Robinson said she expected the company to significantly outperform the industry in online ad revenue growth in 2006 and 2007. The company's digital revenues have jumped from 4 percent of total revenues in 2004 to an anticipated 8 percent in 2006. "In 2007, we believe our total digital revenues will grow approximately 30 percent, or more than $80 million, mainly due to organic growth," she told analysts.

The Times' two-pronged strategy for digital expansion includes not only that "organic" growth, the creations from Zimbalist's team and others, but also "inorganic" growth, the revamping of the company's portfolio through acquisitions of small and mid-size Internet companies.

In March 2005, the Times Company purchased About.com for $410 million, its largest acquisition since it bought the *Boston Globe* from the Taylor family for $1.1 billion in 1993. On the site, an amalgam of consumer information, "guides" create content that offers advice on topics ranging from decorating candlesticks to planning trips to the pediatrician. (One seasonal entry on "Sex Tips for Surviving the Holidays" counseled, "Sex talk often gets lost around Christmas time, maybe because stress, too much alcohol, and spending time with your extended family are not the greatest aphrodisiacs.") Visitors can also send in their own questions.

The Times has attempted to heighten the quality of information on the site, replacing 200 of the 588 independent contractors who serve as guides; up to 100 additional guides are anticipated this year. Although About.com represented only about 2.5 percent of the company's $740 million in revenues in the third quarter of 2006, executives are encouraged by its growth. Ad revenues from January to November for About.com were up an estimated 51 percent from the same period a year earlier; its operating profit margin for the year was 38 percent as of September.

When we spoke in December, Michael Golden cited a recent Yahoo! column that listed About.com as the second-best Internet acquisition behind MySpace. "When we bought it, there were a lot of people in the company that thought it was outside our space," Golden acknowledges, but he says the information it provides, while not news, is useful to millions of consumers every day. "With a few notable exceptions of individual opinions," he says laughing, in an apparent oblique reference to Elmasry's opposition to the site as untested and overpriced, "I think the jury's in on this one, and it was a great acquisition."

In August, the Times Company bought Baseline Studio Systems, an online subscription database for information on the film and television industries, for $35 million. In September it picked up Calorie-Count.com—as its name suggests, a site featuring weight-loss tools and nutritional information—for $900,000. In each of these acquisitions, the Times saw an opportunity to profit from and improve the product as well as a chance to add value to its company. About.com, for example, brings in search engine expertise.

"One of the challenges for a smaller newspaper is, 'How do you own your own community in a digital era?'" Sulzberger says. "One small way to tell, perhaps, is when you Google, when you type in the name of your town or city in Google, where does your newspaper come up?" He wants the Times' community newspapers to appear among Google's leading entries, and hopefully even as No. 1 (he concedes the *Gainesville Sun* will probably always lag behind the University of Florida football team). He thinks the new acquisitions can help achieve that goal.

Former Times Vice Chairman and General Counsel James Goodale played a key role in the company during its first major acquisition, that of Cowles Communications properties including three Florida newspapers, *Family Circle* magazine, and a Memphis TV station, in 1971. "We thought it was very risky because we hadn't done it before, but it really wasn't as risky as it is today," Goodale says, referring to the Times Company's Internet acquisitions. "You just don't know, when you buy a publication on the Net that's only three or four years old, what the hell it's going to do."

But he believes the Times is right to try. "I think they've got to do exactly what we did. They've got to find a stream of income that they can live off of in order to make sure the *New York Times* print newspaper is there," diversifying to protect the core.

Media analyst Ed Atorino thinks the Times could have a growing impact on the Internet. "They want to leverage the brand, leverage their information base," he says. "Anything related to the Web is the way these guys have to go."

In her November report, Morgan Stanley's Lisa Monaco was less sanguine. She noted that About.com has "performed well" under Times ownership and that the Times Company has succeeded in driving traffic to its Web sites. "However, to-date revenues and profits online have been rather insignificant. So, it's hard to see how or what would drive an acceleration in online growth to the levels where it can offset the loss on the print side," she wrote. "Moreover, we think that competition for ad dollars from the Yahoo!'s and Google's of the world is only going to intensify."

It is, perhaps, a tad disconcerting, even a little amusing, to think of the mighty New York Times Company, monopolizer of Pulitzers, owning Internet sites with names like Calorie-Count.com. But it's also a reflection of the urgent need for newspaper companies to adapt in a disruptive era. "The truth is in some ways that's a tough burden for the New York Times Company to bear," says Mark Jurkowitz, associate director of the Project for Excellence in Journalism. Because of "what that brand stands for in the world of dead trees and print, even if they are making intelligent, far-sighted moves, it may be shocking to people."

Increasingly, the Times Company stands for news and information in print and digital forms. Aside from its 17 percent interest in New England Sports Ventures, which owns the Boston Red Sox, Fenway Park, and most of New England Sports Network, a regional cable outlet, nearly all of its holdings are related to dispensing information; even the NESV investment can be seen through that prism with the inclusion of the cable network. It has no equivalent to Kaplan, the Washington Post Company's wildly successful test-preparation company, nor, Sulzberger says, does it want one. "God bless Kaplan," he says. "It was a great decision by the Grahams to get it and then to make it what it is. . . . But we're looking for properties more aligned to the sort of core purpose of the New York Times Company." In other words, news and information.

As it steps up its focus on Internet video, the Times is getting out of the traditional television business. In September, it sold its

50 percent ownership interest in the Discovery Times Channel, a digital cable outlet, back to partner Discovery Communications, recording a loss of $8 million. That same month, the Times Company announced that it would sell its nine local TV stations.

Although both moves involve television, executives describe them as unrelated. "It's hard for an individual local station in a market like Memphis, Oklahoma City, Norfolk, Fort Smith [Arkansas] to really distinguish itself," Golden says. The one in Scranton, Pennsylvania, led its market, but "it didn't create a huge payoff. It didn't create the financial return that a newspaper with that dominance would have in its marketplace," and, given the current and emerging competition, "We didn't see a clear path that these assets were going to be worth more in 10 years than they are now." In January, the Times Company agreed to sell its broadcast group to Oak Hill Capital Partners, a private equity firm, for $575 million.

Times executives proudly cite their award-winning programming on the Discovery Times Channel, which extended *New York Times* journalism to a new platform and garnered three Emmys and other awards. But it never gained traction in the exploding cable frontier. "Those digital channels are very, very tough," Golden says. "We did all the things right, but the audience was very small."

Still, Golden and Sulzberger say the partnership was valuable because it allowed the company to build its "video muscle," as Sulzberger puts it. Although Web video has taken a different direction than long-form TV journalism, he says that was not a foregone conclusion. "It did jump-start us in the video world. It sent the signal to the newsroom that we are serious about this."

Michael Oreskes, now executive editor of the *International Herald Tribune*, was tapped in late 2000 to be a *Times* assistant managing editor and its director of electronic news. The former *Times* Washington bureau chief recalls going to lunch with Sulzberger during the Democratic National Convention in Los Angeles and listening to his boss discuss how the company should prepare itself for the Internet age.

"The whole conversation was about, 'How do we develop a video journalism capability in the newsroom of the *New York Times?*'" Oreskes recalls. "It was clear that in order to be a journalistic organization in a new world, you have to be able to present things in video and other forms. Arthur saw that five, six, seven years ago. The television part was about building the skills. It was not about being in the television business. I think he deserves a lot of credit for that. I think it was a visionary thing, and I think it's succeeded."

At the core of the company's changing portfolio and ambitions for a new digital era stands the ink-on-paper *New York Times.*

It's been a rough few years at the nation's premier newspaper, bedeviled by the twin humiliations of serial fabricator Jayson Blair and the Judy Miller imbroglio, then vilified as unpatriotic by the Bush administration and its allies. But you wouldn't know it to hear Executive Editor Bill Keller skewer the competition.

When we talk in mid-December, he begins by citing the three excellent rivals he feels are indispensable reading: the *Wall Street Journal,* the *Los Angeles Times,* and the *Washington Post.* Then he lets loose. The Dow Jones Company, which owns the *Journal,* "seems to be pumping out a lot of smoke to mask a retreat," covering business for business and offering a more "magaziney" approach, Keller muses, leaning chin on hand and looking contemplative. "My sense is that they're hollowing out the reporting behind it. This really struck me between the eyes during the war in Lebanon. . . . Not every day, but a lot of days during the war in Lebanon, they were writing stories that could have been written from their offices in New York. They were smart, analytical, almost op-ed pieces. I mean, I'm not faulting their analysis. But you sensed a real absence of reporting on the ground."

Next up, the Tribune Company's *Los Angeles Times:* "Nobody knows who's going to own it six months from now, and nobody knows what the owner will decide is his business model, so that's kind of hard to say," he stipulates. "But what they have been going through is a fairly relentless cost-cutting exercise driven by people in

Chicago, who all but say it would be just fine if the L.A. Times were the Chicago Tribune. The Chicago Tribune is an OK paper. It's a fine paper. It's not the L.A. Times."

And then the Post: "The Washington Post, you know, has become an education company that happens to own a newspaper," he observes. While professing "unqualified admiration" for Don Graham and Post Executive Editor Leonard Downie, Jr., he says, "the reality they're dealing with is that it's not really a journalism company"; rather, the Post "is one of the properties that the Kaplan Company owns," and is "certainly under a lot of pressure." Its talent is getting "picked away from outside," Keller continues, citing Allbritton's recent coup in luring two of the Post's top political experts to its nascent Web site. He concludes, "They'll probably go hire all the good people from the L.A. Times." (He adds later, "All the good people who are left after we've finished our own hiring.")

His own paper has not been immune to the difficult business environment. The Times Company eliminated about 750 positions companywide between 2004 and 2006; 69 of those were buyouts in the Times newsroom. Later this year, the Times will narrow the width of its paper from 54 inches to 48 inches, as have the Wall Street Journal and other dailies. Executives say the reduction will save about $12 million annually. But so far, Keller says, his paper has avoided compromises in staff and resources that harm news coverage.

In part to lure lucrative advertisers, his team has launched glossy luxury magazines. These include T: The New York Times Style Magazine, which features the Times' first perfume critic; and Key, a high-end real estate publication. Keller says he's invested some of the new revenues, mostly from these but also from weekly section redesigns, into core newsgathering functions, creating an "overdue" computer-assisted reporting unit and adding a few reporters to the Washington bureau.

He says the newsroom has put the tumultuous Miller episode behind it. "I think there ought to be a statute of limitations on the Judy Miller question," he says wryly, "but yeah, I really think we have. It took a long time. It was like a virus in the system, and the Washington bureau felt it probably more deeply probably than anyplace else," not only the legal morass but the "toxic rain" over Miller's WMD coverage and her "operating style, which tends to leave a lot of bruises."

The mood also has brightened after a rancorous period leading up to the midterm elections, when the *Times* became a favorite punching bag for the Bush administration and its "Amen chorus within the Fox News world and Murdochland," in Keller's words. Twice the *Times* defied administration pleas and published national-security stories based on classified information; the first of those, printed after a year-long delay, won a Pulitzer Prize. "It feels like the zeitgeist has shifted a little back in our favor," Keller says, helped in part by recent scoops by the *Times'* Washington bureau, including revelations of one classified memo by National Security Adviser Stephen J. Hadley expressing doubts about Iraqi Prime Minister Nuri Kamal al-Maliki, and another by Donald H. Rumsfeld two days before he departed as defense secretary calling for a "major adjustment" in Iraq.

In August 2005, the *Times* merged its digital and print newsrooms, although Keller says the physical integration will become much more pronounced when the company and newspaper settle into their new headquarters on the west side of Times Square later this year. (The *Times* plans to rent at least five of the 28 floors it had planned to occupy in the 52-story New York Times Tower.) The phased move into the roughly $600 million building is expected to begin in April. Once there, Web producers will be placed on every section desk in the newsroom, and Keller plans to gradually shift more newsroom resources from print to digital.

The *Times* also is working more closely with its Paris-based sister paper, the *International Herald Tribune*. In October 2002, the Times Company forced the Washington Post Company to sell its half-interest in the money-losing paper for $65 million. Now in full control, the Times has bulked up the *IHT*'s editorial staff and positioned the paper to fight for dominance on a global stage. Although the 242,182-circulation broadsheet is still losing money, Golden says that after several years of sharp declines, advertising was up 15 percent in 2004, 17 percent in 2005, and an anticipated 12 percent to 15 percent in 2006. He says the paper is on track to reap a profit at the end of 2007 and for all of 2008.

In November, Keller and Oreskes announced they were dropping the identifiers under bylines showing which of their papers an article originated in. "The *NYT* and the *IHT* will henceforth fly the same flag (which, agate-wise, is no flag)," the two editors wrote in a staff memo.

In a telephone interview, Oreskes adds, "We want to think about the *New York Times* and *IHT* as one 24-hour news organization. Again, this is very much about the Internet. Therefore, it's necessary to work like a global, 24-hour organization. . . . We've moved considerably down the road of coordinating the two and operating more and more as one organization."

One paper still struggling to find its footing in the New York Times Company is the *Boston Globe*. The *Globe* anchors the company's New England Media Group, which also includes Massachusetts' *Worcester Telegram & Gazette* and a 49 percent interest in *Metro Boston*, a frothy free daily aimed at young professionals and commuters.

In Wall Street parlance, this group is a weak performer, beset by circulation losses and declining ad revenue, which plunged 12.4 percent in the third quarter of 2006 compared with the same period a year earlier. The merger of the Federated and May department stores has hurt: Filene's, formerly the *Globe's* largest advertiser, last appeared in the paper in March. In January, the New England Media Group announced it would cut an anticipated 125 jobs, including 19 from the *Globe's* newsroom and opinion pages. Later that month, the *Globe* said it was shuttering its three foreign bureaus.

"In an era in which major metro dailies are suffering disproportionately from the problems of the newspaper economy, the *Globe* has probably suffered disproportionately in that class," says Jurkowitz, a former *Globe* ombudsman and media writer. "For the most part, the New England Media Group has been the worst performing sector of the Times Company on a fairly consistent basis."

On November 22, the *Globe* reported that the Times Company had rejected a proposal to buy the paper from a trio of Boston businessmen—retired General Electric chief executive Jack Welch, ad executive Jack Connors, and Joe O'Donnell, a local concessionaire. "[G]iven how the paper has struggled, the company may be better off selling the *Globe* and focusing its attention on the flagship paper and About.com," Morgan Stanley's Monaco wrote in her report.

But Jurkowitz notes that the Times' commitment in the region extends beyond the *Globe*. "A divorce from New England and a troubled experiment in New England does not simply entail finding a buyer for the *Globe*," he says. He adds that the *Globe* is a proud newspaper with a rich legacy, and a sale now would stain the company more deeply than discarding its local TV stations or even some of its smaller regional papers. "For the newspaper company with the best reputation in the country to have to bail out of New England under the shadow of 'They didn't really do so well with the *Boston Globe*,' that would go right to the core of their reputation."

Even before the January announcement, the *Globe*'s newsroom had not been spared. At the end of 2005, the *Globe* and *Telegram & Gazette* eliminated about 160 jobs through buyouts, more than 30 of those from the *Globe*'s newsroom. The *Globe* jettisoned its non-Washington national staff, and although the 10-person D.C. bureau also covers national news, *Globe* Editor Martin Baron concedes there are fewer general interest national features in the paper.

Unlike the *Inquirer*'s Tierney, though, he didn't sound ready to cede a Katrina-like news event to his sister paper and other national heavyweights—at least when we spoke in early January, before the latest round of cuts. "I don't think that it makes sense for our paper when there's major national tragedy of that sort to say 'hands-off,'" he said. "We are a regional newspaper, but our job is to reflect the interests of this area and the personality of this area. This is an area that has major interest in what's happening around the world, around the country."

He proudly cites his paper's record over the past few years: a 2003 Pulitzer for public service for its coverage of sexual abuse by priests in the Roman Catholic Church; a 2005 Pulitzer for explanatory reporting about stem-cell research; its 2006 series on the Bush administration exporting Christian faith-based initiatives around the world; and its groundbreaking coverage that year of President Bush's "signing statements," documents in which Bush repeatedly has asserted his perceived power to ignore laws when they conflict with his legal interpretation of the Constitution.

In June, the editorial operations of Boston.com merged with the print staff. "We're moving relatively quickly to turn our newsroom into a true multimedia organization," Baron says, adding that although the *Globe* has a partnership with New England Cable News, it needs to develop its own video capability.

In December, Boston.com—which was created to have a look and personality distinct from the print edition—attracted 3.8 million unique visitors, making it the sixth-largest newspaper site. The print edition of the *Globe* ranks No. 13 in circulation, so "that's quite an achievement," Baron says.

He takes a pass, though, when asked if the *Globe* is a better paper today than before the Times Company bought it. "I wasn't here, so it's not for me to say," says Baron, who became editor in July 2001 after serving as an associate managing editor at the *Times* and as executive editor of the *Miami Herald*. He adds that the Times Company has "invested a lot in this market."

Sulzberger bristles when asked to assess his company's stewardship of the *Globe*. "Compared to what?" he asks. He notes the Taylor family approached his father and his father's executive team about buying the paper and cites the recent pressures there, including consolidation in the retail market and the *Globe*'s traditionally heavy dependence on its help-wanted and classified advertising base, another newspaper mainstay under siege in the Internet era.

"Through very rough seas, I think our management, the New York Times Company management, has been good," Sulzberger says. "Not painless, but good." In September, the company named P. Steven Ainsley, who had been president of its Regional Media Group, as *Globe* publisher and head of the New England Media Group. During the last year, Times Company leaders also installed new chiefs of production, advertising, and circulation and marketing at the *Globe*.

When I ask Sulzberger if the Times will own the *Globe* in 10 years, he shrugs and nods, as if an affirmative answer is obvious. So in your mind, that's a certain thing? "There is no certainty in life, so that's unfair," he retorts. "Is it our plan to continue to own and grow the *Boston Globe*? Yes, that is our plan."

Two chroniclers of the Times believe the company's future, and that of its flagship paper, rest squarely on the organization's continuing commitment to journalism.

Susan E. Tifft, who with her husband, Alex S. Jones, exhaustively documented the Ochs-Sulzberger dynasty in *The Trust: The Private and Powerful Family Behind the New York Times*, says it wouldn't be fair to say the *Times* stands alone in its quality journalism. "But I think that the distance between it and the next tier down has gotten much, much bigger," Tifft says. "The distance could get wider between the *New York Times* and everybody else, and it's kind of lonely at the top."

Gay Talese, whose famed 1969 account of the *Times* newspaper, *The Kingdom and the Power*, was reissued in January by Random House, hasn't been a fan of either Keller's or Sulzberger's. In his *New Yorker* piece, Auletta quoted Talese as saying of Sulzberger, "You get a bad king every once in a while."

When I ask Talese to elaborate one year later, he takes a long-term view of the *Times'* enduring power as an institution, if an unbecoming one of its current leaders. "There's so much that's happened on [Sulzberger's] watch in the newspaper that has not been flattering, but maybe that's because there's much more attention paid to media than there was before," Talese says. "He's more a public property than his forebearers, than his father or grandfather. The *New York Times* can have a bad king. We can have bad presidents. Still the Republic goes on. We survived Garfield."

Yet Talese read the entire paper the other day, he remarks, and thought it was fabulous. "It has to give us information in the *New York Times* that we cannot get elsewhere. If it does that and does that and does that, it makes itself very necessary. It does not matter what is on 'Hardball' and Fox News and the bloggers," he says. If it pursues serious work and presents it in a readable way, if it avoids further embarrassments, then "I think it makes itself unique and necessary."

Analysts and shareholders can argue over whether the Times needs a Kaplan of its own, whether it should buy nascent Internet companies, and whether the quality of its "governance" is subpar from a financial perspective. None of that will matter if the *Times* loses its eminence as journalism's North Star. At a time of alarming retrenchment in the industry, its stewards still value that status, even if Wall Street does not.

"I don't think there's another company of our ilk better positioned to succeed," Sulzberger tells me. He's talking about the need for regional papers to own their communities, for the *Sarasota Herald-Tribune* to pop up on Google when a traveler searches for the best restaurants in the southwest Florida city.

What about the journalism? I ask.

"At the core of all of this is journalism," he replies. "Please, if you walk away from this conversation with anything—we are a journalistic organization. It is the journalism that will see us through. . . . If you lose that, you've lost your touchstone."

JOSEPH EPSTEIN

Trapped in Transition

The numbers, the track record, the recent history—it all added up for Joseph Epstein, who attacked the question of newspapers and their future in Commentary. *By any measure, he argued, the industry is responsible for its own decline, presenting a moribund product in a changing media world.*

"Clearly," said Adam to Eve as they departed the Garden of Eden, "we're living in an age of transition."

A joke, of course—but also not quite a joke, because when has the history of the world been anything other than one damned transition after another? Yet sometimes, in certain realms, transitions seem to stand out with utter distinctiveness, and this seems to be the case with the fortune of printed newspapers at the present moment. As a medium and as an institution, the newspaper is going through an age of transition in excelsis, and nobody can confidently say how it will end or what will come next.

To begin with familiar facts, statistics on readership have been pointing downward, significantly downward, for some time now. Four-fifths of Americans once read newspapers; today, apparently fewer than half do. Among adults, in the decade 1990–2000, daily readership fell from 52.6 percent to 37.5 percent. Among the young,

things are much worse: in one study, only 19 percent of those between the ages of eighteen and thirty-four reported consulting a
daily paper, and only 9 percent trusted the information purveyed
there; a mere 8 percent found newspapers helpful, while 4 percent
thought them entertaining.

From 1999 to 2004, according to the Newspaper Association of
America, general circulation dropped by another 1.3 million. Reflecting both that fact and the ferocious competition for classified
ads from free online bulletin boards like craigslist.org, advertising
revenue has been stagnant at best, while printing and production
costs have gone remorselessly upward. As a result, the New York
Times Company has cut some 700 jobs from its various papers.

The *Baltimore Sun*, owned by the *Chicago Tribune*, is closing
down its five international bureaus. Second papers in many cities
have locked their doors. This bleeding phenomenon is not restricted
to the United States, and no bets should be placed on the likely success of steps taken by papers to stanch the flow.

The *Wall Street Journal*, in an effort to save money on production costs, is trimming the width of its pages, from 15 to 12 inches. In
England, the once venerable *Guardian*, in a mad scramble to retain
its older readers and find younger ones, has radically redesigned itself by becoming smaller. London's *Independent* has gone tabloid,
and so has the once-revered *Times*, its publisher preferring the euphemism "compact."

For those of us who grew up with newspapers in our daily regimen, sometimes with not one but two newspapers in our homes, it
is all a bit difficult to take in. As early as 1831, Alexis de Tocqueville
noted that even frontier families in upper Michigan had a weekly
paper delivered.

A. J. Liebling, the *New Yorker's* writer on the press, used to say
that he judged any new city he visited by the taste of its water and
the quality of its newspapers.

The paper to which you subscribed, or that your father brought
home from work, told a good deal about your family: its social class,

its level of education, its politics. Among the five major dailies in the Chicago of my early boyhood, my father preferred the *Daily News*, an afternoon paper reputed to have excellent foreign correspondents. Democratic in its general political affiliation, though not aggressively so, the *Daily News* was considered the intelligent Chicagoan's paper.

My father certainly took it seriously. I remember asking him in 1952, as a boy of fifteen, about whom he intended to vote for in the presidential election between Dwight Eisenhower and Adlai Stevenson. "I'm not sure," he said. "I think I'll wait to see which way Lippmann is going."

The degree of respect then accorded the syndicated columnist Walter Lippmann is hard to imagine in our own time. In good part, his cachet derived from his readers' belief not only in his intelligence but in his impartiality. Lippmann, it was thought, cared about what was best for the country; he wasn't already lined up; you couldn't be certain which way he would go.

Of the two candidates in 1952, Stevenson, the intellectually cultivated Democrat, was without a doubt the man Lippmann would have preferred to have lunch with. But in the end he went for Eisenhower—his reason being, as I recall, that the country needed a strong leader with a large majority behind him, a man who, among other things, could face down the obstreperous Red-baiting of Senator Joseph McCarthy. My father, a lifelong Democrat, followed Lippmann and crossed over to vote for Eisenhower.

My father took his paper seriously in another way, too. He read it after dinner and ingested it, like that dinner, slowly, treating it as a kind of second dessert: something at once nutritive and entertaining. He was in no great hurry to finish.

Today, his son reads no Chicago newspaper whatsoever. A serial killer could be living in my apartment building, and I would be unaware of it until informed by my neighbors. As for the power of the press to shape and even change my mind, I am in the condition of George Santayana, who wrote to his sister in 1915 that he was too old to "be influenced by newspaper argument. When I read them I form perhaps a new opinion of the newspaper but seldom a new opinion on the subject discussed."

I do subscribe to the *New York Times*, which I read without a scintilla of glee. I feel I need it, chiefly to discover who in my cultural world has died, or been honored (probably unjustly), or has turned out some new piece of work that I ought to be aware of. I rarely give the daily *Times* more than a half-hour, if that. I begin with the obituaries. Next, I check the op-ed page, mostly to see if anyone has hit upon a novel way of denigrating President Bush; the answer is invariably no, though they seem never to tire of trying. I glimpse the letters to the editor in hopes of finding someone after my own heart. I almost never read the editorials, following the advice of the journalist Jack Germond who once compared the writing of a newspaper editorial to wetting oneself in a dark-blue serge suit: "It gives you a nice warm feeling, but nobody notices."

The arts section, which in the *Times* is increasingly less about the arts and more about television, rock 'n' roll, and celebrity, does not detain me long. Sports is another matter, for I do have the sports disease in a chronic and soon to be terminal stage; I run my eyes over these pages, turning in spring, summer, and fall to see who is pitching in that day's Cubs and White Sox games. And I always check the business section, where some of the better writing in the *Times* appears and where the reporting, because so much is at stake, tends to be more trustworthy.

Finally—quickly, very quickly—I run through the so-called hard news, taking in most of it at the headline level. I seem able to sleep perfectly soundly these days without knowing the names of the current presidents or prime ministers of Peru, India, Japan, and Poland. For the rest, the point of view that permeates the news coverage in the *Times* is by now so yawningly predictable that I spare myself the effort of absorbing the facts that seem to serve as so much tedious filler.

Am I typical in my casual disregard? I suspect so. Everyone agrees that print newspapers are in trouble today, and almost everyone agrees on the reasons. Foremost among them is the vast improvement in the technology of delivering information, which has combined in lethal ways with a serious change in the national temperament.

The technological change has to do with the increase in the number of television cable channels and the astonishing amount of news floating around in cyberspace. As Richard A. Posner has written, "The public's consumption of news and opinion used to be like sucking on a straw; now it's like being sprayed by a fire hose."

The temperamental change has to do with the national attention span. The critic Walter Benjamin said, as long ago as the 1930s, that the chief emotion generated by reading the newspapers is impatience. His remark is all the more pertinent today, when the very definition of what constitutes important information is up for grabs. More and more, in a shift that cuts across age, social class, and even educational lines, important information means information that matters to *me*, now.

And this is where the two changes intersect. Not only are we acquiring our information from new places but we are taking it pretty much on our own terms. The magazine *Wired* recently defined the word "egocasting" as "the consumption of on-demand music, movies, television, and other media that cater to individual and not mass-market tastes." The news, too, is now getting to be on-demand.

Instead of beginning their day with coffee and the newspaper, there to read what editors have selected for their enlightenment, people, and young people in particular, wait for a free moment to go online. No longer need they wade through thickets of stories and features of no interest to them, and least of all need they do so on the websites of newspapers, where the owners are hoping to regain the readers lost to print. Instead, they go to more specialized purveyors of information, including instant-messaging providers, targeted news sites, blogs, and online "zines."

Much cogitation has been devoted to the question of young people's lack of interest in traditional news. According to one theory, which is by now an entrenched cliché, the young, having grown up with television and computers as their constant companions, are "visual-minded," and hence averse to print. Another theory holds that young people do not feel themselves implicated in the larger world; for them, news of that world isn't where the action is. A more flattering corollary of this is that grown-up journalism strikes the young as hopelessly out of date. All that solemn good-guy/bad-guy reporting, the taking seriously of *opéra-bouffe* characters like Jesse Jackson or Al Gore or Tom DeLay, the false complexity of "in-depth" television reporting à la *60 Minutes*—this, for them, is so much hot air. They prefer to watch Jon Stewart's *The Daily Show* on the Comedy Central cable channel, where traditional news is mocked and pilloried as obvious nonsense.

Whatever the validity of this theorizing, it is also beside the point. For as the grim statistics confirm, the young are hardly alone in turning away from newspapers. Nor are they alone responsible for the dizzying growth of the so-called blogosphere, said to be increasing by 70,000 sites a day (according to the search portal technorati.com). In the first half of this year alone, the number of new blogs grew from 7.8 to 14.2 million. And if the numbers are dizzying, the sheer amount of information floating around is enough to give a person a serious case of Newsheimers.

Astonishing results are reported when news is passed from one blog to another: scores if not hundreds of thousands of hits, and, on sites that post readers' reactions, responses that can often be more impressive in research and reasoning than anything likely to turn up in print. Newspaper journalists themselves often get their stories from blogs, and bloggers have been extremely useful in verifying or refuting the erroneous reportage of mainstream journalists. The only place to get a reasonably straight account of news about Israel and the Palestinians, according to Stephanie Gutmann, author of

The Other War: Israelis, Palestinians, and the Struggle for Media Supremacy, is in the blogosphere.

The trouble with blogs and Internet news sites, it has been said, is that they merely reinforce the reader's already established interests and views, thereby contributing to our much-lamented national polarization of opinion. A newspaper, by contrast, at least compels one to acknowledge the existence of other subjects and issues, and reading it can alert one to affecting or important matters that one would never encounter if left to one's own devices, and in particular to that primary device of our day, the computer. Whether or not that is so, the argument has already been won, and not by the papers.

Another argument appears to have been won, too, and again to the detriment of the papers. This is the argument over politics, which the newspapers brought upon themselves and which, in my view, they richly deserved to lose.

One could put together an impressive little anthology of utterances by famous Americans on the transcendent importance of the press as a guardian watchdog of the state. Perhaps the most emphatic was that of Thomas Jefferson, who held that freedom of the press, right up there with freedom of religion and freedom of the person under the rights of habeas corpus and trial by jury, was among "the principles [that] form the bright constellation which has gone before us, and guided our steps through an age of revolution and reformation." Even today, not many people would disagree with this in theory; but like the character in a Tom Stoppard play, many would add: "I'm with you on the free press. It's the damned newspapers I can't stand."

The self-proclaimed goal of newsmen used to be to report, in a clear and factual way, on the important events of the day, on subjects of greater or lesser parochialism. It is no longer so. Here is Dan Rather, quoting with approval someone he does not name who defines news as "what somebody doesn't want you to know. All the rest is advertising."

"What somebody doesn't want you to know"—it would be hard to come up with a more concise definition of the target of the "investigative journalism" that has been the pride of the nation's newspapers for the past three decades. Bob Woodward, Carl Bernstein, Seymour Hersh, and many others have built their reputations on telling us things that presidents and senators and generals and CEOs have not wanted us to know.

Besides making for a strictly adversarial relationship between government and the press, there is no denying that investigative journalism, whatever (very mixed) accomplishments it can claim to its credit, has put in place among us a tone and temper of agitation and paranoia. Every day, we are asked to regard the people we elect to office as, essentially, our enemies—thieves, thugs, and megalomaniacs whose vicious secret deeds it is the chief function of the press to uncover and whose persons to bring down in a glare of publicity.

All this might have been to the good if what the journalists discovered were invariably true—and if the nature and the implications of that truth were left for others to puzzle out. Frequently, neither has been the case.

Much of contemporary journalism functions through leaks— information passed to journalists by unidentified individuals telling those things that someone supposedly doesn't want us to know. Since these sources cannot be checked or cross-examined, readers are in no position to assess the leakers' motives for leaking, let alone the agenda of the journalists who rely on them. To state the obvious: a journalist fervently against the U.S. presence in Iraq is unlikely to pursue leaks providing evidence that the war has been going reasonably well.

Administrations have of course used leaks for their own purposes, and leaks have also become a time-tested method for playing out intramural government disputes. Thus, it is widely and no doubt correctly believed that forces at the CIA and in the State Department have leaked information to the *New York Times* and the *Wash-*

ington Post to weaken positions taken by the White House they serve, thereby availing themselves of a mechanism of sabotage from within. But this, too, is not part of the truth we are likely to learn from investigative journalists, who not only purvey slanted information as if it were simply true but then take it upon themselves to try, judge, and condemn those they have designated as political enemies. So glaring has this problem become that the *Times*, beginning in June, felt compelled to introduce a new policy, designed, in the words of its ombudsman, to make "the use of anonymous sources the 'exception' rather than 'routine.'"

No wonder, then, that the prestige of mainstream journalism, which reached perhaps an all-time high in the early 1970s at the time of Watergate, has now badly slipped. According to most studies of the question, journalists tend more and more to be regarded by Americans as unaccountable kibitzers whose self-appointed job is to spread dissension, increase pressure on everyone, make trouble — and preach the gospel of present-day liberalism. Aiding this deserved fall in reputation has been a series of well-publicized scandals like the rise and fall of the reporter Jayson Blair at the *New York Times*.

The politicization of contemporary journalists surely has a lot to do with the fact that almost all of them today are university-trained. In *Newspaper Days*, H. L. Mencken recounts that in 1898, at the age of eighteen, he had a choice of going to college, there to be taught by German professors and on weekends to sit in a raccoon coat watching football games, or of getting a job on a newspaper, which would allow him to zip off to fires, whorehouse raids, executions, and other such festivities. As Mencken observes, it was no contest.

Most contemporary journalists, by contrast, attend schools of journalism or study the humanities and social sciences. Here the reigning politics are liberal, and along with their degrees, and their sense of enlightened virtue, they emerge with locked-in political views. According to Jim A. Kuypers in *Press Bias and Politics*, 76 percent of journalists who admit to having a politics describe themselves as liberal. The consequences are predictable: even as they employ their politics to tilt their stories, such journalists sincerely believe they are (a) merely telling the truth and (b) doing good in the world.

Pre-university-educated journalists did not, I suspect, feel that the papers they worked for existed as vehicles through which to advance their own political ideas. Some among them might have hated corruption, or the standard lies told by politicians; from time to time they might even have felt a stab of idealism or sentimentality. But they subsisted chiefly on cynicism, heavy boozing, and an admiration for craft. They did not treat the news—and editors of that day would not have permitted them to treat the news—as a trampoline off which to bounce their own tendentious politics.

To the degree that papers like the *New York Times*, the *Washington Post*, and the *Los Angeles Times* have contributed to the political polarization of the country, they much deserve their fate of being taken less and less seriously by fewer and fewer people. One can say this even while acknowledging that the cure, in the form of on-demand news, can sometimes seem as bad as the disease, tending often only to confirm users, whether liberal or conservative or anything else, in the opinions they already hold. But at least the curious or the bored can, at a click, turn elsewhere on the Internet for variety or relief—which is more than can be said for newspaper readers.

Nor, in a dumbed-down world, do our papers of record offer an oasis of taste. There were always a large number of newspapers in America whose sole standard was scandal and entertainment. (The crossword puzzle first appeared in Joseph Pulitzer's *New York World*.) But there were also some that were dedicated to bringing their readers up to a high or at least a middling mark. Among these were the *New York Times*, the *St. Louis Post-Dispatch*, the *Washington Post*, the *Milwaukee Journal*, the *Wall Street Journal*, the now long defunct *New York Herald Tribune*, and the *Chicago Daily News*.

These newspapers did not mind telling readers what they felt they ought to know, even at the risk of boring the pajamas off them.

The *Times*, for instance, used to run the full text of important political speeches, which could sometimes fill two full pages of photograph-less type. But now that the college-educated are writing for the college-educated, neither party seems to care. And with circulation numbers dwindling and the strategy in place of whoring after the uninterested young, anything goes.

What used to be considered the serious press in America has become increasingly frivolous. The scandal-and-entertainment aspect more and more replaces what once used to be called "hard news." In this, the serious papers would seem to be imitating the one undisputed print success of recent decades, *USA Today*, whose guiding principle has been to make things brief, fast-paced, and entertaining. Or, more hopelessly still, they are imitating television talk shows or the Internet itself, often mindlessly copying some of their dopier and more destructive innovations.

The editor of the London *Independent* has talked of creating, in place of a newspaper, a "views-paper," one that can be viewed like a television or a computer. The *Los Angeles Times* has made efforts to turn itself interactive, including by allowing website readers to change the paper's editorials to reflect their own views (only to give up on this initiative when readers posted pornography on the page). In his technology column for the *New York Times*, David Carr speaks of newspapers needing "a podcast moment," by which I take him to mean that the printed press must come up with a self-selecting format for presenting on-demand news akin to the way the iPod presents a listener's favorite programming exactly as and when he wants it.

In our multi-tasking nation, we already read during television commercials, talk on the cellphone while driving, listen to music while working on the computer, and much else besides. Some in the press seem in their panic to think that the worst problem they face is that you cannot do other things while reading a newspaper except smoke, which in most places is outlawed anyway. Their problems go much deeper.

In a speech given this past April to the American Society of Newspaper Editors, the international publisher Rupert Murdoch catalogued the drastic diminution of readership for the traditional press and then went on to rally the troops by telling them that they must do better. Not different, but better: going deeper in their coverage, listening more intently to the desires of their readers, assimilating and where possible imitating the digital culture so popular among the young. A man immensely successful and usually well anchored in reality, Murdoch here sounded distressingly like a man without a plan.

Not that I have one of my own. Best to study history, it is said, because the present is too complicated and no one knows anything about the future. The time of transition we are currently going through, with the interest in traditional newspapers beginning to fade and news on the computer still a vast confusion, can be likened to a great city banishing horses from its streets before anyone has yet perfected the automobile.

Nevertheless, if I had to prophesy, my guess would be that newspapers will hobble along, getting ever more desperate and ever more vulgar. More of them will attempt the complicated mental acrobatic of further dumbing down while straining to keep up, relentlessly exerting themselves to sustain the mighty cataract of inessential information that threatens to drown us all. Those of us who grew up with newspapers will continue to read them, with ever less trust and interest, while younger readers, soon enough grown into middle age, will ignore them.

My own preference would be for a few serious newspapers to take the high road: to smarten up instead of dumbing down, to honor the principles of integrity and impartiality in their coverage, and to become institutions that even those who disagreed with them would have to respect for the reasoned cogency of their editorial positions. I imagine such papers directed by editors who could choose for me—as neither the Internet nor I on my own can do—the serious issues, questions, and problems of the day and, with the aid of intelligence born of concern, give each the emphasis it deserves.

In all likelihood a newspaper taking this route would go under; but at least it would do so in a cloud of glory, guns blazing. And at least its loss would be a genuine subtraction. About our newspapers as they now stand, little more can be said in their favor than that they do not require batteries to operate, you can swat flies with them, and they can still be used to wrap fish.

RICK EDMONDS

Fighting the Vortex

❧ ❧

The Project for Excellence in Journalism, funded by the
Poynter Institute, has been diligent in its annual mea-
surement of the media. For the past two years the
prospects have been grim for the newspaper part of that
business. Despite some bright spots, cost cutting has
taken a toll, revenues from Internet efforts are begin-
ning to decline, and changes in the world of retail sales
continue to threaten key advertising sources. Still, as
this excerpt from co-author Rick Edmonds's newspaper
section of the latest report notes, newspapers retain the
vast proportion of their audiences and remain key pro-
ducers of information.

Newspapers have a tough time making the case that their business is
headed in the right direction. The year 2006 was terrible in many re-
spects, and there seems little prospect that 2007 will be much better.

The best that the industry can hope for is that some easing of
costs—both paper and people—will improve earnings and that they
can demonstrate continued strong growth in the range of their online and niche offerings and in ad revenues in the new media.

Even that last seems in doubt. Online revenue growth came in
just below 30 percent in 2006 after years of 30 percent-plus growth.
The rate is expected to fall to 22 percent in 2007, and for the first

time newspaper sites are not maintaining share in total Internet advertising growth.

The grim 2006 picture contained these elements:

- Pre-tax earnings at print newspapers were off about 8.4 percent compared with 2005, and that was not an especially good year either. At companies with television holdings, that was softened by the predictable windfall of Winter Olympic and election advertising.
- Ad revenues were flat, despite contributions from online and niche publications that continue to grow at an average rate of 20 to 30 percent. Optimistic industry sources are predicting a slightly more positive 2007 for advertising. Most analysts, however, forecast that ad revenues will be down by 1 to 2 percent.
- After seeing their share prices drop an average of 20 percent in 2005, publicly traded newspaper companies lost another 14 percent of value in 2006. One of the gainers for the year was Tribune—but that came on speculation that it would be sold at a premium early in 2007.

There will be some good news on costs in 2007, though it comes with a caveat. Newspapers have been downsizing everything from their staff counts to the dimensions of the paper to the breadth of their coverage and the range of their circulation area. All of that flirts with the danger of chasing away readers from an inferior product. Executives argue that they must live within means, but some are also cutting way back on business-side staffing and circulation promotion, which will likely further depress circulation.

One unambiguous bit of good news is that newsprint prices, after three consecutive years of 10 percent increases, had softened by the end of 2006 and were expected to be flat or down in 2007. With smaller papers, a typical company can save 7 percent on newsprint spending.

Looking for more fundamental reasons for hope, we find two. A year ago we noted that the impending sale of Knight Ridder was a likely "lose-lose" proposition—dooming the thirty-two papers to more deep cuts under new ownership or the industry to a sort of no-confidence vote if no buyer materialized.

In fact the McClatchy Company, with a strong record of commitment to editorial quality, came away with twenty of the papers. All twelve of the papers McClatchy chose not to keep, in turn, found buyers among private companies and investor groups. But the fact that only one public company came forward did signal some lack of interest in newspapers generally. And some of those local and private owners have indeed made deeper cuts at the papers they purchased.

The drama over newspapers' appeal continued with turns at another company, Tribune, in 2006 and early 2007. With Tribune on the block, a trend may be emerging in which private investors see better possibilities for newspapers than Wall Street does.

Then there are indications that the industry is making progress toward a wholehearted commitment to transformative online growth. Paul Ginocchio, one of our analyst sources, said after listening to company presentations during the December 2006 Media Week investors' meetings that he could now see at least the potential outline of a successful turnaround.

But the biggest question remains whether the economic model of the Internet can change as the audience moves more heavily to that platform. Until it does, it seems reasonable to foresee the economics of the newspaper business—even with an ever-larger online component—as one of erosion and shrinking horizons.

WHAT AILS ADVERTISING?

In the golden era of the newspaper business financially, from the 1960s well into the 1990s, newspapers had three big things going for them. The first was a lock on the highly profitable classified advertising business. The second was page after page of department-store advertising—John Wanamaker in Philadelphia, Woodies in Washington, D.C., Dayton's in Minneapolis, and dozens more. The third was the leverage to raise rates aggressively even as circulation was beginning to slide because of the numbers, the attractive demographics of newspapers' readership, and their near-monopoly pricing power.

You will find vestiges of all three in newspapers circa 2006–2007. But all three of those pillars are now badly eroded.

Classifieds are subject to massive competition from electronic companies like Google, Yahoo, Monster, and Craigslist, plus an assortment of sites for autos and real estate.

The traditional department store has been progressively weakened by the growth of Wal-Mart, a very light newspaper advertiser, and other discount retailers. Remaining department stores have been consolidating over the last quarter-century, notably in the merger of Federated and May stores, carried out over 2005 and 2006.

Stronger competition and faster circulation losses eat at newspapers' ability to raise rates at will.

Here is a breakout of how those advertising troubles played out in 2006.

RETAIL

The department-store herd has been thinned dramatically. Some of the big-box stores—Best Buy and Home Depot—are at least reliable sources of insert income. In 2006 the Federated and May consolidation led to double-digit-percentage losses in local retail advertising in some markets.

Despite that, the overall picture for local retail advertising in newspapers is not so bad. The Newspaper Association of America found that spending on such advertising was up just under 1 percent from 2004 to 2005. In the first three quarters of 2006, spending on retail looks flat.

CLASSIFIEDS

Classified advertising has a more complicated set of troubles. From competition from online listing entities to companies connecting directly to the consumer through their own sites, skipping the middle man altogether, to the free pricing of Craigslist, classified advertising has entered a new era.

The online giant Monster Inc. built a huge business in employment listings through the late 1990s and early 2000s while newspapers were sitting on their heels. The industry finally countered with its own national service—CareerBuilder—which now edges Monster in volume but not profits. At the end of 2006 Yahoo, with its Hot Jobs (No. 3 in online job classifieds) signed an agreement with two hundred papers. Monster, too, has begun to make newspaper affiliations.

After massive declines in ad revenue from employment classifieds in the 2000–2002 recession, the sector bounced back some in 2004 and 2005. But employment classified again declined in the second and third quarters of 2006, down 6.5 percent and 10 percent year-to-year, respectively. That leaves the marketplace unsettled headed into 2007, but this much is clear: the industry has lost its preeminent position.

Automotive classifieds had an especially bumpy 2006. One of Detroit's responses to the deep losses of the domestic manufacturers has been to eliminate some local dealerships and reduce the advertising budgets of those that remain. Direct online-to-consumer communications, where car buyers can sample everything from interior color schemes to prices, have become a big factor in the business. (A current Toyota TV ad touts the website rather than the cars themselves.) New marketing dollars are sure to flow that way in years to come. Automotive classifieds have declined since 2004, and those declines accelerated through the first three quarters of 2006, hovering near 15 percent.

Real estate classifieds were a bright spot in 2006, up about 20 percent year-to-year through the first three quarters, as a big inventory of properties stayed on the market for months at a time. But as real estate heads from slowdown into downturn in 2007, the industry will be pressed to stay even in that category.

For those three big categories of classified advertising and the smaller "other" (general merchandise and services), the industry faces killer competition from the communitarian-minded Craigslist. From a modest local start in San Francisco in 1995, it has expanded to 450 cities worldwide and posts 14 million new classifieds a month. Most listings are free. The service is now among the top 10 in monthly page visits and clearly has achieved the mass to do the job for a great many buyers and sellers.

National advertising was also weak in 2006, contributing particularly to the poor performance of large regional newspapers and of the *New York Times*, where the important movie advertising category has fallen considerably from its 2000 peak. Year-end spending in 2005 was down 18.5 percent from that 2000 high, representing a loss in revenue to newspapers of over $230 million.

Another major source of national ad revenue is transportation advertising, which accounts for about 15 percent of the category (down from about 19 percent in 2000). As in the case of movie ads, newspaper revenue from transportation ads also fell, by 18.5 percent, from 2000 to 2005, representing a revenue loss to newspapers of over $265 million.

There is a bright element in this dismal picture, however. Coupon spending, which currently accounts for approximately 17 percent of national advertising, has increased by just over 17 percent from 2000 to 2005.

AD RATES

On pricing, the industry has a pair of problems. Online is competitive and priced accordingly. Google search produces results (and premium bid pricing for top placements) that the industry cannot currently match.

Even in the face of falling circulation, newspapers raised their stated rates in 2006 and have said they plan to do so again in 2007. But the higher rates may paint a misleading picture—some advertisers are simply choosing to take less space, something that is evidenced by the decline in total print ad revenue for 2006.

Discussions of newspaper economics are often thin on new trends in the advertising industry. At the moment, advertisers are moving their budgets not only online but also to nontraditional direct-to-the-consumer marketing. One example is Procter and Gamble, a bell-cow in consumer product marketing. It now has its own word-of-mouth agency, Tremor, with 800,000 registered panelists who agree to sample products and then talk them up to friends and acquaintances. The Web makes such "viral marketing" far more powerful.

In the face of all this, newspapers need to protect their share of flat traditional-media budgets, continue to grow online, and invent some new lines of e-commerce—all three at once.

MAKING THE BEST OF IT

While advertising has not declined at the same pace as circulation, there are parallels to the two stories. Repeated reports hammering newspapers for circulation losses tend to overlook the 50 million-plus buyers and 120 million-plus print readers on an average day.

On the advertising front, all the challenges and losses may obscure something about the enduring financial muscle of newspapers: Taking into account the loss of some advertising and the simultaneous arrival of new business, newspapers annually are holding on to the vast majority of their advertising base.

Loyalty and inertia play a role; local advertising practices don't turn on a dime. So does the perceived effectiveness of newspapers, especially when advertising a store's sale prices. The Newspaper Association attempted to highlight those elements with a campaign hailing newspaper advertising as "a destination, not a distraction." The study, by MORI research, includes a barrage of survey statistics on how many readers consider advertising a welcome information resource. The "distraction" is a thinly veiled dig at television, where blocks of commercials are a repetitive irritant increasingly vulnerable to being zapped by TiVos and other DVRs. In short, newspaper ads, executives believe, still have distinct advantages, especially as the landscape of options becomes more cluttered.

Newspapers also continue to field the largest advertising sales force in most communities. We are told anecdotally that there has been a steady effort to upgrade salespeople and particularly managers, recognizing that simple order-taking will not suffice. With the boom of online and niche publications, those salespeople now have a portfolio of products to sell.

Newspaper pricing practices also help. Advertisers earn big discounts if they commit to a fixed-amount annual contract. That can help lock up budgets against other alternatives.

CAN ONLINE EDITIONS RESCUE NEWSPAPERS?

Since newspapers typically have the best-trafficked websites in their markets, and the sites' ad revenues have grown at a 30 percent rate for five years now, it would be appealing to think that readership and advertising will simply transfer gradually to the Web. Thus could the expensive news-gathering function and newspapers' public service mission be preserved, and without the cumbersome costs of printing and delivering the paper.

Unfortunately, after all that growth, online typically still contributes only 6 or 7 percent of ad revenues. So while developing the new platform, papers can ill afford to take their eye off the ball of a print operation that constitutes 94 percent of the business.

As we noted last year, Rick Edmonds of the Poynter Institute, a co-author of this chapter on newspapers, in January 2005 ran a rough projection estimating that it would take online a dozen years to pass print as a revenue source, assuming continuation of the trends of 2003 and 2004. Built into that model, in other words, online would have to continue to grow by a third each year. Print revenue would grow modestly, by 3 percent.

Two years later, it probably makes sense to adjust downward the assumption that print will grow at 3 percent a year for a dozen more years.

But it also seems overly optimistic, absent some surge from new and unanticipated lines of business, to think that online can keep up that 33 percentage growth.

Partly that's just the law of large numbers. As the base gets bigger, even substantial gains are not as large a percentage (a phenomenon that soured Yahoo's earnings reports in 2006).

More mature newspaper Web operations, particularly those of the national papers, are now growing annually in the 20 to low 30 percent range. Gannett executives told analysts in December that USA Today.com would end 2006 with 25 percent revenue growth and was estimated to grow 18 to 20 percent in 2007.

Industry online growth fell just below 30 percent in 2006, and the Newspaper Association forecasts that it will grow just 22 percent in 2007. That is still robust growth, but not a third a year. So it still seems reasonable to expect that the industry is a decade or more away from seeing online business contributing half of revenue.

What can newspapers do to maximize sustained online growth? The consensus strategy heading into 2007 is to get more people to visit and more often (especially with breaking-news updates), and to stay longer (especially with new multimedia and interactive features). More page views can equate to more advertising opportunities.

A second strategy is to redesign, reduce clutter, and create better display space for advertising. The industry's current mix depends lopsidedly on classified (roughly 75 percent). But some speculate that the mix could shift as national and regional advertisers gradually develop the capability for integrated campaigns that include more online display advertising, some of it now in video or even interactive video.

A shift of readership from print to online cuts several ways for newspapers. The commitment of time and attention is so much less that online readers do not command the premium rates print can charge. Paul Ginocchio, a Deutsche Bank analyst, estimates that a print reader is worth $350 a year to a newspaper, an online reader 10 to 15 percent of that.

Since only the *Wall Street Journal* and the *New York Times* charge for all or part of their daily content, newspapers are losing circulation revenue every day, month, or year that a potential reader opts instead for the free Web version.

On the other hand, in theory there should be a critical mass of Web audience that will allow newspaper companies to save at least on paper costs and perhaps on printing and delivery capacity.

So the potential profitability of news websites theoretically is high but also conjectural. One can envision a scenario in which lucrative Web operations carry costs for a newsroom that serves both the site and a slimmed-down and more targeted print edition. But it is just too early to predict that. Nor is there evidence that papers are using the savings from online production and distribution to reinvest in news staff.

Donald Graham, CEO of the Washington Post Company, has a reputation for plain speaking on the topic. He noted in a December 2006 presentation to investors that the *Post* already gets 11 percent of revenue from online (nearly double the norm) and reaches a huge national and international audience who are not served by the print edition. But even with those "strong cards to play," he concluded, "I simply have no way to tell you" what combined newspaper print and online revenues will be like in five or ten years. Extrapolating from the last several years doesn't work because trends could easily change, he said.

COLLABORATIONS

What was new at the end of 2006 was joint ventures with both Yahoo and Google—a sign that the industry had gotten past wringing their hands about the huge upstart competitors and started figuring out ways to make money together.

In the Yahoo deal, put together by Dean Singleton, two hundred newspapers will partner with the online giant. Initially that will mean placing online classifieds through Yahoo's Hot Jobs (third in listings behind Craigslist and Monster). But the partners envision later sharing content and mounting an initiative to build local search advertising (essentially the equivalent of Yellow Page listings for specific goods or services). That would combine using Yahoo's technology and the newspapers' advertiser contacts within their markets to ramp up an emerging base of new business.

The venture is open on the same terms to any other newspapers that wish to join. Media General, owner of twenty-five newspapers (with a circulation of over 850,000), did so weeks after the initial announcement. The deal is being celebrated as "transformational" by several of the participants, and could be so if it opens a new front on local search, which Google dominates. The market analyst Gordon Borrell estimates that local paid search and e-mail advertising will be the hot growth areas online in the next four years, and that newspaper sites are in danger of losing share unless they strengthen their effort.

The Google deal is entirely different: a ninety-day trial in which Google is placing ads from its base of search clients into fifty newspapers with digitized "bid" pricing. Initially it was for so-called "remaindered" space in which newspapers typically place house ads, but it has been expanded to guaranteed placements. The buzz at the December investment meetings where major media companies talk to Wall Street analysts was that Google had met its three-month revenue projection in the first three weeks.

Each of those experiments is new enough that the results cannot be predicted (nor were the revenue splits disclosed). But they add one more piece of evidence that the industry is no longer committed in wishful fashion to doing all the traditional things the traditional way.

If all goes well, the deals might help increase ad revenues as well as pave the way for licensing content to Google and Yahoo, a far more realistic prospect for newspapers than charging local customers directly for content.

"NEWSPAPER NEXT" AND THE NEW BUSINESS MODEL

If one thing seems inevitable, it is that the newspaper industry is moving toward a new business model, though no one seems certain what that will be. The turmoil of 2006 prompted many proposals.

The one attracting the most attention was a year-long $2 million project of the American Press Institute entitled "Newspaper Next" and based on work by Clayton Christensen and others at the Harvard Business School.

In essence, the Harvard team concluded in a report released in September, all of the above—the print edition, existing online sites, niche publications, and acquisitions—may not be enough.

Newspapers were urged instead:

• To be much more committed to a systematic approach to innovation, scoping out unmet "jobs to be done" for consumers and advertisers in their communities.

• To settle for projects that can be started quickly on a modest scale and be readjusted if the initial plan is flawed, as it likely will be.

• To consider a broad cooperative industry-wide effort to sell and place national online advertising.

One of six pilot projects, at the *Dallas Morning News*, involved setting up a website for mothers, with lots of informative listings on camps, after-school programs, and the like. The appeal to a set of advertisers is obvious if the targeted audience is assembled. The idea is catching on fast. By the December investor meetings, Gannett and Journal Communications announced that they had similar sites up, running and off to a fast start at the *Indianapolis Star* and *Milwaukee Journal-Sentinel*, respectively.

Another pilot paper, *The Oregonian*, sought to tap into the "nonconsuming" youth population of Portland and learned that its potential audience primarily demands local and entertainment information. The newspaper is developing a product to meet those needs.

The *Boston Globe*, like the *Richmond Times-Dispatch*, is focusing on marketing, using search engine marketing (SEM) programs for its website that guarantee advertisers with small budgets a certain number of clicks from high-potential customers.

Yet another of the pilot papers, the *Desert Sun* in Palm Springs, California, asked employees to take a close look at the pages of their own paper to identify what they read regularly. Executive Editor Steve Silberman found that his reporters consumed little of their own product, and when he asked them to write in a way that they would be more inclined to read, the result was that stories shrunk in length.

Ultimately the "Newspaper Next" project's strategy is to encourage newspapers to experiment outside their core news product to compete with cheaper alternatives, or what Christensen refers to as "disruptive" products that are proliferating online and as niche publications. Such changes may seem radical to some or a sign of desperation in a beleaguered industry to others. But as one of the organizers remarked, the motivation for change shouldn't be fear but enthusiasm. For now, it may be both.

CONCLUSION

What are the chances of the industry's making a successful transition to a new business model? Newspapers are embracing transformation as a concept and a slogan. The "Newspaper Next" project even provides models of what new lines of business could look like.

Still, a pessimist might note the number of competitors that have emerged from nowhere so far this decade—Google and Craigslist siphoning off ad dollars; Wikipedia, My Space, and YouTube capturing audience and attention. Isn't it reasonable to expect more of the same new ventures at regular intervals in coming years?

There is a case too, however, for a more positive long-term picture. Newspapers remain the preeminent source of news, recycled by aggregators and blog commentators. The aggregators, at least, are now signaling that they may prefer cooperation to a duel that continues to diminish newspapers' capacity.

PHILIP MEYER

The Wrong Way to Make Money

◆ ◆

Philip Meyer's The Vanishing Newspaper *is filled with dark news about the newspaper business. But one nugget in the book suggests that private ownership and a business plan based upon a 6 percent return could be the salvation of the industry. Newspapers really aren't that troubled, Meyer argues, they're just accustomed to making too much money.*

I learn'd to love despair.

—Byron, "The Prisoner of Chillon," 1816

To appreciate how the locale for Byron's poem serves as a metaphor for the American newspaper industry, drive a short distance north of Montreaux, Switzerland, and visit the Rock of Chillon. It sits on the eastern edge of Lake Geneva, and it was fortified in the ninth century. In the twelfth century, the counts of Savoy built a castle on the rock. With the lake on the west side and a mountain on the east, the castle commands the north-south road between. Any traveler on that road had to choose between paying a toll to the owner of the castle, climbing the mountain, or swimming the lake. It was such a sweet deal that the lords of Savoy and their heirs clung to that rock for three centuries.

For generations, U.S. newspaper publishers were like the Savoy family. Their monopoly newspapers were tollgates through which information passed between the local retailers and their customers. For most of the twentieth century, that bottleneck was virtually absolute. Owning the newspaper was like having the power to levy a sales tax.

But new technology is bypassing the bottleneck. Just as today's travelers can fly over Chillon or bypass it in a power boat or on an alternate road, today's retailers are finding other ways to get their messages out. Newspapers have been slow to adapt, because their culture is the victim of that history of easy money. For perspective, consider the following comparison: in most lines of business there is a relationship between the size of the profit margin—the proportion of revenue that trickles to the bottom line—and the speed of product turnover. Sell a lot of items, and you can get by with just a little profit on each one. If sales are few, you'd better make a bundle every time.

Supermarkets can prosper with a margin of 1 to 2 percent because their buyers consume the products continually and have to keep coming back. Sellers of diamonds or yachts or luxury sedans build much higher margins into their prices to compensate for less frequent sales. Across the whole range of retail products, the average profit margin is in the neighborhood of 6 to 7 percent.

In turnover, daily newspapers are more like supermarkets than yacht dealers. Their product has a one-day shelf life. Consumers and advertisers alike have to pay for a new version every day if they want to stay current. Absent a monopoly, newspaper margins would be at the low end. But when they owned the bottleneck, the opposite was true. Before technology began to create alternate toll routes, a monopoly newspaper in a medium-size market could command a margin of 20 to 40 percent.

That easy-money culture has led to some bad habits. If the money comes in no matter what kind of product you turn out, you become production-oriented instead of customer-oriented. You are motivated to get it out the gate as cheaply as possible. If your market position is strong, you can cheapen the product and raise prices at the same time. Innovation happens, but it is often directed at making the product cheaper instead of making it better.

Before newspapers were controlled by publicly held companies, their finances were secret. A few retailers may have noticed that a publisher's family took flying vacations to Europe while they drove theirs to the local mountains or the beach, but publishers were usually careful not to flaunt their wealth. It is unwise to arouse resentment from one's own clientele.

When newspaper companies began going public in the late 1960s, the books opened, and Wall Street was delighted with what it saw. Analyst Patrick O'Connell, in an industry review prepared for E. F. Hutton clients in 1982, ticked off the advantages enjoyed by newspapers:

• Competition in selling was increasing the size of the advertising market, and newspapers had consistently received 28 to 30 percent of total advertising dollars in the previous two decades.
• Newspapers were practically immune from the profit-eroding effects of inflation because they could "pass cost pressures along through prices very efficiently."
• With their strong cash flows, newspaper companies could finance growth with their own money and avoid the uncertainties of fluctuating interest rates.

Looking at the previous decade, O'Donnell noted with satisfaction that "aggressive pricing met little resistance, especially in one-newspaper markets where retailers have few other means of access to their customers." (Note his use of the word "aggressive" to describe increasing prices. In other industries discussed in business literature, aggressive pricing is *lower* pricing. That's because most industries are competitive, and a price cut is aggression against the competition. Newspapers, being mostly monopolies, direct their price aggression against their customers instead of each other.)

At the same time, newspapers were using technology to bring their costs down. Production costs decreased in the last quarter of the twentieth century as the change to cold type and automated typesetting was completed. Circulation costs diminished when newspapers pulled back their "vanity circulation" in areas not considered important by the advertisers in the newspapers' retail trade zones. Administrative costs went up. And news-editorial costs became more flexible.

In 2001, a typical newspaper of one hundred thousand in circulation would have an expense breakdown like this (dollar amounts are in millions: percents are of revenue):

News-editorial	$5.36	11.4%
Advertising	4.00	9.4
Circulation	5.68	11.1
Production	3.99	8.0
Newsprint and ink	6.43	13.9
Administration and depreciation	12.43	25.4
Gross profit	10.98	20.8
Total	55.48	100

The revenue side was much simpler: Industry-wide, advertising accounted for 82 percent of newspaper revenue in 2000 and circulation was the other 18. That was a shift from a 71–29 division in mid-century. Within the three main categories of advertising—national, retail, and classified—the latter grew in relative importance. Here is media economist Robert Picard's analysis of the change between 1950 and 2000:

	1950	2000
Retail	57%	44%
National	25	16
Classified	18	40

That, as Picard suggested, is a whole new business model. And it is a less stable model. Classified advertising, because it includes help-wanted, real estate, and automobile advertising, is especially subject to changes in the business cycle.

Wall Street sees the cyclical nature of the newspaper business as a major drawback. The financial analysts who advise institutional investors make their reputations on their ability to predict the future. So they prefer companies whose growth patterns are steady year in and year out.

THE NEUHARTH SOLUTION

It was Gannett's Al Neuharth who found a solution to this problem. Under his guidance, Gannett accumulated monopoly newspapers in medium-size markets where the threat of competition was remote. Neuharth motivated his publishers to practice earnings management. They held earnings down during the good times by making capital investment, refurbishing the plant, and filling holes in the staff. And they boosted earnings in the bad times by postponing investment, shrinking the news holes, and reducing staff.

Gannett papers played Al's money game vigorously enough to produce a long period of steady quarter-to-quarter growth that satisfied the analysts' lust for predictability. Any long-term costs to these behind-the-scenes contortions did not bother them. Neither, for that matter, did the fact that some of the growth was unreal, because analysts and accountants alike are accustomed to looking at nominal dollar values rather than inflation-adjusted dollars. Neuharth's glory days were also a period of high inflation, and that helped to mask some of the cyclical twists and turns.

The price of Gannett stock soared. Managers of the other public companies saw what was happening and began to practice earnings management, too. One of the devices was the contingency budget, which was more like a decision tree than a planning tool. An editor is told how much he or she can spend on the news product in a given year provided that revenues remain at a certain level. If revenue falls below expectations, leaner budget plans are triggered at specified points on the downward slope.

Neuharth's showmanship worked just long enough to raise everyone's expectations about the value of newspapers. Today, despite some heroic efforts, not even Gannett can match Neuharth's record of "never a down quarter." Inflation is no longer high enough to mask the fluctuations in real return. Readers are drifting away. Advertisers are exploring other routes for their messages. In 1946, at the dawn of the age of television, newspapers had 34 percent of the advertising market. In the second half of the twentieth century, newspaper share of the overall advertising market fell from almost 30 percent to close to 20 percent.

Picard reminded us that, despite loss of share, newspapers still made more money than ever, primarily because the size of the advertising market grew, even after inflation was taken into account. However, it did not grow as much as gross domestic product. Newspapers, by raising prices and reducing cost, did well, but newspaper advertising as a share of GDP fell from seven-tenths of a percent to half a percent in the half-century. Charging more for delivering less is not a strategy that can be carried into the indefinite future. So where will it all end? To envision the future, it helps us to think about the readers.

The readership decline was first taken seriously in the late 1960s, when new information sources began to compete successfully for the time of the traditional newspaper reader. Competition spawned by technology began long before talk of the electronic information highway. Cheap computer typesetting and offset printing led to the explosive growth of specialized print products that could target desired audiences for advertisers. Low postal rates combined with cheap printing and computerized mailing lists spurred the growth of direct mail advertising. In short, the owners of the traditional toll road have been in trouble for some time.

Some observers draw a line on the chart of newspaper decline, use a straightedge to extend it into the future, and foresee the death of newspapers. The reality is likely to be quite different. There is room for newspapers in the nonmonopoly environment of the newspaper future. They will not be as profitable, and that is a problem for their owners—whether they are private or public shareholders—but it is not a problem for society.

Imagine an economic environment in which newspapers earn the normal retail margin of 6 or 7 percent of revenues. As long as there are entrepreneurs willing to produce a socially useful product at that margin—and trust me, there will be—society will be served as well as it is now. Perhaps those entrepreneurs will not be the same ones who are serving us now, and that is not necessarily a concern to customers—except for one problem.

The problem is that there is no easy way to get from a newspaper industry used to 20 to 40 percent margins to one that is content with 6 or 7 percent. The present owners have those margins built into their expected return on investment, which is related to their standard of living.

It is return on investment that keeps supermarket owners content with 2 percent margins. And it is return on investment that makes newspaper owners, whether they be families, sole proprietors, or public shareholders, want to preserve their 20 to 40 percent. All of the money that they have sunk into the industry, whether by buying newspapers or spending on buildings and presses, has been cost-justified on the basis of that fat profit margin.

Look at this way. If I sell you a goose that lays a golden egg every day, the price you pay me will be based on your expected return on investment (ROI), which needs to beat what the bank would pay on a certificate of deposit, but not by much. In negotiating the price that you are willing to pay me (and at which I am willing to sell), we'll both look for an expected ROI that compares favorably with other possible investments. And the reasonable assumption will be that the goose will continue to produce at the same rate.

Fast forward a bit. Once safe under your roof, the goose drops its production to one golden egg a week. That makes you a major loser.

Now, it's still a pretty good goose. You can resign yourself to the reduced income, or you can sell it to a third somebody who will be proud to own and house and feed it. And that new owner can, of course, get the return on investment that you were hoping to receive by simply paying one-seventh of the price you paid.

What happened to the rest of the goose's value? I captured it when I sold it to you on the basis of the seven-day production schedule. The third owner is a winner, too, because he gets a fair return on his investment. Society is OK because there are plenty of other sources for golden eggs. The only loser is you.

Avoiding the fate of the second owner of the goose is the central problem facing newspaper owners today. They know they have to adjust to the reduced expectations that technology-driven change has brought them. They just don't know how. To understand the range of possible adjustments, consider two opposing scenarios laid out by business strategist Michael E. Porter:

Scenario 1. The present owners squeeze the goose to maintain profitability today without worrying about the long term. This is the take-the-money-and-run strategy. Under this scenario, the owners raise prices and simultaneously try to save their way to profitability with the usual techniques: cutting news hole, reducing staff, peeling back circulation in remote or low-income areas of less interest to advertisers, postponing maintenance and capital improvement, holding salaries down.

It can work. A good newspaper, some sage once observed, is like a fine garden. It takes years of hard work to build and years of neglect to destroy. The advantage of the squeeze scenario for present-day managers is that it has a chance of being successful in preserving their accustomed standard of living for their career lifetimes. Both advertisers and readers are creatures of habit. They will keep paying their money and using the product for a long time after the original reasons for doing so have faded. When the bad end finally comes, the managers who locked the company into the strategy can say, "It didn't happen on our watch." Porter calls this strategy "harvesting market position."

Scenario 2. The present owners—or their successors—will accept the realities of the new competition and invest in product improve-

8

ments that fully exploit the power of print and make newspaper com-
panies major players in an information marketplace that includes
electronic delivery. "Rather than viewing a substitute as a threat, it
may be better to view it as an opportunity," Porter says. "Entering the
substitute industry may allow a firm to reap competitive advantages
from interrelationships between a substitute and a product, such as
common channels and buyers." The movement of newspaper companies into Internet distribution of news and advertising is a good example, because it exploits the newspaper's experience at creating
content in the new distribution medium.

It was that prospect, in fact, that took my old outfit, Knight Ridder, into an experiment with electronic delivery of information way
back in 1978. It offered hope of reducing the burden of high variable
costs in the newspaper business. (A variable cost is one that increases
with each unit of production, as opposed to fixed costs that are expressed in units of time. As circulation increases, the cost of
newsprint, ink, and transportation rises in direct proportion. For an
electronic distribution system, the analogous costs are basically the
same whether a hundred or a million consumers read your content.)

Under the second scenario, newspaper companies would build,
not degrade, their editorial products. And there is a way to profit
from the interrelationship between the old technology and the new.
Tufts University political scientist Russell Neuman hints at it in
"The Future of the Mass Audience." There is a way for newspapers
to preserve at least some of their monopoly power. He calls it the
"upstream strategy." Find another bottleneck further back in the
production process.

Originally, the natural newspaper monopoly was based on the
heavy capital cost of starting a hot-type, letterpress newspaper operation. That high entry cost discouraged competitors from entering
the market. Today, computers and cold type have made entry cost
low, but the tendency toward one daily umbrella paper per market
has continued unabated. That is because the source of the monopoly involves psychological as well as direct economic concerns. In

their efforts to find one another, advertisers and their customers tend to gravitate toward the dominant medium in a market. One meeting place is enough. Neither wants to waste the time or the money exploring multiple information sources. This is why the winner in a competitive market can be decided by something as basic as the amount of classified advertising. One paper becomes the marketplace for real estate or used cars. Display advertisers follow in what, from the viewpoint of the losing publisher, seems a vicious cycle. From the viewpoint of the winner, of course, it is a virtuous cycle.

Neuman's thesis is that the competitive battle across a wide variety of media and delivery systems will make content the new bottleneck. "What is scarce," he says, echoing Herbert A. Simon, "is not the technical means of communication, but rather public attention." Getting that attention depends on content. He cites the victory of VHS over Betamax for home video players. Betamax had superior technology, but the buyers of VHS were attracted by the content because the manufacturer made sure that the video stores had VHS tapes.

How would that principle apply to newspapers? If the argument is correct, the most effective advertising medium is one that is trusted. If, as Hal Jurgensmeyer proposed, we define the newspaper's product not as information so much as influence, then we have an economic justification for editorial quality. The quickest way to gain influence is to become a trusted and reliable provider of information.

TRUST AS THE BOTTLENECK

Trust, in a busy marketplace, lends itself to monopoly. If you find a doctor or a used car dealer that you trust, you'll keep going back without expanding the effort or the risk to seek out alternatives. If Walter Cronkite is the most trusted man in America, there can be only one of him. Cathleen Black, when she headed the Newspaper Association of America, was getting at the same idea when she exhorted her members to capitalize on the existing "brand name" standing of newspapers. Brand identity is a tool for capturing trust.

And newspapers are in a good position to win that role of most trusted medium based on their historic roles in their communities. Under Scenario 2, they would define themselves not by the physical nature of the medium, but by the trust that they have built up. And they would expand that trust by improving services to readers, hiring more skilled writers and reporters, and taking leadership roles in fostering democratic debate.

Which scenario are we moving toward—harvesting the goose, or nurturing it and integrating it with new technology? The signals are mixed. During the new century's first recession, they tilted toward the harvest scenario. Reporters, once secure in their jobs, now hold what Herbert Gans has called "contingent employment." When the *Duluth News-Tribune* discovered it was not meeting the year's profit goals set by parent Knight Ridder, it decided that it could meet its community service responsibilities with eight fewer reporters, and out the door they went. Layoffs, closing bureaus, and shrinking news holes became commonplace.

On the other hand, the public journalism movement represented an effort to build civic spirit in a way that would, if carried out over a long period of time, emotionally bind citizens to the newspaper. Whether very many newspapers will spend the money to wholeheartedly practice genuine public journalism remains to be seen. The harvesting scenario produces visible and immediate rewards while its costs are hidden and distant. The nurturing scenario yields immediate costs and distant benefits.

The dilemma cuts across all media and forms of newspaper ownership, but publicly held companies bear a special burden because of Wall Street's habit of basing value on short-term return. Take the case of Knight Ridder. With total average daily circulation of 4 million, its newspapers would bring a total of $7.2 billion if sold separately at an average value of $1,800 per paying reader. (McClatchy paid the Daniels family more than $2,400 per unit of circulation for

Raleigh's *News & Observer*, but Raleigh is a better than average market.) With 82.3 million shares outstanding at the early 2003 price of $64 per share, the entire company, including its nonnewspaper properties, was valued by its investors at only $5.3 billion, or $1.9 billion less than the break-up value.

How would a successful takeover bidder tap that potential $1.9 billion? By selling the papers to harvest-oriented publishers who would slash costs and build the bottom line with a bare-bones product. And how can public companies avoid such takeovers? One way is to do the harvesting themselves.

That's in the near term. Now stretch your time horizon beyond anything seen by Wall Street and imagine the final stages of the squeeze scenario. A newspaper that depends on customer habit to keep the dollars flowing while it raises prices and gives back progressively less in return has made a decision to liquidate. It is a slow liquidation and is not immediately visible because the asset that is being converted to cash is intangible—what the bean counters call "goodwill."

Goodwill is the organization's standing in its community. More specifically, it is the habit that members of the community have of giving it money. In accounting terms, it is the value of the company over and above its tangible assets such as printing presses, cameras, buildings, trucks, and inventories of paper and ink. I asked two people who appraise newspapers for a living, John Morton of Washington, D.C., a former analyst, and Lee Dirks of Santa Fe, a newspaper broker, to estimate the proportion of a typical newspaper's value represented by goodwill. Both gave the same answer: 80 percent. That leaves only 20 percent for the physical assets.

This is vital intelligence for an entrepreneur interested in entering a market to challenge a fading newspaper. As an existing paper cuts back on its product and its standing in the community falls, there must come an inevitable magic moment when a competitor can move in, start a paper, build new goodwill from scratch, and end up owning a paper at only 20 percent or one-fifth of the cost of buying one.

Such a scenario is overly simplified, of course. The entry of competition could be just what it takes to get the existing paper to switch to a Scenario 2 strategy. But the newcomer would have a tremendous advantage, and that is its lower capitalization. Because its outlay is only the cost of the physical plant, one-fifth the value of the existing paper, the challenger can get the same return on investment with a 6 percent margin that the old paper's owners get with a 30 percent margin. Voilà! A happy publisher with a 6 percent margin! Because this publisher is building goodwill from scratch, he or she can cheerfully pour money into the editorial product, expand circulation, create new bureaus, heavy up the news hole, and do the polling and special public interest investigations that define public journalism.

This dream is not so wild. Remember Al Neuharth. One of the factors that propelled him to the top at Gannett was his astuteness in recognizing a parallel situation in east central Florida. Rapid population growth stimulated by space exploration had created a community that needed its own newspaper. He founded *Florida Today* for significantly less than the cost of buying an existing paper. The only obstacle is finding the right time and place — plus an opposition that is greedy and either shortsighted or slow-footed enough to continue squeezing out the old margins in the face of a challenge.

To old newspaper hands, the prospect of battles between the newspaper squeezers and the newspaper nurturers has a definite charm. Some of us old enough to remember the fun of working in competitive markets would line up to work for the nurturer against the squeezer. But the threat to companies that are liquidating their goodwill might come from another direction. It might not come from other newspaper companies at all.

The race to be the entity that becomes the institutional Walter Cronkite in any given market will not be confined to the suppliers of a particular delivery technology. How the information is moved —

copper wire, cable, fiberglass, microwave, a boy on a bicycle—will not be nearly as important as the reputation of the creators of the content. Earning that reputation may require the creativity and the courage to try radical new techniques in the gathering, analysis, and presentation of news. It might require a radically different definition of the news provider's relationship to the community, as well as to First Amendment responsibilities.

It is fashionable to blame Wall Street for the bind in which newspaper companies find themselves. However, not all investors and analysts have a narrow, short-term orientation. Analyst O'Donnell, writing more than two decades ago, observed that quality journalism "can be expensive, but it helps a paper build an image that attracts talented employees both in news and other departments. We have spoken to employees in press rooms, for example, who take great pride in working on a newspaper that wins national awards . . . the perceived 'quality' of a paper can be a critical factor in morale and is not to be underestimated . . . readers' perceptions of the value of the product are substantially related to the quality of the news coverage."

Analysts and investors make their money by spotting trends and taking investment positions in them before their competitors do. If journalistic quality is to have value on Wall Street, we will have to make the case that it is a leading indicator of profitability. If it is, savvy investors will find out eventually. The free market makes it inevitable. But the market sometimes takes a very long time to work its will, and we should not expect existing newspaper organizations to help very much. Their inherent conservatism, a consequence of their easy-money history, places them at a disadvantage in attempts at innovation. The pressures to harvest their market position by squeezing out the historic margins in the short term have made them inflexible. But if influence is the product, sooner or later some business entity will find a way to package and sell it, and the castle that it builds on its rock will shelter the best and the brightest creators of content.

RACHEL SMOLKIN

Tribune Company:
Synergy's Broken Promise

Behind Tribune Company's plan in purchasing the Los Angeles Times and its holdings was the idea that synergy, the buzzword of the era, and a big national advertising footprint would lead to strong returns for investors. It became clear within a few years that the plan would not work. Rachel Smolkin addressed the issue.

Howard Schneider resigned as *Newsday's* editor two years ago, but he hasn't lost his zest for a story. Forty minutes into an expansive interview about the Tribune Company and its "synergy" strategy, he gets excited. "To me that's the lead," he tells me, "that Tribune did have the answer, I can't say The Answer, but certainly directionally had the answer and had the assets and a vision of sorts, but for all the reasons we've discussed—a flawed business plan, lack of execution, a failure to invest, lack of will and lack of staying power—they didn't see this out."

Tribune's 2000 purchase of Times Mirror, including *Newsday*, the *Los Angeles Times*, the *Hartford Courant*, and the *Baltimore Sun*, gave it both newspapers and television stations in the top three markets of Chicago, Los Angeles, and New York. Tribune executives touted the tantalizing possibilities of synergy, the notion that cooperation between TV and newspapers in these markets and others would reap editorial, promotional, and advertising windfalls. Tribune's leaders envisioned these regional media powerhouses forming a cross-country chain that would compete for lucrative national advertisers as well.

The day after the acquisition announcement, the *Boston Globe* quoted Tribune's then-chairman and CEO, John W. Madigan, as proclaiming the creation of "the premier multimedia company in America." In the *Courant*, Madigan said his company's "presence will be defined by taking what are essentially local market media companies, and putting them together into a major, national footprint." One year later, delivering the keynote address at the Bear Stearns Media, Entertainment and Information Conference, Madigan called the Times Mirror acquisition a "fabulous opportunity," and asserted: "It is no different than the AOL/Time Warner merger, except that it's not as large!"

AJR shared the optimism of Tribune's executives; its May 2000 story "Tribune's Big Deal" examined the Chicago-based company's ambitions to distribute its content via print, TV, Internet, and radio, and discussed its desire to "create a network of regional media hubs in Los Angeles, Chicago, and New York that will be irresistible to national advertisers." The story observed, "Sounds like the Tribune Company 'got it' far earlier than most."

But Tribune's exhilarating hopes have gone largely unfulfilled. Despite faithful cross-promotion across platforms and some—albeit often grudging—cooperation among its properties, the synergies have not materialized as expected, nor has the predicted national footprint. The reasons for the underwhelming results are complex, driven in part by bad timing, bad luck, and a bad newspaper economy. Innovative but misguided business assumptions complicated Tribune's strategy, as did the melding of two very different cultures, relentless cost-cutting, and friction over centralized versus local control of Tribune operations.

Six and a half years after Tribune unveiled its purchase of Times Mirror to great fanfare, the company must decide whether to stick with synergy, redefine it, or abandon it. Tribune's stock, which closed at $37 on the last trading day before the acquisition announcement, peaked at $53 in early 2004, then plunged to almost half that by April 2006.

After a blistering outburst about the depressed stock price by the Chandler family of Los Angeles—the same Chandlers who sold Times Mirror to Tribune for $8.3 billion—Tribune's board took action. A special committee of seven independent directors is overseeing management's exploration of what to do next, which could include unloading the company; selling some or all of Tribune's 25 TV stations, its 11 daily newspapers, or the Chicago Cubs; or taking the company private. If the TV stations go, the synergy strategy, at least as it was envisioned in 2000, will disappear along with them.

That vision was at the heart of the Chandlers' complaint. The Chandlers, who became Tribune's largest shareholders after a $2 billion stock buyback in June that they opposed, also occupy three of 11 seats on the board. In a June 13 letter, board director William Stinehart, Jr., one of the Chandler trustees, wrote that the "basic strategic premise of the Tribune/Times Mirror merger was that the cross-ownership of multiple premium major media properties in the nation's three largest media outlets would provide a platform to produce above-industry performance for both its newspaper and broadcast assets and for strong growth in interactive and other media opportunities. This strategy has failed."

Contacted for comment on this article at his law offices in Los Angeles, Stinehart said, "I don't speak to the press," and hung up. The day after the acquisition announcement, the *New York Times* quoted Thomas Unterman, the former chief financial officer of Times Mirror and an adviser to the Chandler family trusts, as saying the profit potential of the joint TV and newspaper cities was "what caught the Chandler family's interest."

Tribune executives had planned to prune Times Mirror newspaper operations perceived as flabby at the time of the merger. But the cost-cutting did not abate after that initial tightening. In 2005, Tribune eliminated 900 jobs—about 4 percent of its workforce—mostly on the publishing side. In its May 2006 stock buyback announcement, the company said it would make cuts worth $200 million over the next two years. Scott Smith, Tribune's president of publishing, told the *New York Times* that $40 million of that would come from newspapers. John S. Carroll, whom Tribune recruited to take over the beleaguered *Los Angeles Times* after the acquisition, left the paper in August 2005 in large part because of unyielding pressures to cut costs. "It seemed to me that there were three pillars on which the acquisition rested," the former *Times* editor says. "Number one, the so-called 'synergy' of owning multiple media outlets in each city; number two, the hope of cashing in on the very large market for national print advertising; the third was cost-cutting. The first two failed. So we've put the whole load on the cost-cutters, and the result has been a ravaging of the Times Mirror newspapers." His blunt assessment came a month before his successor, Dean Baquet, was ousted from the *Times* for his very public refusal to enact further newsroom cuts.

Carroll says the underlying assumptions of the merger "probably weren't a very good idea to begin with, but, in fairness, the company was very unlucky in its timing. With the dotcom collapse right at the time of its purchase, they were operating with a heavy handicap."

The staggering challenges Tribune is confronting are by no means unique within the industry. Knight Ridder is kaput after shareholder pressure forced the company to sell its papers earlier this year. Ad revenues have been stagnant; competition from the Internet is mounting; and circulation is falling. Particularly hard hit have been newspapers in large cities—the backbone of Tribune's synergy strategy. In the six-month period ending in September, the *Los Angeles Times*' daily circulation dropped 8 percent, from 843,432 in 2005 to 775,766 this year. *Newsday*'s fell 4.9 percent, from 431,957 to 410,579.

The TV stations have fared no better, hammered by factors including a new method of measuring audience. In Los Angeles, KTLA garnered an average 204,000 viewers a day during sweeps periods in the first 10 months of 2001; the same period in 2006 netted only 102,000, according to Nielsen Media Research. In New York, WPIX's average viewership dropped to 167,000 from 316,000.

The company also has been battered by difficult circumstances unique to Tribune. Its gamble that the Federal Communications Commission would lift rules barring cross-ownership of newspapers and television stations in the same market has been stymied, first in the courts and then by a bureaucracy slow to issue new rules, creating uncertainty around synergy's core.

Tribune's optimism that it could prevail in an inherited tax dispute between Times Mirror and the Internal Revenue Service proved unfounded; the company is appealing a billion-dollar tax bill in that case.

Tribune also had to set aside $90 million to repay advertisers after revelations of circulation fraud at *Newsday* and *Hoy*, its Spanish-language sister publication, between 2000 and 2004. Nine people, including seven former executives, have pleaded guilty in connection with the scandal, which inflated *Newsday*'s circulation by about 100,000 copies and doubled *Hoy*'s sales. "What we didn't anticipate was revenue falling off so significantly, and we did not anticipate a fraud at *Newsday*," says Jack Fuller, a former president of Tribune Publishing and a pivotal figure in the acquisition. "We bought it, and then the Internet bubble burst, and then the whole industry suffered." Fuller says the circulation scandal at *Newsday* "distracted everybody. It took a lot of energy and time thinking about that subject. It cost a lot to settle with the advertisers who had been lied to. It meant that *Newsday* was a considerably smaller newspaper, had a considerably smaller circulation than it was assumed to."

In an e-mail exchange after we spoke, Fuller added that the anticipated synergies between newspapers and TV were not the biggest factor in the company's expectations for positive financial results early on. In "modeling what we expected from the transaction, the cross-media synergies were considerably smaller than cost savings we anticipated we could get from the *L.A. Times* (and did get, more quickly than we expected). These did not involve editorial, by the way," he wrote. "We also anticipated more than we were able to achieve in national advertising as a result of being able to sell across the top three metropolitan markets in the country (N.Y., L.A., Chicago)."

Tribune denied my requests for interviews with the company's current leaders. In an October 17 e-mail, Tribune spokesman Gary Weitman cited various factors for turning down the requests, including "disclosure problems, strategic review under way, quiet period with earnings on Thursday, and scheduling issues."

Instead, Weitman later offered a short statement, which did not answer the questions I had posed but said in part: "We believe that owning newspapers and television stations in the same market gives Tribune an edge over its peers, especially as it relates to news coverage and promotion." It didn't mention advertising there but did in the next sentence in connection with the Internet: "In addition, the benefits of our newspapers and, increasingly, our TV stations cooperating with our Interactive division are very significant from a news content and advertising standpoint."

Tribune Chairman and CEO Dennis FitzSimons was asked about synergy at an October 24 off-the-record employee meeting at *Newsday*. He "totally backed away," a staffer recounts, replying that he wasn't CEO at the time of the merger (he was then Tribune's executive vice president and president of Tribune Broadcasting), and that each property has to do what makes sense for it. "The energy on synergy, the excitement and enthusiasm about synergy just wasn't there," the staffer says. Another staffer recalls FitzSimons saying that if Tribune forced synergy, properties might comply but engage in "malicious obedience" and allow it to fail. "The fact that the synergy strategy so far has not proven out is no reflection whatsoever on the people who adopted it," says Robert Torray, president and chairman of the Maryland-based investment management firm Torray LLC, which owns more than 2 million shares of Tribune. Torray, who says he's close to FitzSimons, adds: "Things have changed a lot. The media business has been weak. Television has been weak. Radio has been weak. These are things that were completely unforeseeable. I think it's just one of those—we're in a transition period that could not have been foreseen five, six years ago."

Hindsight is always clearer than foresight, and the Tribune Company was unquestionably star-crossed in the timing of the acquisition. But some of the more than 35 journalists, analysts, and advertising experts interviewed by AJR raised questions about the fundamental business plan guiding the acquisition. The strategy of enticing advertisers with a Los Angeles–Chicago–New York model may have rested on a flawed assumption: Newsday is located in Long Island, not Manhattan, and has the bulk of its circulation and resources there.

Anthony Marro, who preceded Schneider as Newsday's editor, respected Fuller and was pleased at the prospect of Tribune ownership. He'd increasingly felt that the Chandlers—with the exception of the legendary L.A. Times publisher Otis Chandler—weren't committed to the newspaper business. His publisher, Raymond Jansen, wasn't hostile to the transaction either, but he was dubious that the sales strategy would work. "He told other people at Newsday that he was skeptical that they could generate additional revenue from selling in those three markets," Marro says. "I know that he was very skeptical of it right from the start. . . . His feeling was in the case of Newsday that it got all of its national advertising not because it was in New York, but because it wasn't in New York." (Jansen declined to comment for this article.)

The three-market strategy had additional problems. Rishad Tobaccowala, chief innovation officer for Publicis Groupe Media, one of the world's largest marketing and ad agencies, says that advertisers look for local, regional, or national opportunities to target particular audiences. "There's no one who says, 'I happen to have the top three markets as my market,'" he says. Tribune "can't get national advertising because they don't really have a national footprint. They just have three or four key markets. . . . What am I buying if I put the three newspapers together? What am I buying special? Nothing."

Tobaccowala, who is also CEO of Denuo, a Chicago-based Publicis consultancy for emerging technologies, doesn't think Tribune executives talked enough to marketers and advertisers before the acquisition, or if they did, they didn't ask the right questions. "I think they were very insular. The hope was if they supplied it, there would be demand. . . . This is an idea that probably made sense for 4 or 5 percent of the market, but it probably didn't make sense for 95 percent of the market," he says. "I don't know if anybody actually paid attention to the market. In hindsight, I'm wondering what the hell they were thinking."

Bob Shamberg is CEO of Newspaper Services of America, a Chicago-based company that places print ads for retailers such as Home Depot, Safeway, Sears, BMW, and Qwest Communications. "Larger advertisers aren't looking for one buy, one bill," he says. "They're looking at, 'Who's going to reach my target audience most effectively?'" Like Tobaccowala, Shamberg says advertisers need a compelling reason to opt for a package instead of making the best individual media buys they can. "Based on the fact that it doesn't appear that they have struck too many deals, they clearly did not come up with a sufficient incentive to sell the package."

In September 2005, a Deutsche Bank report explored strategic options that might brighten Tribune's performance on Wall Street, including buying Knight Ridder. "While some of Tribune's woes are event-specific (e.g., the *Newsday* circulation scandal) or partially out of Tribune's control . . . we believe that the market has grown increasingly skeptical of Tribune's overall strategy of owning both TV

and newspaper in top 30 markets," said the analysis by Paul Ginocchio, David T. Clark, and Matthew Chesler.

"In our view, the Top 30 market focus makes sense. . . . We are
far less convinced on the TV/newspaper dual ownership and convergence front. As several top-level newspaper executives (including
a respected CEO) have told us, 'the jury is still out on convergence.'
While convergence may be working in Tampa for Media General,
the benefits in other co-ownership markets is ambiguous at best. We
(and seemingly the market) are unsure that Tribune newspapers
gain much from the company's ownership of TV stations."

What advertising synergies did materialize tended to benefit the
TV stations. Bob Gremillion oversees Tribune's southern Florida assets, the *South Florida Sun-Sentinel* and WSFL-TV. In addition to
enthusiastic cross-promotion between the two properties, newspaper
sales managers or account representatives often bring a TV sales rep
on calls to introduce them to clients. Newspapers more often deal
directly with clients, whereas TV stations typically have to work
through advertising agencies.

"The newspaper actually helps the TV station with client access,
client contact, and is responsible for a fair amount of revenue that
goes to the TV station," Gremillion says. "It doesn't work in reverse
very much because newspapers have all the clients that want to be
in the newspaper."

South Florida was not part of the Times Mirror acquisition, but
Vinnie Malcolm, vice president and general manager of KTLA in
Los Angeles, echoes Gremillion's observations. Malcolm says joint
sales calls between his team and the *L.A. Times'* peaked about a year
ago, but it's "much harder to move the needle" in adding advertisers
to the newspaper because the *Times* already dominates its market.
"Our [advertising] base is smaller on the broadcast side."

Edward Atorino, a media analyst at the New York–based brokerage firm Benchmark Company, says that Tribune's strategy has
yielded some benefits on the Web, but in terms of the synergies between KTLA and the *Times*, or WPIX and *Newsday*, "the success has

been minimal. They simply haven't had much synergy." He adds that in Chicago, where the company owns the *Chicago Tribune*, the Cubs, WGN-TV, WGN radio, and the news cable channel CLTV, it's "a different story. They dominate Chicago media, and synergy is very effective."

Atorino isn't sure whether problems replicating that success have stemmed from fragmented large markets, or the execution of strategy, or geography: *Newsday* is in Long Island and WPIX is in Manhattan; KTLA is in Hollywood and the *Times* is in downtown L.A. "Dennis FitzSimons didn't buy Times Mirror; John Madigan did," he notes. "Dennis took over, and the bottom was already falling out of the bag, so to speak. . . . You can't blame top management because there was a crook down in *Newsday*." From the beginning, Tribune executives faced an uphill battle in marrying two very different newspaper company cultures—a vital component for successful synergy. Some former Times Mirror editors chafed at the notion that they should use other outlets' stories or work with their sister newspapers and television stations. On many fronts, Tribune executives initially responded by adopting an evolutionary approach, urging cooperation rather than ordering it.

"It would have been, I suppose, much easier to command that we were going to collapse foreign bureaus and collapse Washington bureaus and so forth, but that's not what we did," says Gerould Kern, vice president of editorial for Tribune Publishing, who has urged all the papers to share content and work together. "We've had tremendous positives come out of that. Every newspaper has a richer vein of journalism to draw on than it did before."

The measured approach frustrated *Newsday*'s Schneider, who embraced Tribune's strategic vision of trying to add value across its media platforms as the proper path in a transformative media environment. "In New York, where *Newsday* and WPIX were the major assets, the execution was based on a very evolutionary philosophy. We were aggressive on promotions but slow on the editorial side," he says. "We should have been more aggressive on working together."

When synergy did not net the anticipated successes on the business side, Schneider felt the company lost its focus. "There was fuzziness about the mission editorially, a go-slow philosophy, and the failure to recognize that there would be some additional resources needed," he says. "It was not only a way to reduce resources."

Even Chicago, generally touted as a synergy success story, disappointed Schneider. Although he was impressed by the vigorous cross-promotion among media outlets there, "I didn't see any breakthrough kinds of work across all those areas."

James O'Shea, the former managing editor of the *Chicago Tribune* who succeeded Baquet as *Los Angeles Times* editor in early November, says there are problems, albeit surmountable ones, with cross-platform cooperation. "There's a clash of cultures that I think people tend to underestimate," he says. "We're a very competitive group of people." In addition, television stations tend to favor faster, flashier fare—what O'Shea calls the "bang-bang stories"—than their print counterparts. He recalls that a joint project with WGN about potholes in Chicago did work well, but only because of a special effort by both partners. O'Shea says cooperation was further hampered by the fact that not all the editors "were on the same page, particularly John Carroll. I don't say this as 'It's his fault.' I think he had a genuine philosophical difference of the prevailing view of synergy, of how these things would work together." But O'Shea adds, "When you had the biggest paper in the group saying they didn't want to play, that was a major impediment to making the whole thing work."

Carroll says he never heard "synergy" defined very precisely and isn't exactly sure what it is. But whatever it is, he's not a fan.

Take the Times' spasmodic efforts to cooperate with KTLA. "We were being exhorted to work with KTLA, and we did a few things, but if you looked at KTLA, it didn't have much in common with the *Los Angeles Times*," Carroll says. "One Sunday there was a very slick advertising brochure about KTLA distributed in the Sunday paper, and it had profiles of their journalists, some of whom were exceedingly good-looking. One of the first pieces of information they had about the journalists was their sign of the zodiac. I thought, 'How in the world do you blend this with *Los Angles Times* journalism?'"

He adds tartly, "I suppose we would have been good synergists if we had started listing the zodiac signs of our reporters."

Carroll, who had been editor of the *Baltimore Sun* before taking over the *Times,* resisted what he viewed as pressure to "blur the provenance" of stories from sister papers by publishing it in the *Times* and labeling it as though it were staff copy. He also strongly believed that the *Times,* as one of the nation's premier papers, should be almost exclusively staff-written. "At one point, a very high-ranking person told me that people at one of the other papers were having morale problems because we didn't publish their stories," he recounts. His reply: "I can't take responsibility for morale problems at any paper other than my own."

Carroll, now the Knight Visiting Lecturer at the Joan Shorenstein Center on the Press, Politics and Public Policy at Harvard University, was equally obstreperous about Tribune's efforts at a group-wide launch of "Your Money," a Sunday section produced by the *Chicago Tribune's* business news department that offers user-friendly financial stories and tips.

No one directly asked Carroll to publish the new section. Instead, the request was put through the *Times'* business editor, who took it to him. But Carroll says he later learned his decision to forgo the section was "considered extremely bad form." He adds: "The section turned out to be lousy. It was an embarrassment to all the papers that ran it. I've heard from their editors, from a number of editors, about how chagrined they were to have it in their Sunday papers." Kern considers the section a success that tapped into the publishing group's talent and gave many papers a new resource. "It has helped with advertising as well. The banking and investment sector of advertising was doing quite well for us, and this became a channel that was attractive to those advertisers. What's lost in that? I think there's a lot that was gained."

He says the section expands and contracts in each market depending on advertising; some newspapers run four or five pages, others only a few. The *South Florida Sun-Sentinel* in Fort Lauderdale uses portions of the package. "We haven't done this thing wholesale throughout our newspapers," Kern says. "I completely understand that local origination is really important if you've got the resources to do it."

Kern also oversaw the company's relocation of all its Washington bureaus into one space in late 2005. The combined center is an architectural triumph that preserves each bureau's individual identity and privacy while also offering shared spaces. Among those is a joint news desk, alternatively described to me as the "control room of the Starship Enterprise" and an "avant-garde martini bar," where editors gather two or three times each day. Journalists' initial fears that Tribune would simply toss everyone into one common area never materialized. One of the company's goals for the relocation was to reduce duplication of "routine" stories. Kern compared the first six months of this year with 2003 and concluded that duplication has been cut in half, while the level of content-sharing in the newspaper group has gone up 50 percent.

But those efficiencies have come at a steep price for a group of papers with a tradition of outsized ambitions in their national and foreign coverage. While the *L.A. Times* and *Chicago Tribune* each absorbed about a 10 percent reduction before the move, the midsize and smaller papers were hit much harder. *Newsday's* renowned Washington bureau dropped from 14 people to six; the *Hartford Courant's* fell from five to one. After *Baltimore Sun* editor Tim Franklin objected, his bureau dropped from 10 to seven—an even larger cut had been considered.

Rafael Lorente, a former Washington correspondent for the *Sun-Sentinel* who left in July 2005 to join the University of Maryland's Philip Merrill College of Journalism as a visiting professor, says the cuts confirmed everyone's fears about synergy. "Everybody was always afraid that it was about budget cuts, and they told us it wasn't, but everybody was afraid it was, and that's what it turned out to be about." He adds that journalists in the Washington bureau generally get along well. "Had synergy been about cooperation, you probably could have gotten something decent out of it."

Lorente says the cuts shortchange the rich, community-based reporting that each correspondent delivers for his or her own newspaper. He had carved out a niche with his Haiti and Cuba coverage, cultivating national security sources and breaking a nationally important story about President Bush's Cuba commission in 2004. "L.A. is never going to care about Haiti the way Fort Lauderdale does, and I can't blame them," Lorente says. "The 'little papers' went out of their way to do things that were sort of value-added, to do stuff that the big papers might overlook, and it didn't do them any good."

After a much-remarked-upon period of friction between the *L.A. Times* and the *Chicago Tribune*, the two papers have established a partnership that will become increasingly visible next year if the Tribune Company, or at least its publishing group, remains substantially intact. "In the coming year, we're going to start a much more coordinated way of covering foreign and national news," Kern says. "The headline is L.A. and Chicago are going to form the basis for daily coverage for the network of foreign bureaus, and everyone is free to do enterprise." He describes 2007 as a transition year and says he hopes the new setup will improve foreign coverage by giving papers more flexibility.

Two Tribune papers, the *Chicago Tribune* and the *Sun-Sentinel*, have Cuba correspondents. Kern says the company is still developing the right strategy for its Cuba coverage; he expects to keep the status quo for now.

Newsday, which has garnered more Pulitzer Prizes for international reporting than either L.A. or Chicago, is planning to phase out its bureaus in Beirut and Islamabad, the last outposts of a proud legacy. The *Baltimore Sun* is losing its remaining foreign bureaus in Moscow and Johannesburg. Its correspondent in Jerusalem will become part of the Tribune network, most likely reporting to Chicago or Los Angeles rather than Baltimore.

"Honestly, it's been painful," Franklin concedes. "The *Sun* has a rich tradition of foreign correspondents going back 120 years. The bureaus have been a source of pride for the newspaper." He says the *Sun* remains committed to international reporting, but it will be largely project-focused.

O'Shea says journalistic synergy freed his reporters at the *Chicago Tribune* from writing some routine process stories, enabling them to focus more on projects such as Cam Simpson's 2005 series "Pipeline to Peril," which exposed how some subcontractors deceived and coerced foreigners into working on U.S. bases in Iraq. The series won the George Polk Award for International Reporting. But it's hard to replace the depth of knowledge and unique perspective that each paper's overseas correspondent can offer, as *Newsday*'s Mohamad Bazzi demonstrated so deftly during the Israel-Lebanon crisis, and the *Tribune*'s two correspondents in Cuba have illustrated with their reporting on a secretive regime.

Deborah Nelson, the former investigations editor at the *L.A. Times*' Washington bureau, thinks the *Tribune*'s move toward consolidating its foreign and national coverage is a "really bad idea," but "they've been able to slip it in." Nelson, who left the *Times* this summer to join the Philip Merrill College of Journalism full time, calls the Washington setup "just one baby step away from a monolithic bureau" and cites the blurring of bylines and efforts at coordinating news coverage as further examples of "baby steps" toward a single news report. "By doing it so slowly," she says, "it can happen, and one day it's too late to stop it."

The cuts in Washington and in the *Tribune*'s foreign bureaus are a small but potent symbol of company-wide tightening. The *L.A. Times* had 5,300 employees when Tribune took over; the staff now hovers at about 2,800. Although the newsroom was not hit nearly as hard as other departments, the editorial staff fell from about 1,200 to 940.

In a mesmerizing eruption of internal tensions, *Times* publisher Jeffrey M. Johnson was forced out October 5, three weeks after he and Baquet publicly rebuffed their bosses' orders for more cuts. "Newspapers can't cut their way into the future," Johnson told his paper. "We have to carefully balance economic realities with serving our readers."

While anxious journalists have focused on the struggles over staff cuts and the autonomy of each paper's news operation, a related issue is playing out behind the scenes, one that could have major ramifications for the company's synergy strategy moving forward.

Joel Sappell, executive editor of L.A. Times Interactive and an assistant managing editor for the print edition, says the company is confronting a mixture of Web issues that raise fundamental questions about centralized versus local control and where the appropriate middle ground should be.

"As much as you see cutting at the newspaper, I've seen an equally controversial issue on the Web side of Tribune, another level that's equally roiling," he says. "While the newspapers are experiencing these pangs of centralization, so are the Web sites. . . . It's the other story at Tribune right now, and it's a very, very high-stakes one. There's a sense of urgency mixed with desperation mixed with uncertainty that doesn't always make for easy decision-making." In the Chandlers' scathing June letter, their disdain for the Tribune Company's Internet strategy was unsparing, citing "a history of cost-cutting and retrenchment in these areas, its failure to purchase and invest in such businesses at the pace of comparable companies with more successful interactive businesses and its decision to limit local interactive growth initiatives at the newspapers in favor of a 'one size fits all' corporate approach."

The statement Tribune provided for this article listed five bullet points for Tribune Interactive "growth strategies." Among them was: "Provide national advertisers with a single point of entry and consistent ad placements across our network, enabling them to reach extremely targeted or broad national audiences." Another was:

"Improve our technology to provide users with the highest-quality news and information, including video and user-generated content, on a platform that allows to [sic] quickly roll out new features and functionality across our sites."

Metromix, Tribune's entertainment Web site that debuted in Chicago, has expanded into Baltimore and Orlando, and Tribune executives want to bring it to other markets as well.

"Wow, have you seen that new Web site with the edgier-than-thou 'tude?!" *Sun* columnist Laura Vozzella wrote sardonically in November 2005. "Baltimore.metromix has a take on Charm City that out-alternatives the alternative weekly. . . . But here's the real shocker: This rebellion is brought to you by Tribune Company, the *Sun*'s corporate parent. (And I mean that in the most corporate and parental sense of those words.)" She added that like similar sites linked to other Tribune markets, baltimore.metromix will be directed by an "executive producer"—based in L.A.

A Metromix expansion that creates consistent, targeted content would be attractive to advertisers, says Jeff Marshall, senior vice president and managing director of Starcom IP, a digital marketing group owned by Publicis. "If they can replicate this all across the different markets, they have the ability to capitalize on local advertising and national advertising. Right now it's mostly local." Marshall spoke with Tribune sales staff over the summer about the idea. "They said they've been talking about that and working on it," he recalls. "We talked about Metromix as a brand: Is that the right brand, or should it be a different brand?"

Tribune also is pressing forward with the Gen3 Project, a company-wide initiative to develop standardized templates for all of its newspaper Web sites. Individual papers could choose from an array of models. News of Yankees pitcher Cory Lidle smashing his plane into a Manhattan high-rise might have received a banner headline and a large photo on Newsday.com and more understated treatment on latimes.com.

Sappell describes Gen3 as "controversial among some editors in the constellation of Tribune sites" because of the difficulty in bal-

ancing the company's wish to create efficiencies with individual papers' desire to craft unique Web sites that appeal to local readers. But
he does see potential for the standardized system to free local Web
designers to focus on more creative initiatives. "This is not being
done through fiat," Sappell says. "There is participation by all the
Tribune Web sites on this . . . but ultimately the decision has been
made, and we're participating in a made decision."

L.A. *Times* leaders wanted to expand two features on their Web
site, but were frustrated by delays in securing cooperation from
Chicago to move forward, according to three sources familiar with
the discussions. The first piece, a destinations section, would focus
on vacation spots popular with southern California travelers, including Mexico, Hawaii, and San Francisco, and would allow readers to
place airline or hotel reservations. The second feature, a Calendar
section, was envisioned as the premier listings service in Southern
California, an interactive space for neighborhood goings-on.

"The controversy has kept us from being able to develop either
up to now," a *Times* executive said in October, adding that the fight
over the Web initiatives contributed to the tension that led to Johnson's removal. Eventually, a deal was brokered under orders from
Tribune Publishing president Scott Smith and Tribune Interactive
president Timothy Landon, who were acting with FitzSimons' support. The *Times* dispatched three product developers to Chicago for
the summer to assist with projects that were a higher priority for Tribune Interactive before getting the go-ahead for its dual Web initiatives, first destinations and then Calendar, sources said.

Asked about launching a local version of Metromix, Sappell said
in October that the site was being developed for Los Angeles, and
"then the question is how Calendar and Metromix coexist. The answer is supposed to be that Metromix would appeal to a younger
reader. But obviously there's a lot of concern among everybody on
the Chicago side and the Los Angeles side about how these two can
coexist."

Sappell also is working with KTLA to provide local breaking
news video on both the station's site and latimes.com. In October,

he said he soon planned to launch two daily two-minute newscasts produced by KTLA's staff for latimes.com as well as "commuter-casts" offering traffic updates during the evening rush hour.

Early next year, he expects to expand his Web site's video coverage of live events. Each day, the *Times* will work with KTLA to identify breaking news stories that can be streamed live onto both the newspaper and television station Web sites. The *Times* will subsidize KTLA's costs to deliver the video streams, and the two properties will share revenues.

When Tribune advanced the notion that it should be able to package "content" in different ways and across different mediums, it plunged into the vanguard of a philosophy that is only now taking hold industry-wide. Newspaper companies have finally accepted that an era of transformation is upon them and that to survive they must find new outlets for disseminating their news and "brand."

John Morton, a newspaper analyst and *AJR* columnist, says that synergy hasn't brought the benefits that Tribune anticipated, and he doesn't think that it will until the advertising environment brightens and the rules about cross-ownership of TV and newspapers are finalized. But he rejects the notion that synergy is a failure. When I point out that many advertisers apparently aren't interested in the cross-media packages Tribune is selling, he replies, "That's old thinking, though. The [media] companies that are going to do best are going to offer lots of options. There is going to be a convergence of information providers. Whoever owns the most horses in the race is going to be better off in the end."

O'Shea offers this observation about synergy between newspapers and the Internet: "As we evolve into the future, if we don't learn to make that kind of thing work, we're doomed. If we don't figure that out as an industry, I think there's going to be a lot of very, very small newspapers."

Whether Tribune chooses to salvage or sell the company, its turbulent synergy experiment holds important lessons for the rest of an industry struggling to find its place in a new-media world. When should media companies try to lead advertisers toward new ways of buying, and when do innovative sales strategies founder? How much control should a media conglomerate exert over individual properties? When does a centralized Internet strategy make sense as a way to attract national advertisers and increase efficiency, and when does it slow innovation, stifle creativity, and stymie revenue opportunities at the local level? Is there any reason for a newspaper company to own television stations, or do strategic partnerships with outside stations work as well as those within a single company? With more newspapers handing video cameras to staffers, what can TV stations add?

Schneider, now dean of the journalism school at Long Island's Stony Brook University, adds a few questions of his own: Is the primary goal of synergy to drive readers from one platform to another—to cross-promote—or is the true motivation to add value to the journalism, making that company's brand synonymous with quality? Does a company have the nerve to stay focused if it hits a rough patch?

Is it willing to add resources strategically, or is synergy really a euphemism for tamping down ambitions at once-proud papers?

"At its best, I always felt at the heart of this there was something very exciting, very dynamic, very worthwhile," Schneider says. "I think we may have had the right plan. That's the real tragedy. We didn't execute it; we didn't follow through; we didn't have the resources; we didn't have the staying power." He adds: "When newspaper companies go through hard times financially, and they're subject to such pressures from Wall Street, they begin to throw stuff off the ship, and there's a willy-nilly quality about this. They're cutting just to stay afloat. . . . They abandon their strategies prematurely. It's not just a Tribune issue."

(Editor's Note: Chicago real estate developer Sam Zell bought Tribune Company early in 2007 in a complex financial deal.)

NEIL HICKEY

Money! Money! Money!
The Profits-versus-Quality War

Money does indeed make the world go 'round. But what happens when the drive for profits collides with the social responsibilities of institutions that play a role stretching beyond business formulas? In an article that would help define the conflict that cut journalism to its heart, Neil Hickey examined the costs-and-profits tensions in 1998.

Some random testimony from the far-flung precincts of journalism:

"If a story needs a real investment of time and money, we don't do it anymore." The speaker is a forty-something reporter on a mid-size Illinois daily. "In assignment meetings, we dream up 'talker' stories, stuff that will attract attention and get us talked about, tidbits for busy folks who clip items from the paper and stick them on the fridge." He adds ruefully: "Who the hell cares about corruption in city government, anyway, much less dying Bosnians?"

• A prominent network television newsman complains: "Instead of racing out of the newsroom with a camera crew when an important story breaks, we're more likely now to stay at our desks and work the phones, rewrite the wire copy, hire a local crew and a free-lance producer to get pictures at the scene, then dig out some file footage, maps, or still photos for the anchor to talk in front of, or maybe buy some coverage from a video news service like Reuters, AP, or World Television News. If we had our own correspondent and camera covering the story, we'd damned sure get something nobody else had, and be proud of it. But everything now is dollars and cents. When you're worried about how much it's going to cost, and you have to justify your decisions to your bosses, people are less willing to take risks. The journalism that gets on our air just isn't good enough, and it's a damned shame."

• A radio news director laments that his big-city station is cutting its news staff to the bone, virtually eliminating local news, and grabbing national news from a satellite-delivered network feed. "That immediately shows a big gain in cash flow, so the owner can sell the station for a huge profit to one of the big chains, whose owners care nothing about public service to this community. One more journalistic voice is being killed off in the pursuit of profits. It's very sad."

• The editor of a profitable national magazine who's been ordered to reduce his budget 10 percent a year says: "OK, the first year I'll cut stuff I probably should have cut earlier anyway. Next year I'll have to reduce the number of editorial pages in every issue. In the third year, for damned sure, it's got to be people that will have to go: editors, writers, fact-checkers, art department staff. Then I'll hit a wall. Sooner or later I will have so cheapened the product that it will just go out of business. That's simple arithmetic."

A new era has dawned in American journalism. A *New York Times* editor describes its hallmark: "A massively increased sensitivity to all things financial." As competition grows ever more ferocious; as the audience continues to drift away from traditional news sources, both print and television; as the public's confidence in news organizations and news people continues to decline; as mainstream print and TV news outlets purvey more "lifestyle" stories, trivia, scandal, celebrity gossip, sensational crime, sex in high places, and tabloidism at the expense of serious news in a cynical effort to maximize readership and viewership; as editors collude ever more willingly with marketers, promotion "experts," and advertisers, thus ceding a portion of their sacred editorial trust; as editors shrink from tough coverage of major advertisers lest they jeopardize ad revenue; as news holes grow smaller in column inches to cosmeticize the bottom line; as news executives cut muscle and sinew from budgets to satisfy their corporate overseers' demands for higher profit margins each year; as top managers fail to reinvest profits in staff training, investigative reports, salaries, plant, and equipment—then the broadly felt consequence of those factors and many others, collectively, is a diminished and deracinated journalism of a sort that hasn't been seen in this country until now and which, if it persists, will be a fatal erosion of the ancient bond between journalists and the public.

"It's the biggest story in American journalism," says Ray Cave, former managing editor of *Time*. Regrettably, it's also the least reported story in American journalism.

Sandra Mims Rowe, editor of the *Oregonian* of Portland and former president of the American Society of Newspaper Editors, told the ASNE convention in April that reporters "wonder whether their editors have sold out journalistic values for business ones. They long for the inspiration provided by leaders with abiding passion for the gritty world of journalism." She added that in some companies, "the talk has shifted to financial and marketing imperatives to such an extent that journalists have concluded their owners are blindly driven by Wall Street, and unconcerned about the quality of journalism."

In March, *Los Angeles Times* media reporter David Shaw wrote that while newspaper readership has been on the skids for more than thirty years and competition from cable TV news, the Internet, and magazines is on the rise, "stockholders and stock analysts have been demanding newspaper profit margins equal to—and in some cases greater than—those generated in earlier, less turbulent times."

Television's corporate chieftains, says Walter Cronkite, show little understanding of "the responsibilities of being news disseminators." They expect the news departments to generate the same sort of profits that entertainment programs do—an impossible task. The newspaper business isn't much different, he says. "Stockholders in publicly held newspaper chains are expecting returns similar to those they'd get by investing in industrial enterprises."

The "tabloidization" of TV newsmagazines is strictly geared to ratings and profits. "A major tragedy of the moment," Cronkite maintains, is the use TV newsmagazines are making of the valuable prime time they occupy. "Instead of offering tough documentaries and background on the issues that so deeply affect all of us, they're turning those programs into television copies of *Photoplay* magazine." News executives know better, Cronkite says, and are "uncomfortable" with what they're doing. "But they are helpless when top management demands an increase in ratings to protect profits."

News chiefs themselves perceive that the press is perilously compromising quality in pursuit of gain. Nearly half the nation's editorial and business-side executives surveyed in a January *Editor & Publisher* poll think press coverage in general is shallow and inadequate, and fully two-thirds say newspapers concentrate more on personalities than important issues. J. Stewart Bryan III, CEO of Media General, Inc., and publisher of the *Richmond Times-Dispatch*, told *E&P* that serious news is being sacrificed to profits as papers reduce news holes and produce softer stories. Said he: "I don't think we can put the bottom line ahead of our commitment to quality."

Journalistic values haven't completely disappeared, says Kurt Andersen, columnist for *The New Yorker* and former editor of *New York* magazine. "But they've been significantly subordinated to the general ascendancy of market factors, especially the maximizing of short-term profit." Magazine editors, he points out, "are much more explicitly responsible for business success than in the past. I'm not saying it's black and white; some of that has always been there. It was light gray, now it's dark gray."

Even Brenda Starr, the comic strip reporter, has gotten into the act. She lamented: "Sometimes I think newspapers care more about profits than they do about people."

After scores of wide-ranging interviews conducted over several months with editors, reporters, publishers, media analysts, academics, and labor officials, *CJR* concludes that—more so than at any other moment in journalism's history—the news product that lands on newsstands, doorsteps, and television screens is indeed hurt by a heightened, unseemly lust at many companies for ever greater profits. In the service of that ambition, many editors are surrendering part of their birthright to marketers and advertising directors, and making news judgments based on criteria that would have been anathema only a few years ago.

But haven't media barons always wanted to prosper, like any other businessmen? Winston Churchill, an unrepentant Tory, once said: "It is a socialist idea that making profits is a vice; I consider the real vice is making losses." Journalism isn't philanthropy—no profits, no press. Some recent tendencies, however, alter the landscape:

• More Americans than ever are shareholders in public companies of all kinds, and corporate executives, including those at media corporations, are sensitive to the vastly expanded interests of those investors.

• Top managers in media own ever larger piles of stock options—often a heftier source of income than their salaries—and thus have a direct, personal interest in their companies' profit picture. Higher profits mean a higher stock price and a bigger payoff when they cash in their holdings. Says a TV producer: "The more they can squeeze out of their people, the richer they'll be in the end."

• In an age of rampant consolidations and mergers, clamping down on operating costs and budgets—no matter the effect on news coverage—can fatten the bottom line and make a company a more attractive takeover target, with the consequent heavy windfall to major shareholders.

• Bonuses tied to profits tempt both editorial and business-side executives to trim costs, often to the detriment of news processing.

At the University of Iowa, three professors—John Soloski, Gil Cranberg, and Randy Bezanson—are embarked on an eighteen-month project (funded by philanthropist George Soros's Open Society Institute) studying how ownership structures of newspapers are affecting journalistic function; and examining journalists' complaints that their interests and readers' interests are being sacrificed for the interests of shareholders. "Publicly traded media companies are in a vicious circle they can't break out of," says Soloski, director of the university's journalism school. A huge percentage of their stock is owned by institutions—mutual funds, retirement funds, insurance companies—which care little about the quality of the journalism of the companies they invest in. "Those financial institutions are graded weekly, monthly, quarterly on their own performance. So they pass that pressure along—and it's a lot—to those media companies." They in turn pressure their editors and publishers to raise their stock price by whatever means necessary. The land rush to go public in the 1980s and 1990s has had its residual effect: investors and analysts demand the kind of profits that often can be attained by mid-level papers but are tougher for big-city dailies.

In 1990, when Geneva Overholser, editor of the *Des Moines Register*, was named Gannett's "editor of the year," she offered these thoughts in her acceptance speech:

> As we sweat out the end of the ever-increasing quarterly earnings, as we necessarily attend to the needs and wishes of our shareholders and our advertisers, are we worrying enough about . . . our employees, our readers, and our communities?
>
> I'll answer that: no way. . . . We fret over declining readership and then cut our news holes. . . . We fret over a decline in service to our customers, and then pay reporters . . . wages that school districts would be ashamed of. . . . [O]ur communities are crying out for solutions, and newspapers can help—newspapers that are adequately staffed, with adequate news holes. But not newspapers where underpaid people work too hard, and ad stacks squeeze out editorial copy.

Too often by far, being an editor in America today feels like holding up an avalanche of pressure to do away with this piece of excellence, that piece of quality, so as to squeeze out just a little bit more money.

Other signs of the profit-pressure syndrome were apparent three years ago when a dramatic series of shutdowns, layoffs, strikes, and the emotional departures of top editors afflicted the newspaper industry. The Times Mirror Company killed the *Baltimore Evening Sun* and *New York Newsday*. Knight Ridder Inc. slashed 300 full-time jobs at the *Miami Herald* and won major labor concessions in return for keeping the *Philadelphia Daily News* going.

Some of the biggest editors in the business have quit rather than make budget cuts that they felt would devastate editorial. As editor-in-chief of *Reader's Digest*, Ken Tomlinson grew weary of repeated demands to chop editorial costs up to 10 percent annually, year after year. In late 1995, management ordered a company-wide reduction of roughly 25 percent, largely by inducing many edit people to retire. Tomlinson didn't want to be remembered as the editor who carried out this action. So he told CEO Jim Schadt, "I've found a way for you to take a giant step toward your goal. Eliminate my salary." And so Tomlinson retired at fifty-two. (He now raises racehorses in rural Virginia; Schadt's strategy failed to ease the *Digest's* continuing problems, and he later resigned under pressure.)

That same year, James M. Naughton resigned as executive editor of the *Philadelphia Inquirer*. Among his reasons: "unrelenting pressures" on the newsroom. (And talk about pressure: half the respondents in an AP managing editors poll call their jobs "highly stressful." Their median workweek: fifty-two hours.) Last year, Maxwell King said upon resigning as the *Inquirer's* editor: "When I look at big newspaper companies across the board, the question that occurs to me is, 'Are they all too intent on taking profit now and not intent enough on investing in content for the future?'" The paper was under orders from Knight Ridder to ratchet up its profit margin from 8 percent in 1995 to 15 percent last year.

The *L.A. Times'* David Shaw put the problem succinctly:

Today, many newspaper owners insist on high quarterly dividends . . . thus depriving the papers of money that could be invested in improving quality; there is little question that the shift from individual and family ownership to public ownership has increased the demand for higher short-term profits. In order to make their stock attractive to investors, newspaper companies promise higher profits every year (if not every quarter). That sets up unrealistic expectations. . . . When revenues inevitably decline, even temporarily—because of recession, higher newsprint costs or other factors—most publicly held newspapers feel they must still increase profits. So they cut costs—and, ultimately, quality.

Money is one big reason that newsrooms at America's papers have an older and less satisfied workforce than ever before—more graying heads and reading glasses than fresh faces. Forty-four percent are 40 or over, says an ASNE survey. Between 1988 and 1996, the percentage of journalists 30 and under dipped from 29 percent to 20 percent. More journalists than ever are planning to quit the business before retirement age. The most oft-cited reason: money. (Average base pay at papers having 30,000 to 75,000 circulation: $23,000.) But "working conditions" and "stress" are now a close second and third. The number of journalists rating their papers as "excellent" has dropped dramatically, and most think that newspapers will be "a less important part of American life" in ten years' time. Over half of ASNE's sample said their newsroom budget had declined in the previous five years, and 71 percent called it inadequate.

Meanwhile, the revolutionary Telecommunications Act of 1996 set the stage for huge, disruptive changes in broadcasting. Its deregulatory effects and the resultant seismic shift to corporate gigantism has been at the public's expense, especially in the way the nation's information needs are met.

One example: the act removed all limitations on the number of radio stations any one company can own nationally and greatly increased the number a single entity can operate in any single city. That triggered an unprecedented wave of buyouts and consolidations in the radio industry (with 16,000 stations nationwide), which have left listeners with a less-than-nourishing news diet in many places. (CBS, the biggest owner of radio stations, has 155 in its stable.) At many stations, including CBS's flagship in New York, all-news WCBS-AM, anchorpersons and sports reporters routinely read commercials as part of their duties, an activity that seriously blurs the line between journalist and huckster. But it saves stations the cost of hiring an announcer to intone that advertising copy. And with fewer street reporters, writers, and editors than in past years, many stations are reduced to parroting news from the morning's papers.

Local radio and TV news in many cities have indeed suffered "crippling cutbacks as group owners trim staffs to enhance their bottom lines," says Louis C. Adler, former WCBS news chief, now a professor at Connecticut's Quinnipiac College. The agglomerating of radio stations in pursuit of economies of scale by rich corporations has left listeners in many communities with diminished service. In Connecticut, for example, three New Haven stations—WELI, WAVZ, and WKCI—now belong to Texas-based Clear Channels Communications. A second Texas company, SFX Broadcasting, is grabbing WPLR, WTNH-TV, and control of WYBC and WBNE-TV. In the 1970s, at least four locally owned radio stations in New Haven County had street reporters scouring the area for news. Now there's one, WQUN. Thus, says Adler, deregulation in broadcasting benefits "corporations whose allegiance is not to listeners or viewers but to stockholders who demand an ever-increasing return on their investment, a demand satisfied by cutting costs, reducing jobs, and generally sacrificing public service on the altar of greed."

At the major print newsmagazines, *Time* and *Newsweek*, the trend over ten years, 1987–1997, shows a distinct tilt toward more crowd-pleasing cover subjects and away from straight domestic and foreign news—in the effort to snare the interest of impulse buyers at the newsstand and thus boost revenue. (Reporting foreign news is expensive: a U.S. correspondent stationed in pricey posts such as Hong Kong, Paris, or Moscow can easily cost $500,000 a year in pay, perks, and expenses.)

In 1987, *Time* published eleven covers relating to foreign news—and only one in 1997. Its domestic hard-news covers dwindled from twelve to nine. Thus the overall total for straight news covers dipped from about 45 percent of the total ten years ago to only 20 percent last year. Studying the list of *Time's* 1997 cover choices, one sees stories on Ellen DeGeneres, Steven Spielberg, Generation X, the pop singer Jewel, Brad Pitt in a movie about Buddhism, Bill Cosby and the death of his son, plus "What's Cool This Summer," "Turning Fifty" (with a cover photo of Hillary Clinton), "How Mood Drugs Work . . . and Fail," and "The Most Fascinating People in America." *Newsweek* pitched in with 1997 covers on TV cartoon shows, Jon-Benet Ramsey, Bob Dylan, Deepak Chopra, plus "The Young Kennedys: A Dynasty in Decline," "Does It Matter What You Weigh? The Surprising New Facts About Fat," "The Scary Spread of Asthma and How to Protect Your Kids," "Behind the Mask: The Dark World of Andrew Cunanan . . . Versace's Life, Death and Legacy," "Buy? Sell? How to Invest Now," and a "Special Edition" on "Your Child from Birth to Three." Both *Time* and *Newsweek* ran covers on Princess Diana two weeks in a row, giving them the biggest newsstand sales in their histories.

How come all this emphasis on soft news and lifestyle issues? There are at least two reasons, says Norman Pearlstine, editor-in-chief of Time Inc., the nation's most successful magazine publishing company.

First: The economy is thriving, "so there's probably less concern with what has traditionally been the hard news story."

Second: With the collapse of communism and the end of the cold war, "it's not surprising that the country has turned more inward. There's always been a balance between educating your reader and serving your reader, but we're not getting a lot of demand for international coverage these days in broad consumer publications." Addressing a readership the size of *Time*'s (domestic circulation: 4 million), "you obviously balance telling them what you think they ought to read with giving them what they want to read, and that balance has clearly shifted away from international news in the last decade."

Pearlstine recalls that in 1995, his first year at Time Inc., among the magazine's five worst-selling covers were: two on Bosnia, two on Senator Bob Dole, and one on Social Security. (Among the bestsellers: "How Did the Universe Begin?", "Is the Bible Fact or Fiction?", and "Mysteries of the Deep.")

For the recent May 18 issues of *Time* and *Newsweek*, two stories competed for the cover: India's detonation of a nuclear device, and the death of Frank Sinatra. Sinatra won both covers. Ten years ago, says Pearlstine, the decision probably would have gone the other way.

"The great threat today to intelligent coverage of foreign news," Seymour Topping, former managing editor of the *New York Times*, told *CJR*, "is not so much a lack of the public's interest as it is a concentration of ownership that is profit-driven and a lack of inclination to meet responsibilities, except that of the bottom line." In newspapers, foreign news has declined drastically as a percentage of the news hole. In the newsweeklies, Hall's Magazine Editorial Reports found that from 1985 to 1995, space devoted to international news slipped from 24 percent to 14 percent in *Time*, from 22 percent to 12 percent in *Newsweek*, and from 20 percent to 14 percent in *U.S. News & World Report*. The evening TV news programs, according to the Shorenstein Center at Harvard, gave 45 percent of their time to foreign affairs in the 1970s and a mere 13.5 percent in 1995. Result: the public is being drastically shortchanged in its capacity to learn what's going on in the world outside the U.S.'s borders.

Many news executives tiresomely argue that, in the late 1990s, all the research indicates that the public doesn't want to know about the rest of the world; that it's narcissisticly fixated on life at home in the

United States—its economy, celebrities, scandals, fads, and folk-ways. Media companies aim to feed that appetite.

But, says Ray Cave, it's no good to say that people now are not interested in consequential news. "The general public has never been truly interested in it. But we delivered it, like it or not. By so doing, we piqued public interest in the very matters that must, to some degree, interest the citizens of a democracy."

In network television, the audience for evening news broadcasts continues to dwindle. Competition grows fiercer for larger slices of a smaller pizza, and the quality of those broadcasts has suffered as they, too, offer more lifestyle stories and soft news in search of bigger audiences. In 1980, 37.3 percent of tuned-in homes viewed the three network news programs every night; that slid to 24.3 percent in 1996–1997.

The *NBC Nightly News* with Tom Brokaw has been the dominant newscast for almost two years. Staffers at CBS News and ABC News say that's because it has lowered its aim, too often substituting lifestyle and soft features for hard news in a transparent tactic to increase audience, raise advertising rates, and meet the profit expectations of its powerful parent, GE, the nation's most successful conglomerate. NBC News denies the charge.

But the temptation is great in every news medium to sweeten the product for easier consumption. A survey by the Project for Excellence in Journalism of some 4,000 stories on the three network news programs, on newsmagazine covers, and on the front pages of major papers from 1977 to 1997 concludes that celebrity, scandal, gossip, and other "human interest" stories increased from 15 percent to an astonishing 43 percent of the total.

Indeed, an irreversible rot in the hulls of all three of the old-line networks (in entertainment as well as news) has TV executives scurrying for new ways to build viewership and counter the threat of cable, the Internet, pay-per-view, and home satellite services. The ABC and CBS networks are operating in the red, and ratings-leader NBC's profit is melting from $500 million last year to about $100 million. "It's a time of total transition," CBS boss Leslie Moonves told the *New York Times* in May. "It's all ugly."

Ironically, all three networks are looking expectantly to their news divisions to help slow the decay. How? The major networks this fall will air TV newsmagazines six nights a week—up from two in 1983. Why? They're much cheaper than most entertainment shows to put on the air; the networks own them outright, unlike sitcoms and dramas, which they lease from outside producers; and those programs get respectable ratings. NBC's *Dateline* is expanding to five nights a week. ABC is fusing *20/20* and *PrimeTime Live* into a three-times-a-week event. CBS hankers to make *60 Minutes*—its all-time most-successful series—a twice-weekly program.

Those unprecedented schedule shifts will bring more news-and-feature programming to network audiences than ever before, but there's a flaw in the strategy. The soup will be thinner than ever. Reporters, producers, editors, and crews will be stretched over more working hours a week. The pool of story ideas inevitably will become more polluted and noxious for series that already have gone down the low road in search of ratings: e.g., Diane Sawyer's interview with Michael Jackson and former wife Lisa Marie Presley; *Dateline NBC*'s piece on Baywatch babe Pamela Anderson; *PrimeTime Live*'s chat with sometime O. J. Simpson girlfriend Paula Barbieri. *60 Minutes*'s executive producer Don Hewitt firmly opposes expanding his series to other nights, convinced that the program's quality can't possibly be maintained if diluted. But in CBS's no-holds-barred effort to squeeze more juice out of its prize property he'll almost surely be overruled.

Hewitt is fond of saying that *60 Minutes* ruined it for everybody in news, proving as it did that a news program could be a colossal money machine, and perking managers' hopes that comparable riches could be extracted from all news broadcasts. CNN, as well, takes the rap for the broadcast networks' scorched-earth news budget cuts: Ted Turner established his all-news cable channel in a right-to-work state (Georgia), hired all nonunion journalists and staff, paid them far less than the going rates at ABC, CBS, and NBC, and built a hugely successful worldwide news organization. Corporate bosses at the broadcast networks mused: "Why can't we be as lean, mean, and successful as CNN?" They've been trying.

Ever since Mel Karmazin took over as CBS president (and heir apparent to chairman Michael Jordan), drastic fiscal strategies have been bruited in the corridors of the erstwhile Tiffany network, none of them favorable for the news division. The most attention-grabbing: CBS Corp. would sell off its money-losing CBS Television Network—which, essentially, is merely a program supplier to local stations—while retaining its very profitable station division. It consists of eighteen valuable owned-and-operated outlets.

The fate of CBS News in such a deal is shrouded in uncertainty. Traditionally in the television industry, separating a network from its owned stations is a heretical, risky notion. But as Merrill Lynch analyst Jessica Reif Cohen points out, such ancient, entrenched theorems may be ready for the dustbin of history: "New CBS management is very aggressive," she writes, "toppling a variety of broadcast traditions in order to build shareholder value and willing to explore a large number of strategic options."

Indeed, Karmazin, who has no background in news, is the broadcast industry's model hero for cost-cutting schemes. When he arrived at CBS, *60 Minutes* humorist Andy Rooney told the *Minneapolis Star Tribune*: "Nothing good has happened around here for so long I can't imagine [Karmazin's accession] is going to be good. . . . The emphasis is so much more on money than content in every decision that's made that it's discouraging to be here."

Time was when the evening news programs assigned crews to cover (as one veteran puts it) "everything that moved"—every viable news story every day all over the world. The end began with the buyouts and downsizing of the mid-1980s. More and more coverage came from local stations and independent newsfilm services, and at far less expense. That shift allowed the networks to close many bureaus at home and abroad. Frequently sacrificed, though, was the incisive, polished authority that the best TV news correspondents had brought to the reporting of important news.

Even as TV news operations cut budgets and spread their staffs thinner and thinner to the detriment of news coverage, they continue to pay "star" performers princely sums in the conviction that those engaging faces and voices are their last bulwark against even further audience defection. Thus, Rather, Brokaw, Jennings, Sawyer, and Walters each receive compensation in the $7 million a year range for their putative appeal in attracting viewers—a talent that transcends the quality of the programs they inhabit. CNN's Larry King, host of cable's top-rated, celebrity-infested interview program, is also a $7 million-a-year property. "With everything that's included in the deal, I'll be in the same ballpark as the network guys," King said proudly when the contract was signed in May. Said CNN president Tom Johnson: "Larry's ratings were up sharply last year, and he's had a great first quarter. . . ."

That was good news for King, all right, but simultaneously CNN parent Time Warner cut almost a fourth of the staff—70 jobs out of 300—at its Headline News cable channel, thus saving about $2 million but leaving cable news viewers the poorer for it. A few weeks earlier, TW chairman Gerald Levin predicted the company would increase its cash flow by 16 to 18 percent annually for the next few years. The Time Inc. magazines, collectively, are expected to raise their profits by 15 percent a year.

Obsession with ratings is at an all-time high in television news. One former high-level news producer recalls: "When I first joined the network, you'd probably be fired if you talked about ratings in the newsroom. The newspapers didn't even publish ratings at that time. Nobody ever suggested we do a story because it would get ratings. If somebody from the entertainment side or the promotion department came to us and suggested we do a piece about a lesbian coming out in a prime-time sitcom, we would have yelled 'Forget about it!' It's unbelievable how much of that junk gets on the air."

The question (more relevant than ever) for journalists: Is news what the public is interested in or what's in the public interest? Says Reuven Frank, former president of NBC News: "This business of giving people what they want is a dope pusher's argument. News is something people don't know they're interested in until they hear about it. The job of a journalist is to take what's important and make it interesting."

Closing news bureaus at home and abroad has been one of the more conspicuous effects of cost-cutting ever since ABC, CBS, and NBC changed ownership in the mid-1980s. No broadcast network now has a full-fledged bureau (with correspondent, camera crews, and office staff) anywhere in Africa or Latin America; Europe is covered mostly from London, Moscow, and Tel Aviv. (CNN, on the other hand, maintains twenty-three bureaus outside the United States.)

"Roving bands of free-lance cameramen," says veteran TV news producer Av Westin, "shoot coverage at every crisis spot at home and abroad and sell it to networks and local stations." He calls them "the video equivalent of paparazzi." ABC News closed its San Francisco bureau in April, around the time the news division reportedly was figuring out how to comply with a ukase from parent Disney to cut between $25 million and $50 million from its $625 million budget.

Hour-long, single-subject documentaries on key issues virtually disappeared from broadcast networks years ago—illustrious series such as *CBS Reports, NBC White Paper*, and *ABC Close-Up*. Those programs had been the news divisions' crown jewels. (But occasionally TV news surprises, with a spurt of its old energy. ABC News, for example, is embarked on the most ambitious documentary ever: *The Century*, a $20 million, twenty-seven-hour series to begin next March, a colossal survey of the last hundred years. And CNN in September will launch *Cold War*, a massively researched, twenty-four-segment history. But even series on so grand a scale are expected to pay their own way or even make a profit.)

In the newspaper industry, last year was a watershed for two big reasons: trafficking in papers was at an all-time high; and profits boomed, even as circulation continued to slide. It was dubbed The Year of the Deal: 162 dailies out of 1,509 changed hands, up 37 percent from the year before. Mega-deals abounded: Knight Ridder bought the *Kansas City Star*, the *Fort Worth Star-Telegram*, and two other papers from Walt Disney Company for $1.65 billion; McClatchy Newspapers snared Cowles Media for $1.4 billion. Transactions for the year hit a record $6.23 billion. As of February 1, 81 percent of those 1,509 dailies were members of a chain or group. Gene Roberts, former managing editor of the *New York Times* and now a journalism professor at the University of Maryland, told a press group in California:

> News coverage is being shaped by corporate executives at headquarters far from the local scene. [The shaping] is seldom done by corporate directive or fiat. It rarely involves killing or slanting stories. Usually it is by the appointment of a pliable editor here, a corporate graphics conference there, that results in a more uniform look, a more cookie-cutter approach among the chain's newspapers, or the corporate research director's interpretation of reader surveys that see common denominator solutions to complex coverage problems. . . . As papers become increasingly shallow and niggardly, they lose their essentiality to their readers and their communities. And this is ultimately suicidal.

Alarmingly, only fifty-five American cities now have more than one paper. The sharp decline in the numbers of dailies competing vigorously against each other has damaged the quality and squeezed the amount of reporting in American papers. Studies show that in cities where competition is hot, the news holes tend to be larger and there are more reporters to fill them. "The absence of competition tends to affect the financial commitment of publishers to the news-editorial department," says a forthcoming survey by the Columbia Institute for Tele-Information.

What kind of returns do chains demand to justify high purchase prices? Steven S. Ross, a Columbia Journalism School associate professor, explains: "This is what is historically new. Today, if a paper underperforms, its stock price is threatened and it's vulnerable to takeover. A 25 percent return on gross revenues sounds pretty good to a paper's staff. But the new owner's board says, 'We paid $500 million for that company. How dare they earn only 25 percent?'"

Complaints abound from editors of large chain papers that the investment they require to produce a superior paper is being drained away to meet owners' profit demands. That shows up in large ways and small: when Gannett took over the *Asbury Park Press* in New Jersey, it cut the staff from 225 to 180 and told the theater critic there was no money for him to cover Broadway plays.

A particularly instructive case history is that of the *Patriot-Ledger* of Quincy, Massachusetts. It's a 161-year-old daily that was sold in February to Newspaper Media LLC for about $95 million by the Low family, which had owned it for four generations. The paper actually was worth $70 to $75 million, according to analysts. In need of larger operating margins to service their heavy debt, the new owners decreed that the editorial budget be slashed from $7 million to $5.5 million; 17 to 18 percent of the paper's costs had been devoted to news and editorial, but that was reduced to 10 to 12 percent. The *Patriot-Ledger* serves twenty-six communities near Boston, and had at least one full-time reporter in all of them—several in larger suburbs like Weymouth, Braintree, and Plymouth. Too expensive, said the paper's new publisher, James Plugh. Also: twelve vacancies existed in the newsroom at the time of the ownership change, but Newspaper Media declined to let them be filled. The paper's value to its readers has been grievously undermined as a result of such economies.

Unwilling to function in that new environment, the *Patriot-Ledger's* editor of twenty years (and former president of ASNE), William Ketter, resigned on May 29. Speaking generically of the nationwide profits-versus-quality controversy, Ketter says: "I'm concerned about the prices being paid for newspapers and the need for greater profit margins to meet those financial obligations. The squeezing of editorial budgets is a shortsighted way of dealing with that need. When you start diminishing and degrading the nature of newspapers' content, you run the risk of those papers being less valuable in the marketplace."

Says the *Oregonian*'s Sandra Mims Rowe: "Newspapers don't invest nearly enough in their employees, especially in training and teaching. There are journalists in the streets of every town who cannot report, write, or edit with authority, cannot provide the rich, full, detailed, accurate story the reader wants."

Evidence mounts that the blurring of editorial-advertising distinctions—as the latest technique in profit-building—is compromising news judgments and decisions, resulting not so much in fawning pieces about major advertisers but rather in self-censorship, a reluctance by some editors to take the heat for doing stories critical of space-buyers.

Witness: the highly publicized move by *Los Angeles Times* publisher Mark Willes to involve marketing/advertising executives in the paper's day-to-day editorial decisions, a tactic that continues to draw fire from journalists around the country. The big fear is that if journalists have to worry about advertising and profits, they may self-censor and shrink from producing tough coverage of stories inimical to advertisers' interests. But what Willes has done is being copied at many other papers in this new era of profit worship.

In a self-justifying speech to ASNE in April, Willes pointed out that more than 200 papers have closed in the last twenty-five years; that overall newspaper circulation has declined 10 percent in the last dozen years (while the population has grown 12 percent); that newspapers now attract less than 22 percent of all advertising, down from 27 percent in 1980; that only 58 percent of adults read a daily newspaper, down from 81 percent in 1964; that barely a third of the population cites newspapers as their main source for national news; and that in a recent Gallup poll, Americans ranked the honesty and integrity of newspaper reporters behind police officers and TV reporters, and only slightly ahead of lawyers and building contractors.

If those trends continue, Willes warned, "newspapers will be increasingly marginalized, less important and, therefore, less relevant." For such reasons, he argues, it behooves editors and business-side managers to work together, more closely than in the past, to help assure the good health of newspapers. Willes's diagnosis of newspapers' illness is impressive. But his ideas for the cure alarm many journalists.

The subject of compensation and incentive pay troubles the University of Iowa's Soloski. There are major implications when the bonuses of media executives depend solely on the economic—and not the journalistic—performance of their publications. With a direct interest in his paper's profits, can the editor truly exercise uncontaminated judgment in covering controversial subjects or advertisers that might take offense and defect? The answer is yes, of course, the honest editor can—but she or he must always be aware of the potential for conflict.

Many publishers are increasingly pressing for special sections of their papers as a magnet for advertisers and readers, even though the content of those (continuing or occasional) sections is often frivolous, and creating them places added stress on news staffs. The *Wall Street Journal* has its new Friday section called Weekend Journal, filled with entertainment and lifestyle advice and related advertising. In mid-May, the *New York Times* published a massive sixty-four-page special section on the charms of eastern Long Island, mostly the fashionable Hamptons, with articles on sailing, kayaking, land development, dining, sport fishing, and (of course) the famous showbiz and media folk who summer there—along with a tonnage of advertising from real estate agents, restaurants, clothing boutiques, liquor stores, nurseries, and country inns. (A study sponsored last year by ASNE and the Newspaper Association of America discovered that newspaper advertisements better meet readers' expectations than does the quality of news coverage.)

The questions: Are such sections an editor's vision of a value-added supplement that fills an important editorial need, or mainly a publisher's gambit for a quick-hit spike in revenue? And can those sections be executed without draining resources from the paper's main service?

Such one-time and continuing special sections are a greater strain on papers that don't have the legendary resources of the *Wall Street Journal* or the *New York Times*. But the criterion for success is usually the same: economic, not journalistic. At the *Los Angeles Times*, for example, where the editor of a daily section is yoked uncomfortably with a counterpart from the ad department, a section's survival chances depend heavily on its capacity to generate revenue, not on its journalistic excellence.

A comparable syndrome exists in the magazine industry: special issues, which exploit the value of a title in the effort to squeeze additional income from its brand-name identity. It's an old tactic that's employed with ever greater frequency these days to prettify the bottom line, even as editorial staffs have been pruned and there are often fewer people to take on the task. Can a magazine editor, who presumably occupies a full-time job, effectively oversee these special issues—on the passing of Frank Sinatra, Princess Diana, the Seinfeld sitcom—and still do his main job? "When the driving force is economic and not journalistic," says a senior editor of a national magazine, "the push is coming from the wrong direction. I would rather use that energy and that talent to improve my main product than to create a one-time offshoot. It's all very well to say I can do both, but I'm not sure anybody can, without weakening the core magazine."

The underlying debate continues. Profits. Return on investment. The public's right to know. Shareholder value. Journalistic responsibility. Are the terms incompatible? Not necessarily. Early in this century, the great labor leader Samuel Gompers said: "The worst crime against working people is a company which fails to operate at a profit."

But should news organizations reasonably expect the same profit levels as software companies, pharmaceutical firms, and computer makers? Or should stockholders and owners understand, when they wed their fortunes to those of working journalists, that news is a venture like no other? It's the only business protected by the Constitution of the United States, a status that brings obligations for both the shareholder and the journalist. "I wish investors and owners of media companies could be made to understand the incredible responsibility they've assumed," says Walter Cronkite, "and accept a reasonable return instead of the excessive profits that can be garnered elsewhere."

If that's too much to expect in this era of mega-media conglomerations, a surging economy, a galloping Wall Street, and chronic public dismay about the press, then the mission of journalism in America may be perilously debilitated. The big question: What doth it profit a media company to demand, unremittingly, steadily higher profit margins year after year and, in that very pursuit, lose its professional soul?

JACK SHAFER

Embracing Extinction:
The 1970s and Newspaper Decline

The Press Box columnist for Slate.com, Jack Shafer, has been an astute and acerbic critic of the media business even as his role as an editor and commentator at Slate has grown. In November 2006 he traced the newspaper industry's insecurity back to the 1970s.

A good three decades before the newspaper industry began blaming its declining fortunes on the Web, the iPod, and game machines, it knew it was in huge trouble. In the mid-1970s, two of its trade associations (which have since merged)—the American Newspaper Publishers Association and the Newspaper Advertising Bureau—sought to diagnose the causes of tumbling newspaper readership since the mid-1960s and recommend remedies.

The associations formed the Newspaper Readership Project, which sociologist/marketing specialist Leo Bogart helped direct. Bogart's 1991 book, *Preserving the Press: How Daily Newspapers Mobilized to Keep Their Readers*, portrays an industry that knew exactly what ailed it but refused to adapt to a shifting marketplace. Change a few dates and a few names in a couple chapters from *Preserving the Press*, and you could republish the whole thing as "breaking news."

Bogart and the project rat out the usual guilty parties for falling circulation—radio and television. But they also cite city-to-suburb migration (and the distribution difficulties caused by metro sprawl), growing transience that prevents people from establishing roots that in turn nurture the newspaper habit, and changes in work and commuting patterns as well as the flaccid editorial product in many markets.

The ideas ultimately advanced by the Newspaper Readership Project were so universally accepted that *Los Angeles Times* media reporter David Shaw was already filing a preview of its findings and recommendations in a Page One November 26, 1976, feature. In the lead to "Newspapers Challenged as Never Before," Shaw asks: Are you now holding an endangered species in your hands?

At the time of Shaw's extinction warning, the number of U.S. households and the combined circulation of all daily newspapers was almost at par—about 70 million households versus 60 million in circulation. Today, the number of U.S. households exceeds 100 million, but daily circulation is flat or down a couple million from the 1970s.

Shaw quotes *Times* publisher Otis Chandler saying that he doubts the *Times*—or any other metro daily—is "really essential" to even 50 percent of its readers, something even the most depressed publisher working today would never say. And remember, the *Los Angeles Times* of that era was a circulation lion.

The solutions proposed by *Preserving the Press* and Shaw's article read like the standard prescriptions written today: Make an attempt to "reconnect" with readers, who feel alienated from newspapers. Make coverage more local. Hook kids when they're young. Let readers "sound off" about issues on special pages of the paper. Connect with and hire minorities. Expand the weather report. Introduce or expand op-ed pages. Spice up the design and print more color. Run more lifestyle, consumer, and personal-finance articles. Chase potential readers—and advertisers—into the deep suburbs.

Is there a metropolitan newspaper that hasn't taken all of this medicine? Is there one that isn't taking maintenance doses of these meds today? And yet newspaper circulation continues to dribble down. Shaw reports that newspaper people thought the increases in leisure time would benefit their industry. To a degree, that played out, especially when readers devoted themselves to fat Sunday papers. But as societal wealth increased, Shaw writes, many readers found they could afford other leisure pursuits they found more compelling than reading the news and completing the crossword puzzle: travel, watching movies on VCRs, dining out, making long-distance phone calls, groovin' to a Walkman, and recreational shopping.

Fresh thinking about what ails newspapers arrived in the November 29, 2006, *Wall Street Journal*, where staffer William M. Bulkeley contributed a column titled "The Internet Allows Consumers to Trim Wasteful Purchases." Bulkeley explains how the photographic film industry, encyclopedia publishers, the music industry, and the advertising industry feasted on buyers by forcing them to purchase things they didn't want—prints of all twenty-four shots from their camera or a whole album to secure one favorite song, for example. "The business models required customers to pay for detritus to get the good stuff," Bulkeley writes. But digital cameras, the Web, iTunes, and search-related advertising have stripped those industries of their power to charge for detritus.

Bulkeley could have easily applied the wisdom of his lesson more broadly to newspapers. It's not that the complete gestalt of local, state, national, and international news plus sports, comics, classified, opinion, and hints on fashion, home, entertainment, and food isn't still useful. It is. But given a choice, and the economic means to make a choice, many buyers prefer to make an unbundled purchase. Unbundling the news they want from the news they don't want is what the Web allows readers to do now.

For decades, newspapers—and other media—prospered by exploiting what former hedge-fund manager Andy Kessler calls EPILIT, which is short for Entertainment (or Editorial) and Perishable Information Leading Indirectly to a Transaction. The model works to the media moguls' advantage, he writes, as long as the number of distribution "pipes" (newspapers, TV networks, radio stations, cable channels, phone lines, etc.) can be controlled. When anybody can join the EPILIT party—exactly what the Web encourages—the monopoly profits enjoyed by media moguls suffer. And make no mistake about it, American newspaper publishers sucked every available dollar out of their advertisers and readers when they occupied the commanding heights.

Kessler's cheeky essay from October, "Media 2.Uh-Oh," predicts that because nobody will be able to control the pipes in the future the way they once did, all the media markets will be in play and remain in play for some time. The turmoil experienced most acutely by the newspaper and music industries has now spread to the television industry, which is cutting costs and restructuring. . . .

If you agree with me that the newspaper business has been on a slow, unstoppable train ride to hell for many decades and that the Web has only accelerated its descent, then you'll enjoy another article in yesterday's *Wall Street Journal.*

"Buy This Newspaper!" by editorial-page staffer Holman W. Jenkins, Jr. . . . regards Jack Welch's offer to buy the *Boston Globe,* the coming breakup of the Tribune Company, and Wall Street's snipping at the New York Times Company as "straws in the breeze" portending a time when newspaper companies stop trimming page size and get rid of paper pages altogether for the Web.

What's preventing anybody from going first, of course, is the $45 billion ad market that generates profit margins of up to 20 percent, Jenkins writes. Yes, newspaper Web advertising is growing, but not fast enough to cover the declines in print advertising. A paper gets about one-tenth or one-twentieth the advertising revenue for a Web reader as it does a print reader, he notes.

To thrive, news companies need to convince advertisers to pay much higher rates for readers who "value their time at tens or hundreds of dollars an hour lingering on newspaper Web sites for perhaps half an hour every day, and they're not just channel flicking. They're engaged," Jenkins writes. As I've written before, people may be giving up the newspaper habit, but their appetite for news is growing. The 1.1 million circulation for the print *New York Times* served 25 million unique readers in April via its Web site, according to the company's own logs.

I'm not the type to predict the future, if only because I'm so bad at it. But print editions of newspapers, which saw the endgame coming thirty years ago and did everything they could to forestall it, need to figure out what they're best at and double down in those realms. To give one example, if newspapers think they're in the editorial business, the slimming of the business pages at most dailies indicates that the standard business section is doomed and that the copy should be folded into the rest of the paper to make room for a section the masses really want to read. Sports sections that refuse to retool themselves as the smart supplement to ESPN can kiss their pages goodbye.

If newspapers think they're primarily in the advertising business, they could take Mark Cuban's sharp advice from this week and redeploy their ad staffs to broker Web advertising wherever they can find a place for it, not just on their own Web sites. What they'll probably do instead is form a new intra-industry Newspaper Readership Project.

MICHAEL WOLFF

Glory Days: The Billionaire Solution

❧ ❧

Everyone in trouble dreams of a white knight, and in the newspaper industry the big man on the stallion rides up with bundles of money. Are billionaire owners the solution to the newspaper industry's problems? Should we turn back to the days when the names Mc-Cormick, Hearst, Knight, and Pulitzer defined the ownership of daily papers?

I was invited the other day to stop in for an off-the-record visit with one of the really, really rich men who are lining up to buy the country's biggest newspapers. In addition to his own billions, he had lots of billionaire friends, he said, who were also interested in the newspaper business, and, as a benchmark, he pointed out, the *New York Times* had a market value of only $3.3 billion. So what if, say, the *Times* shareholders—this billionaire was interested as well, albeit for lesser amounts, in *Newsday* and the *Boston Globe* and the *L.A. Times* and the *Wall Street Journal*—were offered a 50 percent, or even 100 percent, pop? I mean, he said, come on.

It was just a market anomaly—the kind that opportunity is made from—that newspapers were suddenly worth much less to mere mortal shareholders than they were to a new, assertive, patriarchal class of multi-billionaires.

This billionaire—an appropriately larger-than-life character, re-markably fit (I re-evaluated my own diet and exercise regimen), in a vast office filled with knickknacks and press coverage and separate seating areas, with, like so many of his fellow billionaires, not enough to do with his great energy—immediately confused my role. In the kind of mix-up that perhaps one might see if he does take over one of these papers, he clearly saw me not as a reporter but as a helper. A collaborator. Indeed, I gossiped handily.

In a way, it was good that he recognized he needed some help (and, possibly, a sign of humility), because, in fact, he knew nothing whatsoever about the newspaper business, or news. Zip. Nada. I am not sure he quite understood that it was a bleak business. I offered that there are many people who believe that the commercial viabil-ity of big-city dailies will be kaput within five years.

He said, with affable certainty, and as though agreeing with me, Oh, but there will always be lots and lots of people who want to read a newspaper.

I pointed out that, actually, only older people read a daily paper—average age: 56.

He said that, in his opinion, when people got married and set-tled down, that's when they'd start reading a paper. Why, he was just talking to X—a famous captain of finance—who agreed with him. In fact, said my billionaire, they would start reading a paper—these hypothetical newlyweds—if, *if*, they could start getting news without all the opinion. Keep the opinion on the editorial page!

Ah.

But, most of all—and here the billionaire's eyes really focused—newspapers had to stop being so anti-business. This country was be-ing ruined by the anti-business press. Sarbanes-Oxley, the federal business regulations destroying our competitive advantage, was all due to the anti-business press!

But what about selling advertising? I asked. It's an ever more competitive and cutthroat world.

He tsked. His view was clear: only the weak-willed and panty-waist could not sell in a difficult market.

Anyway, in short order, the billionaire checked his watch, and I was dismissed, although with the promise of future consultations.

"He doesn't have a clue," I said to one of his aides on the way out. The aide said, brightly, "He's probably the leading expert in buying businesses he knows nothing about."

Out in Chicago, in a far different reality, I was at a meeting of new-media types about the future of news: user-generated, social-network, Web 3.0, intracranial-chip, and so on. Forget newspapers—digital news was about to flatten broadcast too. That was the subject: who'd be the next big brand—the CNN (though it would not be CNN), or the *New York Times* (though it would not be the *New York Times*), or the Google (though it would probably not even be Google)—of the new-news world. Or would the whole idea of news brands die a whimpering death?

It was only happenstance that this meeting about the future of the new news was in Chicago, which is ground zero of the end of old news. That Chicago should be the scene of this last act is a masterstroke of staging. The *Chicago Tribune* has dominated this city for most of the last century. It is one of the city's biggest companies and biggest employers (the entire Midwest media community seems to have worked, at one time, for a Tribune company). The *Tribune's* web of power and influence is bred into the city. The *Tribune* is Chicago. You can't imagine the *Tribune* being taken over by outsiders any more than you could have imagined the *Los Angeles Times*, that bastion of civic back-scratching, being taken over—although, as it happens, six years ago, the *Tribune* itself took over the *L.A. Times*. And, too, there is the great Tribune Tower, mock-Gothic, art-directed, sentimental, rising, near our new-media meeting, over downtown Chicago.

A year ago, institutional shareholders at Knight Ridder, owner of more than 30 daily papers—with Gannett and the Tribune Company, K.R. was part of what's been known in the industry as the three bears—in a display of petulance and impatience and power, forced management to sell the business to the highest bidder (and not so high, at that—$4.5 billion). Almost immediately thereafter, the largest block of shareholders at the Tribune Company (the former shareholders of Times Mirror, the company that had owned the *L.A. Times*) became aggrieved, too, and in a series of push-pull maneuvers forced the Tribune Company—which, in addition to the *Tribune* and the *L.A. Times*, owns *Newsday*, the *Hartford Courant*, the *Baltimore Sun*, many television stations, and the Chicago Cubs—to put itself on the block, where it now teeters, entertaining offers.

Our new-media meeting adjourned for lunch to a downtown club—an odd, out-of-time, red-leather steak-and-shrimp-cocktail club—in the Wrigley Building. It was a huge room, and there wasn't much business. We were there with some amount of irony—or mockery: observing a relic. And, indeed, one of the people in our group, a prince of new media, with heightened relic radar, suddenly singled out Dennis FitzSimons, head of the Tribune Company, among the most anonymous of the anonymous people in the room.

This was a clever celebrity sighting, because the entire point about the CEO of the Tribune Company is that newspaper executives are nameless, faceless, professionally gray people. Dennis FitzSimons, with his out-of-fashion mustache and brownish suit—a former television-station executive and advertising salesperson—was not much different from any executive who ran, say, a public utility, which is what newspapers had become. Personality-less, reliable, bureaucratic, and, until very recently, throwing off lots of free cash flow.

In this public-utility age of newspapers, the institutional blandness which resulted—reporters themselves, once clever and disreputable, became something like public-service employees, seeing themselves with the beleaguered virtue of schoolteachers—helped turn newspapers into a medium for old people (newspapers are for people who remember newspapers). In some sense, newspapers became the inverse of media: designed not to be noticed. Indeed, Gannett, the No. 1 chain, had, not so long ago, spent more than a year searching for a chief executive, looking for a big-deal media type (indeed, reportedly trying to get people such as Sirius Radio's Mel Karmazin and Comcast's Steve Burke interested in the job), but nobody with pizzazz wanted a newspaper company, so Gannett was forced to settle for, in the description of one newspaper insider I know, "Dennis FitzSimons's idiot brother."

This was the cosmic joke: newspapers, once the singular province of big men, great sons of bitches, monsters, Citizen Kane himself—the *Tribune* was run by one of the most outsize of news barons, Colonel Robert McCormick, grandson of a Chicago mayor, co-founder of one of the nation's biggest law firms, isolationist, militarist, show-off, star of the first newsreel, avid and odd personal crusader (spelling reform was one of his hot issues)—had become the land of nobodies.

Which, if you had a comic turn of mind, could now be seen as cyclical capitalism offering opportunity to the somebodies—this grand assortment of the biggest egomaniacs of modern capitalism, with some of its biggest fortunes. There are, among others, music and film impresario David Geffen ($4.6 billion), after the *L.A. Times*; supermarket king and Clinton buddy Ron Burkle ($2.5 billion) and real estate giant Eli Broad ($5.8 billion), bidding for the Tribune Company; America's most celebrated retired executive, former G.E. CEO Jack Welch (some $720 million), going for the *New York Times*–owned *Boston Globe*; and insurance mogul—roughed up by Eliot Spitzer—Hank Greenberg ($2.8 billion), amassing shares in the *New York Times*. For them, money is truly no object. Attention span might be, but not money.

Of course, it could well be that none of these egomaniacs really want to own a newspaper. The opportunity they are most attentive to might not be the actual paper but the currency of saying you might buy the paper—that in itself provides a valuable opportunity.

Hard to believe that David Geffen or Jack Welch might want more publicity—but that is like saying it is hard to believe they might want more money.

Or, and this would be my preferred explanation for some of this newspaper mania, all of these egomaniacs are, themselves, pretty old (which partly explains their restlessness)—Geffen is 63; Burkle, 53; Broad, 73; Welch, 71; Greenberg, 81. That puts them among the more and more rarefied group of people who actually still read newspapers. And because they are billionaires they reasonably might assume that they are at the center of the world, and, accordingly, since they read newspapers, everyone else must read, or want to read, a newspaper.

Or, possibly, these guys are really, as they keep saying, civic-minded ("I believe a newspaper is a civic asset, a civic trust," said Eli Broad recently). But it would not be civic-minded in the usual sense of providing some community virtue or service, but civic-minded in the sense of not being able to imagine the civitas without the dominating force, the everyday feel, the clarion headlines, of a newspaper. If you are above a certain age and interested in civic life and, as important, the power that determines civic life, it's almost impossible imagining going forward without a daily paper. (The corollary for such men is the difficulty of imagining life without being in the paper.) So the idea of the rich man, the mega-rich man, in the newspaper business is likely a nostalgic idea about dominance—synergistic dominance, even: dominant paper, dominant man. His dominance is his civic contribution. The sports-team parallel is a useful one. Rich men buy sports teams as a personal expression of boosterism, and civic engagement, and personal fun. What's more, they believe they can increase the value of these teams—and they often do—by their own energy and public face. They become the No. 1 fan. Likewise, these guys undoubtedly see themselves as cheerleaders of the news.

But the critical flaw with newspapers may in fact be this very idea of dominance. That is, if information is no longer top-down, emanating and controlled from a central source, is a newspaper, then, a little ridiculous? The following comes from Ken Doctor, former managing editor of the *St. Paul Pioneer Press*, whom I met in my Chicago new-news meeting and who has made the savvy transition from participating in the decline of the business—there are 51,000 journalists at U.S. dailies, a number that shrinks by 3 percent annually—to profitably predicting it. In beard and sport jacket—city-room chic—he travels around the country from meeting to meeting giving one version or another of his PowerPoint lecture on the imminent end of the American daily.

Nineteen-fifty marks the high point of newspaper penetration in America: 100 percent of American homes took one or more daily papers. Fifty-six years later fewer than half of American homes get one. At the current rate of decline, no homes will get any newspapers in the not-too-distant future. Morning news, once the monopoly province of newspapers (virtually all evening papers, facing competition from network news, folded in the '60s and '70s), is now overwhelmingly the province of the networks, cable, radio, and the Web. Newspaper readers (as well as broadcast-news audiences) are old and growing ever older (on an actuarial table, you can plot the newspaper's last day). There are, effectively, no *new* newspaper readers. Newspapers have worked best as a direct-marketing medium—introducing seller to buyer—but the Web is better and cheaper. The mainstay of newspaper profits—real estate, auto, recruitment advertising—accounting for as much as 30 percent of them, is migrating almost entirely online. Shopping itself, that other elemental commerce connection of a newspaper ("The principle of free speech owes at least as much to department stores as to the First Amendment," notes Ken Doctor in passing), is ever more an online activity. While circulation steadily drops, and as online price competition becomes fiercer, newspapers have, nevertheless, continued to charge more for ads—a kind of pyramid scheme, which, sooner rather than later, falls in on itself.

This is terminal, and yet big-city dailies, even in this latter stage of industrial decline, are still—having to do with the residual strength of their monopoly position—a mud slide of dough. Margins of more than 20 percent have been, until recently, the norm (even in this terrible year, the industry average is still 17 percent). Now this erodes every day, and beating this horse will, at some point, become hardly worth the effort. But between now and then is someone's opportunity. This is—one of the things billionaires understand better than the rest of us—arbitrage: the discrepancy between present value and future value.

The newspaper business is almost entirely about straddling this discrepancy. What do you do before the lights go out?

So there's cut-and-gut. Otherwise known as managing for cash. As the market deteriorates, you produce your paper ever more cheaply. Gannett has been a reliable cutter-and-gutter. Most of its papers are in smaller markets, so if there's been a fuss it's been hard to hear.

The Tribune Company has had a different strategy. It's used the free cash flow of its papers to buy other local media. The idea has been to balance the declining market share of newspapers with radio, VHF, cable. But this synergy play has produced less return than even the newspapers themselves. Hence the Tribune Company has also moved toward cutting-and-gutting. But it's harder to cut in top-tier markets than in mid-tier: you hear the fuss. This fall, both the editor and the publisher of the *L.A. Times* effectively went on strike when asked to make newsroom cuts—bad press that's helped push the Tribune Company toward its dissolution. A reporter at the Tribune's *Hartford Courant*, Rinker Buck, wrote a widely circulated attack on the ethics, intelligence, and competence of Tribune management; dozens of *Newsday* staffers have also publicly lambasted FitzSimons over newsroom cuts. Likewise, the buyers of the *Philadelphia Inquirer* and the *Philadelphia Daily News*—a local group of wealthy marketing executives who are trying to implement a version of this cut-to-size strategy—find themselves pilloried across the industry they hope to be taken seriously in, as well as faced with a strike by the Newspaper Guild.

Then there's the more gentlemanly version of cut-and-gut, as practiced at the *New York Times*, the *Washington Post*, and the *Wall Street Journal*. This involves literally cutting inches off the paper and from the news hole, as well as slashing budgets and staff. But the premise here is that saving these papers, helping stabilize the health of these papers, justifies the incremental losses—pay no attention to the fact that ever more increments will need to be sacrificed to maintain stability.

And then there's the Hail Mary Internet pass. This is the most hopeful strategy and, too, the iffiest, with the *New York Times* its most dedicated adherent. The premise is that technology (for which newspapers have no natural disposition) and good intentions will help create a new digital form for news and a new-news business. Since no clear form or adequate business model exists for online news delivery, it is almost impossible to handicap the chances for who might succeed here (given the uncertainty, the odds, objectively, are not good for anyone).

So without a clear program for how to get from here to when the lights go out, shareholders have been fleeing newspapers, forcing the sale of K.R. and Tribune, and cutting share prices in half over the last few years.

This leaves the billionaire option. In essence, news, or publicity, that true currency of our time, is worth more to newsmakers—and every billionaire is a newsmaker who associates with other newsmakers—than to investors (and perhaps even to news consumers). So at the end of the day theirs will be the winning bid.

For journalists, who as the industry has contracted have become ever more ethically self-righteous, this is the ultimate nightmare scenario (save only for going out of business itself). To be owned and operated by somebody who has juice in the game—who might get value out of what the paper writes or whom it writes about and how—contradicts the whole point of contemporary journalism.

And yet, as my billionaire recognized during my brief visit, there is, too, a mutuality of interest—of sensibility even—between billionaire and journalist. Newspapers may be absolutely ending, but people within an industry, any industry—and these billionaires, accustomed to being written about, are as much involved with newspapers as the people writing about them—are the last to be able to see its absolute end. (Whereas for people outside the industry, especially outside the newspaper industry, *especially* among the growing majority who don't read a paper at all, the end seems to be almost inconsequential.) It's impossible to believe that something that defines your life, something that exists as big as life—like, say, an American car—will just cease to be. (This kind of denial is one of the things that make industrial decline such a glacial process.)

Increasingly, as newspapers come to be seen more and more as a throwback, perhaps something is to be gained by acting the part— there might be a sort of rediscovered glamour. Prior to the rise of newspaper chains, papers were most always patriarchal institutions. (The title of Susan Tifft and Alex Jones's 1991 book about the Binghams, the star-crossed family that bought the *Louisville Courier-Journal* and the *Louisville Times* with its fortune in the 1920s, is *The Patriarch*.) These were semi-feudal worlds of authority and privilege (arguably, part of the reason newspapers began their decline was that the overbearingness of the various newspaper patriarchs tended to produce ne'er-do-well sons who dissipated the patrimony). Newspapers—in rather direct contradiction to the theoretical values of the journalists who worked for them—have classically been about power and influence and settling scores (in the ideal formulation, the proprietor gets the editorial page to exercise his primal needs, while the news pages remain more pure) and, not least of all, gaining advantages in real estate deals. Newspapers often bullied their way to centrality in a community. They were a kind of Mafia, a kind of protection racket—you don't play nice with me, you don't advertise with me, I mess with you.

Actually, it is not impossible to imagine, in this age of so many billionaires, that competing billionaires would want competing papers. That you can't be an effective or prideful billionaire without your own paper. New York City has the most robust newspaper market in the nation because billionaire Mortimer Zuckerman's break-even-ish *Daily News* competes against billionaire Rupert Murdoch's certainly-money-losing *New York Post*.

Even the more fundamental worry of journalists, that billionaires are cheapskates (no doubt they are), might be, in this circumstance, unfounded. The cheapskates in Philadelphia aside (and their problem seems to be they just weren't rich enough to buy a paper), Murdoch has spent his way at the *New York Post* into being *Murdoch*—which is worth much more than the millions he's losing on the *Post* every year (Murdoch, doubling-down, reportedly might be a buyer of the Tribune Company's *Newsday*, on Long Island).

Of course, the Internet is a bitch. On the other hand, the Internet is an inefficient way for a big man to throw his weight around. A newspaper really is the much more effective bully pulpit.

What's more, given a host of new papers—the *Daily Geffen*, the *Welch Globe*, the *Greenberg Times*, the *Broad Journal*, the *Burkle Shopper*—freed from the deadening template of the people who theoretically know how to run newspapers, maybe the people who know nothing at all about newspapers will stumble onto something that makes them shout and sing (Eli Broad recently offered that it might be a good idea if the *L.A. Times* had more pictures of donors at charity events . . . well . . . maybe). Anyway, now is not the time to worry about the unknown. The unknown is the only hope. Make the deal.

MICHAEL SHAPIRO

Heartbreak on Wheels:
The *Philadelphia Inquirer*

*It would almost always cause an argument, but there
was a time only a few decades ago when the assertion
that "the* Philadelphia Inquirer *is the best damned
newspaper in the country" was not only plausible but
defensible. Rolling up stacks of Pulitzer Prizes even as
it buffed its reputation as a writer's paper, the* Inquirer
*made a legend of itself in a very short period of time.
Now that's over, and what lives in its place is one of the
saddest stories in journalism.*

1. PHANTOM MENACE

The events that would transform life at the *Philadelphia Inquirer*
from the merely disheartening into the profoundly terrifying began
to unfold shortly after three o'clock on the afternoon of last November 1 when Sandra Long, a deputy managing editor, appeared outside the glass wall of managing editor Anne Gordon's office waving
a small piece of paper. Long did not look well.

Gordon, who carries herself with an air of relentless purposeful-
ness, was in the midst of explaining why the impending loss of 15
percent of the *Inquirer*'s editorial staff was not nearly so dire a situa-

tion as most everyone else in her beleaguered newsroom believed. "Putting out a great newspaper has nothing to do with numbers," she was saying. "This is an idea game now." Just then Long poked her head in the door. Above her hung a sign that read, "Fight the Good Fight."

"There is," she said, "an emergency." Her voice possessed the gravity of someone bringing word of a loved one's death.

Gordon excused herself and followed Long out into the vast and airy newsroom, where people were still caught between putting out the next day's newspaper and deciding whether the time had come to apply for a buyout and leave.

Gordon returned a few minutes later and said, without obvious concern or alarm, that the largest holder of stock in the *Inquirer's* corporate parent, Knight Ridder, was demanding that the company be sold in order to boost the stock's sagging value. With that, she rose and strode back through the newsroom and into the page-one meeting to decide what the *Inquirer's* 357,000 subscribers would read the following morning: an update on the stalled talks in the city's day-old transit strike; analyses of a possible Jon Corzine administration in Trenton and a Samuel Alito term on the Supreme Court; and, tucked back on the business pages, the *Inquirer's* story about the perilous turn in its own already unsettled fortunes set in motion by a little-known man from Naples, Florida, named Bruce S. Sherman.

By this time the story told and retold in journalistic circles about the *Philadelphia Inquirer* had assumed a familiarity that bordered on the monotonous: a once dreadful and then brilliant newspaper—seventeen Pulitzers in eighteen years!—that might have been great still had it not been for the endless meddling, cutting, and demands for ever greater profits from its corporate masters. The *Inquirer*, it was said in a tone used to describe a handsome friend who has not aged well, was not what it was. Where once it was sparky and filled with surprises, to say nothing of those great, Pulitzer-destined heaves, its pages were now too often filled with dutiful pieces relaying word of further steps in bureaucratic processes. Dispatches from overseas and from across the nation that once carried *Inquirer* by-lines now came via the wires. No one was suggesting that the *Inquirer* had become a bad newspaper, far from it. But it had become duller, yet another newspaper whose occasional highs seemed to come at ever longer intervals. That judgment was rendered both from afar and from within the paper's white tower of a home on North Broad Street.

The *Inquirer* had gone through three editors in the last six years, had by last summer seen its newsroom staff already reduced since 1999 from 600 to 500, and perhaps saddest of all, had gone from being perhaps the most alluring and electric place in the business to work to yet another newsroom where some young reporters wondered whether they would have been wiser to have gone to law school.

And the *Inquirer* was an economic disappointment to Knight Ridder. The paper was still profitable, and still posted margins in the low teens, and together with its sister paper, the tabloid *Philadelphia Daily News*, generated more revenue—$500 million, with about $50 million in profits—than any other papers in the chain. But that revenue was declining, and given a continuing drop in circulation and advertising, the *Inquirer*, the largest of Knight Ridder's thirty-two daily papers, had become another drag on the company's stock, whose value had fallen by 20 percent in the last year and a half.

So it was that weeks before almost anyone at the *Inquirer* heard the name Bruce Sherman, the paper's editor, Amanda Bennett, had emerged from a meeting with her publisher, Joe Natoli, ridden the elevator down from the twelfth floor, and walked into a room where her senior editors had gathered to discuss, once again, how best to adjust to yet another round of cost-saving buyouts. Bennett looked ashen. The paper, she announced, would need to eliminate not twenty-five more positions, as had been expected, nor fifty, as had been feared. Seventy-five people would have to go, which, in all likelihood, meant not only buyouts but, for the first time, layoffs. The room fell silent.

And soon Bennett would do a curious thing. A few weeks later, on the day in September that she and Natoli gathered the entire staff to inform them of the cuts, she told NPR that the magnitude of that loss represented, of all things, "a gift for us." Smaller cuts, she explained, could have been managed by stretching what resources remained. But not so in losing seventy-five people. "We're going," she said, "to have to reinvent ourselves."

With that she established several committees charged with assessing where the paper stood, and where it might be taken. The *Inquirer*, she made clear, could no longer go on as it was. What it might become, however, was far from clear.

Reinvention was not a novel idea at the *Inquirer*. The paper had been reinvented time and again throughout its long history. This attempt, however, would be carried out in an altogether more difficult time for the American newspaper. It was as if a dark cloud had descended over the news business, a mood exacerbated by the journalistic inclination to see the worst in things. On the same day in September that the *Inquirer* announced its cuts, the New York Times Company said it was reducing its newsroom staff by forty-five and that of the *Boston Globe* by thirty-five. Though newspapers remained profitable, and great sources of cash, the coming of the Internet (and with it, free news and classified advertising), the declining readership among the young, and the feared migration of advertisers away from print, had left reporters and editors wondering whether they might be the ones left to turn out the lights.

The *Inquirer* could no longer afford all the many things it had once offered its readers—a meaty Sunday magazine, series and stories from abroad that no one else had, a seemingly inexhaustible stream of investigations. Fewer people felt compelled to subscribe, and those advertisers who still saw value in the *Inquirer* knew it. As more of its readers departed the city for the suburbs, the *Inquirer* could not seem to settle on a way to lure them away from suburban papers that offer all the local news any reader could want. Nothing seemed to stop the stock price from slipping and the profits from dropping and the mood in the embattled newsroom from darkening.

So the fall brought competing imperatives to the *Inquirer*. The staff, and that of the *Daily News*, which was losing twenty-five positions, had until November 4 to apply for a buyout, and those who applied had until the following week to change their minds. The last day of work for those who chose to leave would be November 18 and, with the gallows humor that invariably accompanies dark moments in the news business, the editors on the committee overseeing the transition joked about the prospect of preparing seventy-five farewell mock front pages. In the meantime, Carl Lavin, the deputy managing editor for news, and Nancy Cooney, the metropolitan editor, were dispatched to the newsroom and to the paper's suburban bureaus to spread the word that good and important work could still be done at a stripped-down *Inquirer*. The paper, they were quick to point out, had weeks earlier seized upon and run with a grand jury report identifying predatory priests, devoting pages and many reporters as the story churned and grew—the way the *Inquirer* had done things in the good days. Still, people were anxious, Lavin later said, about everything. About the paper, what am I going to do? About whether this is the kind of paper they want to work at. He and Cooney did their best to be reassuring. Cooney felt that people wanted to believe them.

Meanwhile, the Sunday editor, Tom McNamara, conducted the grim head count, an assignment that he had actually begun in June when Bennett asked him to put together a report on possible staff reductions. McNamara, who also oversaw features, had come to the paper from *USA Today* five years earlier and brought with him ideas about story length, graphics, and content that at times stood in direct refutation to the ethos that had once made the *Inquirer* soar. His view of that ethos, which he believed existed in a time warp, did not make him especially popular. "I was sort of the devil," he joked. But now, some people confessed to him that after years of late nights they wanted to be home in time to have dinner with their children, and that perhaps a buyout might bring the chance to start at something new. Others wondered whether all the cutting was a harbinger of ever-gloomier times for newspapers. As he walked along the long rows of desks that stretched almost a city block, he would find himself thinking: "he's gone; she's gone." He did not believe that the cutting was at an end. He would pass people in the stairwell, say hello, only to be greeted with silence.

By the afternoon of November 1, McNamara was calculating that perhaps forty to forty-five people would apply for the buyout. If he was right, the *Inquirer* would have no choice but to fire thirty people. His section alone stood to lose an art critic, as well as his pop music, movie, and theater writers. Like every other editor at the *Inquirer*, he could try to find replacements from those who were staying, or simply let the jobs vanish.

McNamara's calculations, however, proved well off the mark. By the end of the week ninety-four people would apply for the buyout. But then that was after the newsroom learned that Sherman, CEO of Private Capital Management LLC, was after Knight Ridder to sell. By the end of the week the chain's second and third largest shareholders had joined him in demanding a sale; on the day Sherman's letter was released Knight Ridder's stock rose by $4.62 to $58 a share.

2. BLUE SKIES

Amanda Bennett had been editor of the *Inquirer* for almost three years and had yet to make the paper truly her own. She had come to Philadelphia from the *Lexington Herald-Leader*, where she had been a well-regarded editor. She had run investigative projects and helped win a Pulitzer as a managing editor at the *Oregonian*, and before that had spent more than twenty years as a reporter for the *Wall Street Journal*, where she had also been part of a Pulitzer-winning team. She had written five books. Bennett was fifty-one then and projected a buoyant eagerness. The staff of the *Inquirer* had greeted her appointment with great delight, having grown ever more disenchanted during the seventeen-month tenure of Walker Lundy, whose legacy included sitting in his office on the night of a primary watching not the news but *Judging Amy*. Lundy had left the *Inquirer* with the vague explanation that his financial planner had told him he was in a position to retire comfortably. Bennett was welcomed as a journalist of accomplishment and vision who might even lead the paper back to what it had been when Richard Ben Cramer's return from the Middle East and his Pulitzer were celebrated by bringing a camel into the newsroom.

But that transformation had not yet happened. And though no one could reasonably blame Bennett alone for the malaise that afflicted her newsroom—her arrival was preceded by buyouts in 2000 and 2001—the excitement that had attended her appointment had largely disappeared. Bennett remained an enigma to the staff. Though people did not question her journalistic skills, they nonetheless whispered to anyone who asked about her carelessness with her words, a tendency she was quick to acknowledge. (She had felt compelled, for instance, to explain to the staff that she had not intended to criticize the paper when, in a presentation to Knight Ridder executives, she used a series of cartoons, one of which showed a homeless man sleeping on a bench with a newspaper over his head; this was meant to show the executives what they thought of the *Inquirer*.) She was often absent, closeted in meetings with the business side, trying to manage the newsroom's ever more difficult finances. The staff wanted more from her. By her own admission, she had not yet been able to give enough.

Yet now, at the darkest moment in memory, Bennett had emerged and declared that the time had come to be bold. She established nine committees in the hope that those reporters and editors who had chosen to stay might help devise a new path for the *Inquirer*. One committee explored the possibilities of the Web, and another considered the unpleasant task of stretching resources— deciding whether, say, the cuts in copy editors necessitated creating a universal copy desk, or whether it would still be feasible to send both a reporter and a photographer to cover so many high school football games.

The most intriguing work, however, was being done by the committee mandated to envision the *Inquirer* of the future. The committee was chaired by Chris Satullo, the editorial-page editor. Satullo was fifty-two, bright, serious, and respected in the newsroom. Bennett and Anne Gordon had turned to Satullo after the staff cuts were announced in September, and asked him to preside over a retreat the following week at which newsroom managers could begin making sense of what was about to happen to the paper.

He was a logical choice; Satullo had been an advocate of civic journalism and, in addition to opening his page to debate among ever more "community voices," he had presided over public debates on such issues as the future of school design. The weekend after the cuts were announced, Satullo devised a broad agenda for the retreat: What, he would ask his colleagues, should the *Inquirer* be in 2015?

The editors gathered on September 26. Bagels and coffee were served and Satullo, who had been nervous the night before, knowing how the mood would be, explained how the day would work. He understood that while it was important for people to air frustrations, extended venting would do little good. And so, he asked them to think about the future. He divided the forty assembled editors into small groups and charged them with two tasks: imagining a happy and successful *Inquirer*, and creating a narrative that told how this transformation took place. Most important, the groups would be asked to explain what values animated the newsroom of this new *Inquirer*. He asked that they be optimistic, not cynical.

Still, he could well understand the impulse toward the latter. As it happened, Satullo himself was not necessarily sure he wanted to stay, though he had a daughter who was thinking seriously of a career in journalism, which made him wonder what she might think if he walked away. He had arrived at the paper in 1989, and his tenure had coincided with the paper's decline in circulation, as well as in reputation. This had not surprised him. "I'd been here six months," he later said, "and I had this nagging feeling that this paper is not nearly as good as the people who work here think it is."

The 1990s had been a period of dramatically fewer prizes as well as seemingly interminable discussions about how best to serve the core of the paper's readers, who now lived in the suburbs. The *Inquirer's* circulation map was an editor's nightmare: one big city and two states—Pennsylvania and New Jersey—that included scores of municipalities and more than 200 school districts. Where once the paper had seen itself as a legitimate competitor to the *New York Times* and the *Washington Post*, it now struggled to do battle with some twenty suburban dailies, some of which were quite strong. At times since the 1980s the paper had offered its suburban readers special weekly and then biweekly inserts, then four zoned editions, then five with eight on Sundays, before cutting back to three on weekdays. The staff felt ever more as though they were riding a pendulum, swinging back and forth between trying to offer the most localized coverage before reversing course and instead running broad pieces that attempted to capture the zeitgeist of the region.

Through it all, circulation kept dropping, and the advertising dollars did not flow in sufficient numbers from all the many shopping malls that dotted that maddening circulation map. Although the population of Philadelphia's Center City was growing, the future was not in the city but, as it was for big-city papers across the country, in the towns and villages that surrounded it. Two-thirds of the *Inquirer's* readers now lived in those suburbs, which also generated two-thirds of its ads.

Forty percent of the newsroom budget was spent covering the suburbs—twice as much as was spent covering the city and far more than the 5 percent that went to the national, Washington, and foreign reports. The pressure to offer its many scattered readers local news was not a decision made exclusively at the *Inquirer*. Knight Ridder was a great believer in local news, so much so that when Maxwell King, the paper's editor from 1990 to 1998, visited corporate headquarters he would be subjected to a review of his paper by Knight Ridder executives who wanted to know why he wasn't running more local stories on the *Inquirer's* front page. The executives explained that the readers the chain interviewed in its many focus groups said it was local news that they wanted.

This was true, but only to a point. The *Inquirer* itself did a good deal of market research and what people who sat in on those meetings learned was that readers wanted not just local news; they wanted sports, fashion, dining guides, TV listings, and even news from faraway places. They wanted everything. Yet the mantra from Knight Ridder, heard by editors across the chain, was that if local was paramount it therefore stood to reason that other things were less important and certainly not worthy of the front page. The either/or framing sprang from an unintentionally patronizing view of suburban life. This view held that those who once lived in the city abandoned what interest they had in things that did not bear directly on their lives the moment they relocated to a split-level home with a two-car garage. It therefore stood to reason not only that foreign, national, and Washington stories were of lesser value, but that if the *Inquirer* was to have a local zoned edition in, say, Montgomery County, it was going to carry a Montgomery County story on the front page, no matter how mundane. It was the dateline that mattered because that's what readers said they wanted, or at least what those doing the asking wanted to believe they had heard.

Covering Montgomery County in a way that might generate all that local news meant boots on the ground—reporters who knew the area. This highlighted a conflict: Knight Ridder was determined to keep profit margins above the industry average. But the chain did not present editors like Max King with long-range plans on how to achieve and sustain those lofty margins, other than vague talk about community service and quality journalism. There was nothing concrete—King uses the word "robust"—that would facilitate the budgeting and planning to develop and keep in place a suburban strategy. Years later, Max King would recall his tenure and his trips to headquarters, which were then in Miami. "It felt to me like a ceaseless pressure to help diminish costs and raise the profit margins," he said. He was told that this had to be done "to satisfy the needs of the shareholders." This assumed that the shareholders could, at some point, be satisfied. Knight Ridder looked at the numbers every month. And if the numbers fell short, Knight Ridder had one solution: cut. But that presented a problem: from a revenue-savings perspective, eliminating a foreign or national bureau was inconsequential. There was one place to cut where serious money could be saved and that was the suburbs. But the suburbs were the greatest potential source of revenue.

In 1999, the paper launched what at the time seemed a bold approach, worthy of the *Inquirer*: "the paper within a paper"— a daily section aimed exclusively at readers in Chester County. Eighteen reporters were assigned to the Chester County edition, and such was the excitement about the new approach that seasoned people asked to be part of the experiment. If the Chester County edition could succeed, the thinking went, the same approach could be applied elsewhere and the *Inquirer* could emerge as the definitive voice of the region. The "paper within a paper," however, lasted only until 2001; it was dropped after the expected ad revenue did not materialize. In the view of the editors who worked on it, the business side gave up on the experiment far too quickly. Robert Rosenthal, who was by then the editor and who tended to embrace story ideas with an infectious passion, wrote a memo announcing the section's demise but assuring the newsroom that the decision would not erode the paper. With that he launched yet another reinvention, a review of all the paper's many beats—his task force would eventually come up with 208—so that a leaner *Inquirer* could begin producing stories "that transcend geography." Rosenthal still believed the *Inquirer* could do big and important journalism, in the suburbs and elsewhere.

Knight Ridder, however, made it clear to him that his ambitions for the paper were perhaps overdrawn.

"Well, you know, you created a Cadillac," one corporate executive told him. "And we wanted a Chevy." Rosenthal was fired nine months later.

The paper then embarked on yet another iteration of the suburban coverage, under Rosenthal's successor, Walker Lundy. Lundy, who came from the *St. Paul Pioneer Press*, the Knight Ridder paper in the Twin Cities, was granted approval to hire more than forty reporters, whom he dispatched to the suburbs along with twenty-three city-side reporters. He added two new zones to the existing three, and even people who had worked on devising the defunct Chester County edition allowed themselves to believe that, at long last, the *Inquirer* had a plan for the suburbs. That was in 2002. Lundy quit a year later. Amanda Bennett inherited his plan, but no assurance that she would be able to keep all those people he had hired. For their part, the reporters in those suburban bureaus were not at all sure what their editors wanted them to be doing.

By the end of Satullo's September retreat, people were offering practical suggestions such as how to better incorporate the paper's Web site with its print edition, as well as recommendations that decision making be less hierarchical. More important, the group was able to agree on what this new *Inquirer* would have to be. The paper would have to accept that there were things it could no longer afford to do. Yet for the *Inquirer* to remain the *Inquirer*, it would have to retain what Satullo called the paper's "core values": that it did investigations, served as watchdog, set the region's agenda—all the while maintaining its commitment to accuracy, ethics, and fairness.

All of this sounded good, in the way that mission statements at the end of such gatherings often do. But there was one other point that the editors believed essential: that the paper have "a voice." Not that the paper spoke in its news columns as one, but rather that it told stories in a way that compelled its readers to read on. Voice, of course, is a wonderful quality to possess but difficult to achieve in that it cannot be acquired by asking people what they want to read. Every editor in that room that day understood what it meant to have a voice, and understood that voice gives a newspaper the personality with which it can maintain a relationship with its readers.

Chris Satullo drove home that night feeling far better about the future of his newspaper than he had in days. "The people in that room were all pretty much committed to staying," he said. "I feel as if I'm not a fool to stay. There's no way what we're going through is good or pleasant or intrinsically good for a newspaper. But there's a chance if we can retain the spirit of that meeting we can redeem this moment."

With that he set about conducting similar meetings throughout the newsroom. But when only five people came to the first meeting, he understood "that the staff is still in purgatory."

3. CURSE OF THE GOLDEN AGE

The *Inquirer*'s two-story newsroom is so long and its ceilings so high that conversation feels muted and restrained. The current carpeted newsroom had in 1997 replaced the old and storied newsroom where mice ran free and where the office intrigue unfolded in many corners and nooks. The floor was then linoleum, by decree; James Naughton, executive editor in those days, had banned carpeting in the belief that it would deaden the noise and with it the creative spirit of the place.

Such was life at the *Inquirer* at a time known in the newsroom as the "Golden Age." The Golden Age began some time after 1972, when Gene Roberts was appointed editor, and is generally considered to have ended after 1990, when he retired. That occasion was marked by a very long and expensive party in a downtown hotel at which it was almost possible to forget that although Roberts was only fifty-eight years old he was carrying himself with the weary bearing of an older man.

Roberts had come to the *Inquirer* from the *New York Times*, where he'd been national editor. On his first day of work he entered the *Inquirer* building through a revolving door, only to pass an editor on his way out. The man paused only long enough to tell Roberts, "You're making the dumbest mistake of your life."

The *Inquirer* was, mercifully, no longer owned by Walter Annenberg, who had sold it to John S. Knight three years earlier. Knight had acquired a newspaper famous for very little other than the relentless way it covered the police blotter—a reporter in every precinct house—and the rare distinction of seeing its best-known reporter, Harry Karafin, sent to prison for extorting thousands of dollars from the subjects of his investigations in return for not writing about them.

Knight had spent a lot of money transforming newspapers in Akron, Miami, Chicago, and Detroit and was now prepared to do the same in Philadelphia. Before Roberts, he dispatched John McMullan, who had been executive editor of the *Miami Herald*, to edit the paper, and it was generally understood by the new reporters he hired that McMullan's role was to rid the *Inquirer* of its worst offenders and offenses. He stayed for two years, all the while preparing the newspaper for his successor.

Gene Roberts might well have stayed at the *Times* had Knight not dangled before him a paper so sorely in need of an overhaul. "I thought it would be an interesting thing to do with your life," he said, "to see if you could build a good newspaper."

The *Inquirer* was then running a distant second in circulation and reputation to the *Philadelphia Bulletin*, the dominant afternoon paper whose slogan—In Philadelphia, nearly everybody reads the *Bulletin*—was the theme of a series of cartoon ads in the *New Yorker*. Roberts understood that he was in no position to challenge the *Bulletin* as Philadelphia's paper of record. But he could wage an altogether different sort of newspaper war, transforming his paper into the puckish upstart that, free from the constraints of having to cover everything, could pick its spots. Roberts had freedom, money, and time—he believed it would take years to reinvent the *Inquirer*.

He began to hire and, having briefly flirted with taking a desk in the middle of the newsroom—the better to get a feel of the place— also began looking for the paper's untapped talent. Roberts understood that it was all well and good to talk about changing the culture of the newsroom—"you had to prove that excellence was possible on the paper," he said—but quite another to impose those changes on people who had grown accustomed to the unfortunate ways of the past. The copy desk was a case in point: Roberts reasoned that adding a new editor or two would be counterproductive in that, human nature being what it is, those new editors would adapt to the desk's existing culture. So he broke the desk apart, forming two smaller copy desks and on them installing his new people. They, in turn, were given the better stories to edit—the breaking stories and the trend pieces he wanted to see in the paper. As more editors came to the paper, they were assigned to the newly configured copy desks, where they were imbued with the culture of his *Inquirer.* "We developed a philosophy," Roberts said, "that we'd zig when the others zagged."

That is a refrain heard so often from veterans of the Golden Age that it has become a newsroom cliché—a pity, because the words once carried great power and meaning. The men and women who worked for Roberts talk, wistfully, of the possibilities that awaited them each day when they came to work. They were not guided, they say, by a journalistic sense of "should." Their responsibility was not to be comprehensive but to be different, to be bold and, they admit without hesitation, to please the boss.

That did not happen easily. Roberts was both demanding and inscrutable. He said little—and at times, such as during job interviews, nothing at all. Still, he was very much the editor whom reporters wanted to please—"mostly we decided he was smarter than the rest of us," said Steve Seplow, who came to the paper shortly after Knight bought it. That, however, is only part of it. Roberts understood what reporters needed to make them happy. He recognized that their sometimes-maddening combination of arrogance and insecurity could be harnessed and channeled. He chose not to edit by intimidation—the staff appreciated his refusal to run the *Inquirer* by fear as his old boss, A. M. Rosenthal, ran the *Times*—but by manipulation. He would dispatch reporters to the suburbs, say, not by fiat but by convincing them that the future of American journalism was, in fact, in the suburbs and that that future was very much in their hands.

By the late 1970s, the *Bulletin* had become yet another in a dying breed of afternoon dailies. It was losing readers and money, just as the *Inquirer* was beginning to post annual profits of $10 million and seeing its circulation climb. Roberts saw in this an opportunity to transform his paper further still. The death of the *Bulletin* would rob Philadelphia of its authoritative voice. Roberts intended to fill the void. And so he created the "Alpha Plan."

The Alpha Plan was a year in the making and displayed both Roberts's vision and his savvy. The death of the *Bulletin*, he reasoned, offered his paper's corporate owners their one chance to prove to Philadelphia that they were serious about producing a paper of the highest quality. The chain was then still run by the spiritual heirs of John Knight, who had retired in 1976. Still, Roberts took no chances. He insisted that the wording of the plan be filled with military jargon, the better to please Alvah Chapman, Knight Ridder's chairman and a graduate of The Citadel. The *Bulletin* folded on January 29, 1982, and that day Roberts, who almost never held staff meetings, stood in the middle of the newsroom and announced that the *Inquirer* would immediately hire seventeen reporters from the *Bulletin* and would double its number of foreign and national bureaus. He did not stop there: in the months to come he hired eighty-five people and continued expanding the paper's suburban coverage. By 1984, *Time* magazine selected the *Inquirer* as one of the nation's top ten newspapers—and on some days, *Time* argued, the best.

By the mid-1980s, the *Inquirer*'s profits had soared to over $100 million a year. The paper had so much money and freedom in deciding how to spend it that when reporters took leaves others were hired to take their places. For years Roberts came back from Miami with whatever he wanted. But in 1986 that began to change with the appointment of Tony Ridder, who had been publisher of the *San Jose Mercury News*, as head of the chain's newspaper division.

Since the 1974 merger of the Knight and Ridder chains, John Knight and his lieutenants had dominated the corporation. But Knight's son and heir apparent had died in World War II and his grandson, John S. Knight III, an assistant to the managing editor of the *Daily News*, was stabbed to death in 1975. While Knight was a chain run by newspapermen with journalistic aspirations, the Ridders owned many smaller newspapers of marginal distinction. The Ridders were regarded as prudent, perhaps overly so. The family, for example, owned the *Journal of Commerce*, whose circulation at the end of World War II matched that of the *Wall Street Journal*. In 1951, however, the Ridders, looking to cut costs, decided to drop the *Journal of Commerce*'s stock listings and to focus the news columns on stories of narrow interest—a move so shortsighted that, years later, the *New York Times*' Floyd Norris would include it in his list of the century's dozen worst business decisions. Fifty years later, the *Journal of Commerce*'s circulation stood at 17,000—as compared to the *Journal*'s 1.75 million.

By the mid-1980s, it was no secret that Roberts, a darling in John Knight's chain, had fallen out of favor with those who now ran the chain. Though Tony Ridder never criticized Roberts publicly, the view from Miami was made clear, years later, by Knight Ridder's vice president and corporate spokesman, Polk Laffoon IV. "Our definition of what is good journalism here has evolved from the time Gene Roberts was editing the *Philadelphia Inquirer* in the 1970s and '80s," he told Howard Kurtz of the *Washington Post* in 2001. "We put a lot of emphasis on local news and useful or service-oriented features and news that readers tell us over and over that they want . . . health and nutrition, personal finance, personal technology."

That would suggest that Roberts was not interested in such matters; to the contrary. He was, for just one example, a stickler about television listings. Still, by 1990, the legacy of the Alpha Plan was crippling the paper in ways that could not have been envisioned in 1982. Producing a newspaper of record requires a commitment from those holding the purse strings to the quality of the content. To be perceived as trying to do it on the cheap, to second-guess the vision and the approach, risks jeopardizing the fragile nature of the enterprise.

By 1989, when Ridder became president of the chain, the staff had grown accustomed to seeing Roberts trudge into the newsroom after his monthly budget meetings in Miami. After one especially draining trip, an editor spotted Roberts and asked, "Who won, the Christians or the lions?"

"The Christians," Roberts replied, in his low and languid drawl. "But the lions only have to win once."

By 1990, he had had enough. "God knows I tried," he now says. "But in the end I wasn't going to change anything. And there were forces bigger than me that were propelling the company."

On November 18 last year, the *Inquirer* was preparing to bid farewell to seventy-five people, fifty-five of whom were veterans of the Golden Age. Six had even worked for Walter Annenberg. They were people who had been young together, who, before spouses and children and the inevitable desire to make it home before bedtime, had played cards and gone drinking together and come to see themselves as part of something grand, though ever more distant. It was still possible to find pockets of the Golden Age at the *Inquirer*, such as the investigative team, which was housed in a room in the farthest reaches of the newsroom with a door that the staff could close to keep the darkening mood from seeping in.

It was getting close to five o'clock and Amanda Bennett was in her office, preparing to make a formal farewell. She seemed uneasy. She tucked herself in the corner of a long, blue couch and admitted that she had taken the job knowing that a day just like this one could come. "It would have been naive of me to think it was impossible."

But would the cutting stop?

"I hope so," she said. "I don't know."

She excused herself, the better to prepare for the task to come. She emerged a few minutes later and made her way to the distant corner of the newsroom where the business staff had gathered to bid farewell to Patricia Horn, a reporter who was leaving after only seven years. Bennett approached the gathering but stopped before making her presence felt. She stepped away only to circle back, as if she was not sure where to stand.

Meanwhile, people began moving slowly to the front of the room, where tables were being set up for a buffet dinner. As they drew closer, they began whispering to one another: Gene Foreman is here. Foreman had been Roberts's managing editor, and people crowded around him, shook his hand, and hugged him.

Bennett stepped forward to speak. She held her arms across her chest. "This is such a sad day," she said. She spoke of all the "great journalism from all of you who are leaving," of all the extra phone calls and late nights. "We wish you joy and luck in your new lives."

Then she stepped aside to let the publisher, Joe Natoli, speak.

The staff did not blame Natoli for the buyouts. Many, in fact, spoke with admiration of the way he had come down to the newsroom after they were announced, stopping at people's desks to chat and offer what answers and reassurances he could. He came quickly to the point. "I wanted to spend time talking about growth," he said. "But events have overtaken us and we are where we are to-day." The great room was quiet. "We're in a time of uncertainty un-like any other that I have ever faced in my thirty years in the news-paper business."

And then Natoli said what those who were staying later admitted they very much wanted to hear: "I'm convinced the world needs what we do."

Now it was Bob Martin's turn. He had been at the *Inquirer* for nineteen years and, it turned out, was something of an amateur songwriter. Martin opened a manila envelope and took out a thick sheaf of pages, enough for everyone. On it were the lyrics to a song in which Martin had managed to condense the history of the *Inquirer*. The name of the song, and the refrain the staff sang together, was "We Didn't Miss the Deadline." Martin stepped to the microphone and turned on his boom box. People smiled at the words and everyone was singing.

4. THE LIONS' DEN

Knight Ridder's executives had been scheduled to appear at the annual UBS Global Media Conference, but with the company in play the presentation was canceled. Still, the fate of the chain was very much on the minds of the analysts who gathered on the morning of December 7 in a ballroom at the Grand Hyatt Hotel in midtown Manhattan.

For thirty-three years the nation's most important newspaper executives had come before the analysts, whose standing had grown dramatically since the days when John S. Knight could say with impunity that no one was going to tell him how to run his company. When he took his company public, however, Knight issued only a single class of stock, unlike the Sulzberger and Graham families who maintained for themselves a separate class of stock and with it voting power over their companies. Knight's banker, Goldman Sachs, had recommended that a single class would be more attractive to investors.

From the often-limited perspective of journalists, who assumed that mere profitability would suffice, the relationship between the analysts and the media companies had become an unseemly one in that the power now resided with men and women who appeared not at all interested in the quality of the content but instead looked at the quarterly numbers as evidence of those companies' worth.

Every quarterly statement, in turn, was an occasion for a conference call between the heads of those companies and the analysts, who asked many questions about earnings, revenue streams, and cost containment.

For instance, in the October conference call that took place a few weeks after the *Inquirer* announced its job cuts, Tony Ridder and his chief deputies made clear that they understood that while the chain's small-market papers were showing strong growth in advertising revenue, Philadelphia, in particular, was a problem. Advertising was slipping for movies, airlines, and telecommunications. The fourth quarter did not look promising. Still, steps had been taken to boost ad revenue and to contain costs, especially in San Jose, where the *Mercury News* was losing fifty people, and in Philadelphia. This prompted Frederick Searby of JPMorgan to pose a more cosmic question:

"Do you think there's a rethink in terms of the newspaper model that will continue and how much you really can support at this point from an editorial perspective?"

Tony Ridder offered a narrowly reasoned response. "Well, I think that after we have the staff reductions, I think we will still be generously staffed," he said. "So I think we were overstaffed in those two places and I think this is just bringing them back into line."

Until the afternoon of November 1, it was possible to stand in the newsroom of the *Inquirer* and believe that Tony Ridder was the worst person in the world, but then, that was before people heard of Bruce Sherman. Ridder, the refrain went, cared not a lick about the quality of the papers his chain published, and was so lacking in imagination and the capacity to look into the future that his one solution to all financial difficulties was to cut the payroll.

Ridder had gotten off to a bad start. In the spring of 1987, not long after he became head of Knight Ridder's newspaper division, he came to visit the *Inquirer*. The paper had just won three Pulitzers. Ridder told the assembled editors and managers that while he wanted to congratulate them on the prizes, he wanted to speak with them about "something more important." "Next year," he said, "I would like you to win a Pulitzer for cost cutting."

He had preached this ethic ever since, adhering to a business strategy that focused on the moment. He sold off such ventures as Knight Ridder Financial, which accounted for 20 percent of the chain's revenue but only 5 percent of its profits, and the Information Design Laboratory, where the chain had conducted some of the earliest work on electronic publishing. He became known in his newsrooms as "Darth Ridder." All the while he clung to his arguments that even though his newspapers were jettisoning reporters and editors, they were still staffed above the industry standard—one reporter for every thousand subscribers—and that his newsroom spending had, in fact, gone up. He was said to be deeply hurt when in 2001 his friend, Jay Harris, resigned as publisher in San Jose to protest the cuts Ridder was demanding—just as Harris's counterpart at the *Miami Herald*, David Lawrence, had done three years earlier.

Tony Ridder was now sixty-five years old and enjoyed sailing, outback skiing, and driving expensive sports cars. He also possessed a knack for the leaden touch with the public gesture: at the end of 2005, for instance, his company's compensation board voted to increase his annual bonus from 85 percent to 95 percent of salary. Still, it was hard not to feel a bit sorry for Ridder, who, like so many newspaper executives, was caught in a quandary that was not, strictly speaking, of his own making. Whatever desires and hopes he had for maintaining the high standards of his newspapers were eclipsed by powers greater than his own: the analysts, the shareholders, the money managers like Bruce Sherman. Jack Knight had taken his company public because he wanted the shareholders to invest in his newspapers. Those investors, in turn, were now like those on the staff of the *Inquirer* still pining for the Golden Age—longing for the days when profit margins exceeded 20 percent, and the foresight they had displayed in identifying newspapers as undervalued stocks had proven correct. And like the journalistic veterans of the Golden

Age, the shareholders were disappointed with the man they now held responsible for their diminished fortunes.

But where Ridder's fall assumed a tragic quality was, ironically, in his expressed desire to produce newspapers of quality. Granted, papers like the *Inquirer* were not what they once were. Yet even among the increasingly embittered staff of the *Inquirer*, there was the understanding that good work could still be done. Now, with the company up for sale, people spoke of the possibility of things getting worse, which for many meant Gannett. In journalistic circles Gannett represented a newspaper world of vastly diminished ambitions, of short, shallow stories and the overuse of the word "us."

As more and more names of potential bidders emerged, people at the *Inquirer* began talking, almost prayerfully, of the paper's being rescued by private investors, wealthy enough—the Newhouses, say—to not be Wall Street's slave. It was easy to forget that Walter Annenberg had been just such an owner and had driven the paper well past the point of ridicule.

Bruce Sherman had gone to San Jose last July, at Knight Ridder's invitation. Sherman, as it happened, liked to visit the headquarters of the companies in which he had invested. He believed it important to get a feel for the men and women who ran the companies, to broaden the knowledge he systematically acquired in his exhaustive review of the numbers. Sherman was fifty-seven and was one of the nation's most successful money managers. In the story of Knight Ridder's fall, he emerged as a marvelous counterpart to the patrician Ridder: the accountant from Queens—the "streets" of Queens—who had displayed an early gift at assessing stocks. He told the story of how, after reading the annual report, he calculated that the time was right to sell the ten shares of Polaroid stock that his engineer father had bought at $20 a share for his bar mitzvah; Sherman sold at $180. Sherman's firm, PCM, now had $4.3 billion of the $30 billion it managed in newspaper stocks and had strong positions in, among others, Gannett, Media General, McClatchy, Journal Register, and the New York Times Company.

Whatever questions Sherman put to Ridder, the answers did not please him. He made his disappointment clear in the November letter demanding the sale. Granted, he wrote, the board had taken steps to boost the stock's value "in so far as they went." But Knight Ridder was still burdened by the loss of advertising, and "unexceptional operating margins." The company's "break-up value," he concluded, is "substantially in excess of the current share price."

Sherman was doing what he was paid to do, which was to make sure the companies in which he had placed his clients' money performed. It was not his brief to ensure that Knight Ridder's newspapers were places of great journalistic accomplishment. By taking Bruce Sherman's money, Tony Ridder—and every other media company in which Sherman held stock—had assumed a subservient role in a culture whose values they did not necessarily share.

Tony Ridder had become a metaphor for American newspapers—the man who in trying to please everyone, pleased no one. And for all his trouble he now stood very close to losing his company.

Knight Ridder had set a December 9 deadline for the first round of bids for the company. In the days after Sherman's announcement, analysts were setting the odds at no better than fifty-fifty that someone would want to buy Knight Ridder—given the problems that had led to shareholder revolt. Yet a month later, by the morning of the UBS conference, the names of several prospective suitors had begun to surface, among them two private equity firms, the Blackstone Group and Kohlberg Kravis Roberts & Co. Among the analysts at the conference was Eugene H. Gardner, Jr., who lived and worked in Lancaster, Pennsylvania, a town on the very edge of the *Inquirer's* circulation map. He was not a subscriber. He read the *Wall Street Journal* as well as the *New York Times* online. He also subscribed to the two Lancaster dailies. He saw no need to add a "regional" paper to the mix. He lived too far from Philadelphia to be interested in, say, the listings and restaurant reviews the *Inquirer* carried. There was very little that the *Inquirer*, as it had been conceived in its series of reinventions, could offer him.

Gardner had sympathy for Joe Natoli and Amanda Bennett, and he also had sympathy for Tony Ridder. He was careful to avoid criticizing him, even though he believed that "you cannot cut and cut your way to quality."

As he spoke, Gardner sounded more and more like a man politely declining a dinner invitation. "I can't name a single *Inquirer* journalist for you right now," he said. "That's too bad."

But could the *Inquirer* do anything to make itself appealing to him?

"I want a regional newspaper to appear on my doorstep . . ." he began, thinking out loud. "What would it contain?"

He paused. He took a minute before replying.

"Opinions," he said at last. "And not just regarding what's happening in the city." He wanted writers who compelled him to read. If the *Inquirer* was going to lure him, Gardner went on to explain, it would have to acquire what it now lacked: a voice.

The UBS conference offered a snapshot, of sorts, of the state of the industry. Dennis FitzSimons, the embattled chairman of Tribune Company, assured the analysts that the company was cutting to keep expenses flat: nine hundred jobs had been eliminated in the past year, mostly on the publishing side. Dow Jones followed, but with its profit margins having slipped into the single digits, many of the analysts left the room. Then came Gannett. The analysts flooded back in, as if the exotic dancer had just arrived at a bachelor party. One of them, fairly bursting, asked Craig Dubow, the company's chairman, whether it might be possible for Gannett to boost its margin from its stellar 25 percent to a stratospheric 30 percent. Dubow made no commitments.

With that another analyst asked whether Gannett might make a bid for Knight Ridder. Dubow replied that Gannett would, as always, take a "hard look" at all potential acquisitions.

5. INDIAN SUMMER

After years of nine o'clock, ten o'clock, and lunchtime budget meetings, after months of planning the reorganization of a staff with seventy-five fewer people, after a fall of endless speculation and dispatches on the latest turns in the Knight Ridder sale, Amanda Bennett was ready, as she put it, to "do journalism." She could barely contain her excitement.

In December the various committees had submitted their reports on the *Inquirer's* reinvention, and Bennett had celebrated their work with a champagne toast. Changes began almost immediately. Editors were reassigned. The investigative staff moved from the seclusion of its corner office to a cluster in the middle of the newsroom. And now, in mid-January, Bennett was bringing the newsroom, desk by desk, into the page-one meeting room to hear the long and detailed PowerPoint presentation that Anne Gordon, the managing editor, had prepared on the future of the paper.

It was a moment unlike any other at the *Inquirer.* The potential sale of the chain had, at once, left the newsroom in limbo and effectively removed Knight Ridder from the everyday business of the paper. Bennett had been freed to proceed without corporate interference. She had solicited the collective wisdom and the sensibility of her staff and had discovered, much to her delight, a view of the *Inquirer's* future remarkably similar to her own. It was, in fact, a vision that she had brought with her from Lexington to Philadelphia three years earlier and that now, arguably in the darkest and most unsettled time that anyone could recall, she at last had her chance to try to make happen.

The business desk's turn came in the second week of presentations. The staff arranged themselves around the long conference table and, when that filled up, the chairs around the edge of the room. The lights went dim and on the screen appeared a headline "Newsroom 2006."

For the next forty-five minutes, Bennett and Gordon outlined a plan that called for, among other changes, cutting the number of zones from five to three, and placing an ever-greater emphasis on disseminating the news online. Those and many smaller changes they detailed were in service of a larger goal: the *Inquirer* could not and would not continue trying to be Philadelphia's paper of record. That, in turn, meant that the shrunken staff was now free from the burden of covering everything, and given that freedom, the paper would begin to be filled with the boldly conceived and written pieces that had once been its hallmark. The readers, too, had spoken. The *Inquirer* had conducted yet another round of focus groups in the fall, and the report back confirmed what people had been hearing for as long as they'd been asking: readers turned to the *Inquirer* to read national and foreign stories almost as much as they wanted local news.

The new *Inquirer*, Bennett and Gordon explained, would work to satisfy those readers, though it could not do so in the ways of the past. For one thing, 750,000 people now read the *Inquirer* either in print or online. There was little crossover between the two markets, which meant that it was necessary to satisfy both. The paper itself would no longer be merely reactive to events, filled with news that was, for practical purposes, stale by the time it appeared in the *Inquirer*. Bennett and Gordon wanted the paper to break news—in print and online. The *Inquirer*'s Web site, Philly.com, would become the destination for news breaking throughout the day. The site, which as Gordon put it was now filled with "cul-de-sacs," was being redesigned. Each desk would be given control of its own online content.

As for the newspaper, Bennett and Gordon wanted stories that anticipated events, pieces ready to run when things broke. They wanted intelligently imagined angles. The day's front page offered a case in point: rather than cover the president's speech defending his administration's secret domestic spying, the *Inquirer* instead fronted a story about the competing uses of the Fourth Amendment by the program's supporters and critics.

"We want you to select for ambition," Bennett said. "We want you to select for quality."

The operative verb, of course, was "select." The implication was that, in the absence of being aggressively selective, it was easy to slip into making the default choice of reporting what, in Bennett's view, everyone already knew. In fact, she had felt this way about the paper even before she arrived. "I found the paper very dull," she said. "We were still doing a lot of institutional coverage. We were still clinging to the newspaper of record, and the newspaper of record thing was a noose." There was, she went on, "a lower-than-I-would-have-liked level of storytelling."

She believed that the *Inquirer* was "not tremendously engaged" in the region; it was missing too many stories it should have seized upon, such as strong coverage of the area's extensive medical and pharmaceutical industries. The *Inquirer*, she explained, "was still a very good paper," but one that went about its work guided by "deep and profound habits. We run ourselves ragged to cover everything."

But all this raised the question of what she no longer wanted her paper to cover. It was a question very much on the minds of her staff, as had become clear when Bennett and Gordon made their presentation to the metro desk. Tom Ferrick, a columnist who had been at the paper for thirty years—and who largely agreed with their vision—asked if Bennett and Gordon weren't, in fact, outlining a plan that would mean more work for fewer people.

What precisely, he asked, would the staff no longer cover? Was it to be the case that the young city hall reporter sitting next to him would be expected to file repeatedly to Philly.com several times a day, all the while leaving him ever less time to report and write the more ambitious pieces that the new *Inquirer* was to carry?

Gordon replied that "tough choices" would have to be made. Ferrick was not satisfied. He and Gordon soon ended up in a heated exchange. Ferrick returned to his desk and wrote a memo to Bennett and Gordon, apologizing for his outburst but then pressing for the explanation he was not alone in wanting. "If we try to do everything,

we won't do anything particularly well," he wrote. "The message I
got was: we are going to do it all. In fact, we are going to expand into
online in a major way. The problem with this is that this doesn't give
the necessary guidance to reporters. By telling them to do it all, you
cede the decision on triage to the people in the field. (If the generals won't make the decision, the corporals will.)"

Which, ironically, is precisely what Bennett wanted. She wanted
to believe that as she articulated a vision her staff would understand
what she wanted and would, in turn, themselves make the very decisions that Ferrick was demanding of her.

She could, if she chose, edit by command. "If I say, "Run over
there' they'll run," she said. "But you're not going to get what you
want. I could make a Delphic pronouncement and see it happen
and not want it to happen. When you're trying to make a really fundamental change you've got to make sure that people understand
what that change is. That people have the tools and have the support
of their colleagues. And that they want to make that change." She
began sending Friday memos to the staff on what had worked that
week, and, without saying it in so many words, what had pleased her.

She could already see the change coming, in spots. She had
been happy, for example, to read an e-mail exchange in which a reporter challenged a metro editor who was asking for a crime story.
The reporter argued that that was precisely the kind of story the paper was not going to cover anymore. Some editors, Bennett said, had
grasped the concept more quickly than others. Among them was
Bob Rose, the business editor.

She had hired Rose from her old paper, the *Wall Street Journal*,
whose culture was very much one of leaving some stories untold—
or briefed—in return for pursuing the larger piece that others had
not even thought of. As it happened, that morning, Rose was presented with a story that necessitated his choosing between the paper's traditional ways and Bennett's vision of the future. Ford had announced that it was shutting fourteen plants and laying off 30,000
people, a big story. Tradition would have called for pulling a reporter

off one piece—perhaps a time-consuming enterprise piece—and, in the absence of an auto writer on the staff, asking him to cobble together something for the next day's paper. Rose considered doing just that, and then changed his mind. Without a large piece already conceived and reported about, say, the decline of the American auto industry, without a writer in Detroit or someone in-house with real knowledge of the industry, and without any Ford plants in the area, he decided to leave it to the wires. Instead, he concentrated on two local stories—a scoop on Donald Trump's plan to build a forty-five-story luxury condominium on the Delaware waterfront, and the Food and Drug Administration's decision to allow the sale of prescription diet pills over the counter, one of which was manufactured in Philadelphia. Both stories ran on page one.

Still, it had been one thing for Gene Roberts to edit in his often inscrutable way, leaving his subordinates to decipher his meaning. Roberts had hired 400 people who had come to his *Inquirer* because he had detected in them an understanding of what he wanted. Bennett had inherited a staff hired by Roberts and his successors. Roberts himself had some sympathy for her predicament. "Say you come up with a plan," he said. "My experience is that it's going to take you five years to implement it. You can't implement it without hiring flexibility. After all, your staff has given you your existing newspaper."

Bennett could not hire, and she had set in motion a process that could only be achieved with time. Time, however, given Knight Ridder's imminent sale, was an unknown quantity.

It was not the Golden Age that Amanda Bennett wanted to reclaim—she had neither the money, the large staff, nor, it was now clear, the inclination. But the plan she had envisioned, which even her critics in the newsroom thought a good one, could bring to the *Inquirer* not another reinvention but something far more satisfying: a restoration.

Bennett's *Inquirer* soon displayed a willingness to, as it were, zig when others zagged, when in February it published the cartoons from a Danish newspaper that had so inflamed the Muslim world, and which so many of the big papers chose not to print. The newspaper that Bennett had in mind had existed once before: it was the *Inquirer* before the Alpha Plan, before the death of the *Bulletin*, before the days when it could reasonably challenge the *Times* and the *Post*. The *Inquirer* of the mid-1970s was a renegade. It ignored things. Its stories ran long. It indulged its reporters; it made so many of them so happy that they pushed themselves to do good work and did not want to leave.

Now there were people, especially the newer reporters, who had come to the *Inquirer* from other places, who did not want to believe that they had made a mistake in coming to Philadelphia. They were surrounded by older people who had decided not to leave, and who had known what it was like to work at a great newspaper and wanted to experience that particular joy again. Chris Satullo felt it was important that Bennett and Gordon appreciate just how corrosive the past fifteen years had been to the staff of the *Inquirer* and to be aware, as he put it, of the "scars people carry on their backs."

Meanwhile, in San Jose, Knight Ridder was hosting its suitors. Gannett had tendered a preliminary bid along with McClatchy, Providence Equity Partners, Texas Pacific Group, Madison Dearborn Partners, Spectrum Equity, Thomas H. Lee Partners, and Media News Group, though it was still difficult to tell which firms might actually be secret partners.

The sale and the future were out of Amanda Bennett's hands, and that brought her a certain comfort. "There's nothing I can do about it," she said. She sat on the edge of the long blue couch in her office. Two parakeets chirped in a cage next to her desk. "I'm going to do journalism here. I'm going to try to change this paper into something alive and vibrant and thoughtful."

Anne Gordon appeared at her door. Gordon looked concerned, unnecessarily so. She had brought to Bennett what was, at the moment, the most welcome sort of problem: a question about a story.

Still a Powerful Voice

Do newspapers still have clout? In many cases the honest answer would be no. Their editorial voices no longer dictate political realities, particularly in big-city America. In The Nation, John Nichols tells the story of an America where newspaper voices still matter.

As the November 7 election approached, Jon Tester was getting hit with the full force of Karl Rove's still considerable arsenal. The White House political czar had decided that the way to maintain Republican control of the Senate was to concentrate GOP resources on traditionally "red" states like Montana, where Tester, an organic farmer and state senator, was mounting a populist campaign against scandal-plagued Republican incumbent Conrad Burns. The airwaves filled with attack ads that savaged the Democrat for criticizing the Patriot Act and declared, "Tester is backed by radicals." Former Department of Homeland Security chief Tom Ridge described Tester's championship of civil liberties as "unfathomable, almost inexplicable." Vice President Cheney arrived to paint the Burns-Tester race as a test of "whether this government will remain strong and resolute on the war on terror or falls into confusion, doubts, and indecision." President Bush, who carried Montana by twenty points in

2004, showed up to close the deal, as some pundits began to predict a Burns comeback.

Tester, a darling of liberal bloggers, was not going to be saved by flaming posts now. He needed a trusted Montana voice, or better yet a chorus of voices, to come to his defense. As election day approached, he got it. The daily newspapers of the Big Sky State came out, one after another, with endorsements of the challenger. Conrad Burns may have had the president and the vice president singing his praises, but the *Helena Independent Record*, the *Bozeman Daily Chronicle*, the *Great Falls Tribune*, the *Montana Standard*, and the *Billings Gazette* were telling Montana voters that Jon Tester was one of their own, and that he belonged in the Senate. The Tester camp scrambled on the last Sunday of the campaign to get the word out, sending e-mails that urged supporters to print out a hastily assembled leaflet highlighting the endorsements to pass along to friends, slip under doors, and post on grocery store bulletin boards.

Two days later, Tester bested Burns by about 2,800 votes. How did Tester beat back the full-court press of the Bush White House? Before the election, a local conservative commentator had tried to argue that the newspaper endorsements were no more influential than "visits of luminaries or stars or political mucky-mucks coming in from the national scene," while a prince of the blogosphere, Daily Kos founder Markos Moulitsas, had posted his prediction that the hometown endorsements would still carry weight in Montana. Daily Kos was right. When the votes were counted, it could fairly be argued—and indeed it was—that endorsements from local papers had tipped the seat to Tester and the Senate to the Democrats.

Newspapers may be the dinosaurs of America's new-media age, hulking behemoths that cost too much to prepare and distribute and that cannot seem to attract young—or even middle-aged—readers in the numbers needed to survive. They may well have entered the death spiral that Philip Meyer, in his recent book *The Vanishing Newspaper*, predicts will conclude one day in 2043 as the last reader throws aside the final copy of a newspaper. But, as the Tester win illustrates, the dinosaurs still have enough life in them to guide—and perhaps even define—our politics.

Especially at the local and state levels, where the fundamental fights for control of a nation less red and blue than complexly purple play out, daily newspapers remain essential arbiters of what passes for news and what Americans think about it. For all the talk about television's dominant role in campaigns (less and less because of its importance as a source of news for most Americans, more and more because of campaign commercials) and all the new attention to the Internet, newspapers for the most part continue to establish the parameters of what gets covered and how. Moreover, neither broadcast nor digital media have developed the reporting infrastructure or the level of credibility that newspapers enjoy. So candidates for the House, the Senate, and even the White House still troop into old gray buildings in Denver and Omaha, Louisville and Boston, Concord and Des Moines in search of a forum where they can talk with reporters and editors about issues and where those conversations will, they hope, be distilled into articles and editorials that set so much of the agenda for the political debate at the local, state, and national levels.

Thus, while George W. Bush may say he rarely reads newspapers, he sat down in 2000 and 2004 to talk with individual newspaper publishers and editors in hopes of winning the support of publications in such battleground states as Pennsylvania and Ohio. So did Al Gore and John Kerry. And Illinois Senator Barack Obama, a newspaper junkie, is busily making the rounds as he ponders a bid for the 2008 Democratic presidential nomination. The attention on news pages and support on editorial pages that newspapers can provide is even more important for candidates trying to elbow their way into the competition by raising new issues.

Former senator John Edwards learned this three years ago, after a *Des Moines Register* endorsement focused on his ideas about the disturbing development of "two Americas" and ignited his campaign in Iowa's Democratic presidential caucuses. "We were talking about issues, such as poverty, that didn't necessarily lend themselves to soundbites," explained Edwards, who said his campaign, which eventually finished a solid second in the caucuses, experienced a "massive upsurge" after receiving the endorsement. "When a newspaper that people know says, 'Hey, people should be paying attention to what this guy is saying,' it makes a huge difference."

And it's not only in the heat of a campaign that newspapers help set the agenda. Consider, for example, the *Chicago Tribune's* relentless focus on the injustice of the death penalty, which led a Republican governor to declare a moratorium on executions in Illinois six years ago and, ultimately, to clear death row. Groundbreaking revelations regarding the disputed 2000 presidential election in Florida were uncovered by the *Orlando Sentinel* and the *St. Petersburg Times*. And while there is no question that bloggers raised the alarm about Diebold's dubious voting machines before the 2004 election, newspapers were dramatically more aggressive in picking up on concerns about paperless ballots and election abuses than TV networks or local stations during the 2006 campaign.

This is not to suggest that most newspapers do their journalism as well or as wisely as they should, nor that the role of newspapers is still as vital as it was in the 1950s, when President Dwight Eisenhower, worried about the financial difficulties of the *New York Herald Tribune*, personally wrote millionaire John Hay Whitney and urged him to take charge of the publication because, he argued, it had a "great and valuable function to perform for the future of America." But newspapers remain necessary, at least for now. Unfortunately, necessity does not translate to the sort of profits that contemporary newspaper owners demand—nor to any assurance of the long-term survival of journalism as we know and need it.

Crises like that of the *Herald Tribune* a half-century ago are now the norm rather than the exception. The newspaper industry is in trouble. Big trouble. In 1950 newspapers in the United States had a weekday circulation of 54 million. The circulation figures are roughly the same today, but the number of households has more than doubled. The *Los Angeles Times'* daily circulation was down 8 percent in a single six-month period in 2006, while the *Philadelphia Inquirer* was down 7.5 percent, the *Boston Globe* 6.7 percent, the *New York Times* 3.5 percent, and the *Washington Post* 3.3 percent.

With drops in circulation have come declines in revenues—not because subscriptions provide all that much money but because media companies collect money from advertisers based on the number of homes they reach. Big advertisers long ago began shifting from the printed page to television, but now classified advertising, the meat-and-potatoes of local and regional daily newspapers, has begun migrating at dramatic speed to websites like craigslist.

What's happening is not just a temporary downturn. From 1990, when newspaper circulation peaked at 62.3 million, readership has been in steady decline. That might lead some to the casual conclusion that the Internet is the problem. But as veteran journalist and media writer Ben Compaine explains, "The heyday of newspapers was in the late nineteenth century, as expanding literacy combined with the development of the steam-driven rotary press, a market economy, and wood pulp–based newsprint to make the mass-circulation penny press possible. From the mid-1800s to the 1920s, newspapers were the only mass-circulation daily news and information medium in the media barnyard. That changed with radio. It accelerated with television. The Internet is just the latest information technology that has added to the choices that consumers and advertisers have for obtaining and creating information." All true, but there is powerful evidence that the breaking point for newspapers may finally be coming.

Individual owners and powerful families—who often, though by no means always, settled for reasonable profits in return for the ego boost that went with putting out a quality newspaper—are exiting the stage. Increasingly newspapers are owned by the shareholders of national chains, who do not even know—let alone care about—the names of the papers from which they demand profit margins that are generally twice the average for other industries. Where a local family might have grudgingly accepted a weak quarter and a downturn in revenues, shareholders greet any softness on the bottom line with demands for draconian cuts. If a paper's current managers are unwilling to make them, investors look for more ruthless managers. Investors forced the breakup and sale, in 2006, of the venerable Knight Ridder chain, which owned Pulitzer Prize–winning newspapers like the *Philadelphia Inquirer*, the *San Jose Mercury News*, and the *Miami Herald*. Similar pressures have forced the Tribune Company, which publishes the *Chicago Tribune*, the *Los Angeles Times*, the *Hartford Courant*, and several Florida dailies, to put itself on the block.

In recent months, Morgan Stanley has been pressuring the New York Times Company to alter its voting structure to reduce the influence of the Sulzberger family, which has opted for reasonably high—if often imperfect—journalistic standards over unreasonably high profits. The company's "current corporate governance practices deviate from what is widely considered to be best practice," explained Morgan Stanley Investment Management, owner of almost 8 percent of the Times stock, in asking shareholders to vote at this April's annual meeting in favor of its plan. The Sulzbergers shot back with a statement that the family "has no intention of opening our doors to the kind of action that is tearing at the heart of some of the other great journalistic institutions in our country." But the bosses at Knight Ridder once said much the same thing, and even if the Sulzbergers do manage to maintain one major newspaper in something like its current form, their statement is an acknowledgment that the broader trends are in the wrong direction.

How wrong? Under apparent pressure from Wall Street, the McClatchy chain just sold off what would normally have been a crown jewel among its holdings, the *Minneapolis Star Tribune*, at a rock-bottom price—less than half the $1.2 billion it paid for the largest paper in Minnesota eight years ago. "It was a drag on the bottom line, and we felt we would do better without it," declared McClatchy CEO Gary Pruitt. The new owner, a private-equity firm that owns no other newspapers, is not expected to raise journalistic standards — even if the new overseers claim they'll maintain the *Star Tribune* as the great regional daily it has been for decades. "These buyers aren't in it for the love of journalism, or even for the influence that you get by buying a local paper," argues John Morton, dean of newspaper ownership analysts. "They are in it to make a profit by flipping the paper in five or six years, and the way to do that usually involves a lot of cutting in the meantime."

The *Times*, the *Star Tribune*, and other great newspapers are not going to collapse soon. But their circumstances are evidence of the rapid, and often dire, changes transforming American newspapering into something less than it has been. Owners are moving to satisfy investors by slashing newsroom staff, pressuring unions to accept cuts, dumbing down coverage of important issues, eliminating statehouse, Washington, and foreign bureaus (even the *Wall Street Journal* is getting into the act, with the recent shuttering of its Canada bureau), and generally sucking the life out of what were once considered public trusts — or by selling out to firms that will do the same thing.

The result has been a hemorrhaging of journalism jobs, as reporters and editors join manufacturing workers in the ranks of "disposable Americans." More than 44,000 news industry employees, at least 34,000 of them newspaper journalists, have lost their jobs over the past five years. Roughly 200 jobs have been cut at the *Chicago Tribune* over the past year. The *Akron Beacon Journal*, a Pulitzer Prize–winning Ohio daily that once set the standard in the state for investigative journalism, has slashed newsroom jobs by 25 percent. The *San Jose Mercury News* is in the process of shedding 17 percent of its newsroom positions. And deep cuts are being implemented in Denver, Pittsburgh, St. Paul, Philadelphia, and dozens of smaller cities where traditional beats — labor, farm, federal courts — are disappearing as retiring reporters are not replaced.

The Project for Excellence in Journalism's current report on "The State of the News Media" notes, "In some cities, the numbers

alone tell the story. There are roughly half as many reporters covering metropolitan Philadelphia, for instance, as in 1980. The number
of newspaper reporters there has fallen from 500 to 220. The pattern
at the suburban papers around the city has been similar, though not
as extreme. The local TV stations, with the exception of Fox, have
cut back on traditional news coverage. The five AM radio stations
that used to cover news have been reduced to two. As recently as
1990, the *Philadelphia Inquirer* had 46 reporters covering the city.
Today it has 24."

What that translates to is this: If we assume that *Inquirer* reporters work normal schedules, there are substantial portions of any
given week when fewer than five journalists provide the primary coverage for a city of 1.4 million people. Major news stories are going
untold. Vast stretches of a metropolis are being neglected. And the
reporter-to-population ratio will soon worsen, as plans are implemented to cut up to 17 percent of remaining editorial jobs. More significant, as Ed Herman, professor emeritus at the University of
Pennsylvania's Wharton School and an expert not just on the media
but on Philadelphia, told me last year, the sense of civic connection
that should be nurtured by a great newspaper is instead fraying.
"Newspapers were once thought to bring communities together.
That's not the case anymore," he said, explaining, "People aren't stu-
pid. They recognize when their local newspaper loses interest in
them as anything but consumers of advertisements."

It is the recognition of what is being lost that has inspired journalists to begin speaking up and getting active in ways that have not
been seen since media unions began to organize in the 1930s. The
Newspaper Guild and its parent union, the Communications Workers of America, organized a Day of Action on December 11 to draw
attention to the fact that cuts, often seen only in isolation, add up to
a crisis not just for journalism but for the political and governmental processes of the nation. "That's why we're asking the public to
join us—for democracy's sake—to say no to cutting the jobs of jour-

nalists and all workers whose work supports good journalism," explained Guild president Linda Foley.

Syndicated columnist Molly Ivins puts it best when she says that newspapers aren't dying but committing suicide. "What really pisses me off," she told the journal of the newspaper industry, *Editor & Publisher*, is "this most remarkable business plan: Newspaper owners look at one another and say, 'Our rate of return is slipping a bit; let's solve that problem by making our product smaller and less helpful and less interesting.'" If there has been a model of American newspaper innovation in the past three decades, it's this: Never do something bold, edgy, or intelligent when there is a predictable and useless gimmick into which energy and resources can be dumped for a few years.

At the same time, newspaper owners have poured resources into lobbying for federal policy shifts that would allow them to merge with competitors and create one-newsroom towns. The Newspaper Association of America and industry lobbyists have been pushing for years for the elimination of the Federal Communications Commission's newspaper/broadcast cross-ownership ban, which prohibits ownership by a single firm of a newspaper and television and radio stations in the same market. Newspaper owners argue that with the ban lifted, they could cut costs by having the same journalists produce online and print reports and appear on company-owned radio and TV news programs. In the few cities where the cross-ownership model has been tried, however, there is no evidence to suggest that it produces better journalism or a more informed public. Instead it makes the few remaining reporters busier, leaving them with less time for what *Washington Post* veteran and Pulitzer Prize–winner David Maraniss says is the most important work of journalism: thinking.

Left to their own devices, the current owners of American newspapers are indeed likely to consummate the suicide pact they have entered into with their investors. That should scare the hell out of Americans who recognize that Jefferson was right when he said that good journalism is essential to democracy. It should also get citizens asking the right questions: If newspapers really are fading away, what comes next? And in this period of transition, how do we assure that the vital role that newspapers still play is not lost? As sad as the end of newspapers might be for someone like me, who began writing at age 11 for the weekly newspaper in my Wisconsin hometown, the important question for the great mass of Americans is not, How do we save newspapers? It's, How do we still get a healthy mix of reported news and analysis from a variety of at least reasonably reliable sources?

Local television stations, identified by a majority of citizens as their primary source of news about civic life, are actually covering less political news than they did a decade ago. A new survey of the coverage of the 2006 election season, conducted by University of Wisconsin researchers, established that "local television news viewers got considerably more information about campaigns from paid political advertisements than from actual news coverage." The survey also said that "Local newscasts in seven Midwest markets aired four minutes, 24 seconds of paid political ads during the typical 30-minute broadcast [before the election] while dedicating an average of one minute, 43 seconds to election news coverage."

The Internet certainly devotes more attention to politics. But, for the most part, the information discussed is still gathered by newspaper reporters, and while a few high-profile journalists have begun to migrate from old-fashioned newsrooms to the blogosphere, they tend to arrive as commentators rather than gatherers of news. The web has yet to emerge as a distinct journalistic force—let alone one that speaks with the authority at the local, state, or regional level of a traditional daily newspaper. While the web may someday be home to sites that generate the revenues needed to pay reporters and editors to produce meaningful journalism, that day has yet to arrive in any real sense.

"What is really frightening is that newspapers appear to be dying so quickly that they may disappear, or at least disappear as a serious part of our lives, before we have a replacement for them. That's a grave danger to democracy," says Maraniss. "As flawed as journalism as practiced by newspapers is, we don't have another vehicle for journalism that picks up where newspapers leave off. That's what we should be worried about. Maybe newspapers can be replaced, probably newspapers can be replaced. But journalism can't be replaced—not if we're going to function as any kind of democracy."

European and Asian media owners have been a good deal more creative and aggressive in their response to the changing circumstances of newspapers. And in many cases, though certainly not all, they have been more successful than their American counterparts in maintaining the popular appeal of print publications. European publishers have, for instance, been far more willing to invest in radical redesigns of papers and new printing and distribution systems. And they have long recognized something that is close to unimaginable to those who guide American newspapering: that taking strong front-page stands on issues such as the genetic modification of food and global warming—becoming what the British refer to as a "campaigning newspaper"—does not inspire charges of bias but instead draws readers to groundbreaking journalism.

While the *Chicago Tribune* surely gets high marks for its attention to the death penalty issue, newspapers like Britain's *Independent* embark on dozens of campaigns in the course of a year—even going so far as to give their front pages over to promotions of rallies and protest marches against everything from poverty in Africa to the war in Iraq. But it's not just that European publishers are more engaged and adventurous. European citizens and their governments have a tradition of taking seriously the role newspaper journalism plays in building a civil and democratic society.

In Norway, Sweden, and Finland, where Internet use is high and strong public broadcasting systems provide sound radio and TV alternatives, newspapers are in a dramatically better position than in the United States—in part because of long-standing government commitments to encourage competition, diversity, and quality. In

Norway, for instance, the Media Authority, an administrative body within the country's cultural affairs ministry, uses public subsidies to encourage the development of local newspapers that compete with bigger established papers. The program promotes the development of newspapers in sparsely populated regions and helps sustain publications that may have an ideological following but are not necessarily popular with advertisers. The system is strictly controlled to avoid government censorship or pressures on publishers—in fact, the joke goes that the best way to get government assistance is to start an opposition newspaper. Even large newspapers that have little or no need for the subsidies are influenced by the system, as they find themselves in competition with papers that push the journalistic envelope. The basic requirements to qualify for subsidies provide encouragement to newspapers to invest in journalism. At the same time, key subsidies are not available to newspapers owned by companies that pay stock dividends—a restriction that prevents investors from cashing in on the public largesse.

One by-product of the Scandinavian commitment to newspapers, especially in Norway, has been the development of some of the finest news-oriented Internet sites in the world. If newspapers do eventually slide out of existence, the strength of these websites offers encouraging evidence that journalism will survive. Norway's Schibsted newspaper firm now earns 35 percent of its operating profits from Internet ventures that have built on the reputation of its newspapers to develop the most-visited news websites in Scandinavia. Another Scandinavian publishing house, Orkla Media, owns what is frequently referred to as one of the world's most successful web-only newspapers, Germany's *Netzeitung*. "It's not a blog, a search engine, or an aggregator," explains web journalism consultant Jeff Jarvis in an enthusiastic review of the initiative. "It is a newspaper without the paper, but with 60 journalists reporting the news. *Netzeitung* has not only survived the Internet bubble and a Ping-Pong game of corporate sales, it has acquired other media properties; it is starting an ambitious effort in networked journalism with citizen reporters; and it is set to be profitable [in the near term]."

The point here is not to portray subsidy programs as a panacea. While they seem to have worked well in Norway and a few other countries, their track record in countries like Italy is decidedly more mixed. The lesson from the rest of the world isn't that the United States ought to set up a particular program of subsidies—or borrow any other individual idea. It's that government can in the right circumstances and with the right intentions play a useful role in stabilizing the fortunes of newspapers and in encouraging investments in serious journalism. For instance, allowing Americans to deduct the price of an annual newspaper subscription from their taxes would boost circulation while creating the potential for papers to be less reliant on advertising revenue, and thus less vulnerable to pressures from advertisers. However, even this innovative approach runs the risk, if it were embarked upon in isolation, of reinforcing the bad habits of U.S. media owners.

What America needs are new and better models of newspaper ownership. Instead of letting the FCC open the way for chain newspapers to establish local monopolies by eliminating the ban on cross-ownership, Congress should concern itself with reestablishing competition and innovation by encouraging the breakup of chains and the sale of big-city dailies to local owners who value the role a great newspaper can play in a community. Much has been made of the interest expressed by wealthy newspaper fans like entertainment mogul David Geffen, former supermarket magnate Ron Burkle, and former home builder Eli Broad in buying the *Los Angeles Times*. Broad, a critic of chain ownership who suggests that distant owners of local newspapers ill-serve the communities in which they publish, explains, "I believe a newspaper is a civic asset, a civic trust. I see a role for foundations that are not totally bottom-line oriented somehow being involved in the newspaper industry and/or civic-minded families or others."

Broad's line of reasoning should be encouraged. But the most important aspect of his vision is that reference to "others" who might own newspapers. Civic-minded families may well have a better record of running newspapers than distant investors, but there aren't enough wealthy philanthropists to go around, and besides, they aren't all "civic minded." Foundations and trusts, which control a handful of American newspapers, present a more interesting prospect. While the experience is limited, foundation-controlled newspapers such as the *St. Petersburg Times* do, for the most part, have better journalistic reputations than their competitors. Congress should concern itself particularly with developing policies that would make it easier—through shifts in approaches to taxation, postal subsidies, and the often-abused "joint operating agreements" established in a number of larger cities to help maintain competition—for newspaper employees, unions, and even community coalitions to buy, and perhaps even start, newspapers.

Representative Maurice Hinchey, the New York Democrat who chairs the congressional Future of American Media Caucus, has the right idea when he says Congress should seek to assure that the American people "have easy access to vast sources of news so that they can be well informed with a diverse mix of reporting and opinion." That may sound like a broad goal, but it's the right organizing principle. No matter what the fate of newspapers, developing new models for ownership of institutions that gather, analyze, comment upon, and then distribute the news—be they newspapers, television stations, radio stations, websites, or whatever the product of the next great technological leap—is essential to making sure that journalism survives and thrives.

Much of the current media landscape would have been unimaginable just a few decades ago. Much of what will be is equally unimaginable. What is necessary now is a determination to insure that the media of the future deliver not merely for owners but for workers, news consumers, and democracy. Perhaps newspapers really can survive in a form familiar to those of us who cherish them.

But even if that is not to be, they must survive in a form that fosters a healthy transition from old media to new, and that preserves and, one hopes, improves journalism. The transition need not be tidy. It should embody the experimentation, adventurousness, and glorious failures that our current crop of risk-averse publishers have shunned.

Above all, the debate about the future of newspapers should not be ceded to the investment-driven corporations that have failed so miserably to maintain media that sustain both themselves and democracy. Americans who recognize that newspapers remain, at least for the time being, essential generators of journalism, and that the serious-minded gathering and analysis of news is still necessary for an informed and engaged citizenry, must join reporters and editors in the struggle to assure that even if newspapers do not survive forever, journalism will.

KEN AULETTA

Can the *Los Angeles Times*
Survive Its Owners?

One of the institutions trapped in the center of Tribune Company's failed synergy plans is the Los Angeles Times. *In a brief period of time and under intense pressure from Chicago to cut costs, it lost a string of publishers and popular editors and found itself at the center of a battle between the remnants of the old owners, the Chandler family, and a collection of Chicago executives desperately seeking a solution to the company's problems. Tribune Company was viewed by some as the salvation of the* Times *when it bought the company. By the time Ken Auletta arrived on the scene for* The New Yorker, *the question was, "Can the* Los Angeles Times *survive its owners?"*

By the morning of July 20th, after months of gossip, everyone in the third-floor newsroom of the *Los Angeles Times* knew that John S. Carroll, who had been the newspaper's editor for five years, was going to resign. Through the large glass window of the conference room, the staff could see Carroll, along with the senior editors and the publisher, Jeffrey Johnson, who had rarely appeared in the newsroom. They all looked somber. A few minutes after the meeting adjourned, the staff assembled at the national desk, across from Carroll's office, to hear Johnson confirm that Carroll was indeed leaving.

Tension between Carroll and the Tribune Company, the newspaper's Chicago-based owner, had been growing for a couple of years; Carroll, who is sixty-three and had edited three newspapers, was expected to leave soon, in any case. The departure ceremony was brief; the speakers relied on cliché and euphemism to get through the ordeal. History, the publisher said, would look at Carroll's stewardship as an "incredibly special period"—a reference to the fact that the newspaper had won thirteen Pulitzer Prizes since Carroll's arrival. Carroll, who speaks in a monotone, with a trace of a North Carolina drawl, said, "There have been any number of factors in my consideration, and I'm not going to go into them all." Having worked in newspapers his entire adult life, he'd decided it was time to move on, he said. "Leaving is always hard, and this is hard for me." Carroll then hugged Dean Baquet, the managing editor, whom he had hired not long after he came to the *Times*.

Carroll didn't say much else. When *Newsweek* asked him if the Tribune Company appreciated the journalism of the *Times*, he said, "I want to be candid with you, but I'm going to have to duck on that one." But, to anyone who had followed Carroll's career, and knew about his problems with the newspaper's owners, the reply was in fact candid. As he later told me, he had grown weary of "incessant cost-cutting" by the Tribune Company. He believed that, on the contrary, investing in the newspaper would eventually produce higher profits, which was what the company eagerly sought, and that cutting costs, while it would temporarily improve the bottom line, would erode the paper and might someday destroy it. Carroll and the Tribune Company had been arguing about these issues for five years. The resolution would now be left to his successor.

In March, 2000, the Tribune Company paid $8.3 billion to buy the 116-year-old Times Mirror Company from its controlling shareholders, the Chandler family, who received cash and stock and were awarded four of the sixteen seats on the Tribune board. In addition to the *L.A. Times*, the purchase gave the Tribune Company control of *Newsday*, on Long Island; the *Baltimore Sun*; and the *Hartford Courant*, among other assets, bringing the total number of Tribune daily newspapers to eleven. (Tribune's holdings also include twenty-six television stations; the Chicago Cubs; a quarter of the WB network and a regional sports network; a third of the Food Network; and a television entertainment division.) The biggest prize in this new acquisition was the *Times*, which became the company's largest and most prestigious newspaper. This was something of a sore point in Chicago—the *Chicago Tribune*, founded in 1847, was the company's flagship but had little more than half the readership of the *Times*. In Los Angeles, the newsroom initially welcomed the new ownership. Five months earlier, the paper had been deeply embarrassed when it was revealed that the Times Mirror CEO, Mark H. Willes, a former executive with General Mills, and the newspaper's publisher, Kathryn Downing, had entered into a profit-sharing partnership with the new Staples Center, a sports and entertainment arena, and had then published a special edition of the *Times'* Sunday magazine devoted to the center's opening. The arrangement, which was kept secret from the paper's editor until shortly before publication, gave Staples Center half the advertising revenues for this supposedly independent journalistic enterprise. The *Times* and its top management had been humiliated, and the Tribune Company seemed to promise a new era.

There was optimism in Chicago, too. Ann Marie Lipinski, the editor of the *Tribune*, said, "For the most part, the print journalists were happy that the company was laying down a major bet on the viability of these things we love," meaning newspapers, at a time when "people were looking to divest themselves" of newspapers.

Like most newspaper companies in the United States, the Tribune Company has to confront not only declining circulation and disappointing advertising sales but a belief on Wall Street that newspapers are a poor investment. While the population of the United States increased by 64 percent between 1960 and 2004, daily newspaper circulation dropped by 3.7 million—to just over 55 million. There is something almost prehistoric about using expensive newsprint and elaborate delivery systems, to homes and newsstands, in the age of the Internet.

These concerns have affected newsrooms everywhere. Recently, the New York Times Company announced that it would reduce its workforce by five hundred, including about 4 percent of the news-room at the *Times* and 6 percent at the *Boston Globe*; Knight Ridder said that it would cut 15 percent of the newsroom staff at the *Philadelphia Inquirer* and at the *San Jose Mercury News.* The after-noon newspaper in Birmingham, Alabama, announced in late Sep-tember that it was going out of business, and the Tribune Company is cutting forty-five newsroom jobs at *Newsday.* Personnel reductions have become as common in newsrooms as they are in American factories.

In Chicago, the reasons for buying Times Mirror were clear. There were opportunities "for significant cost savings at the *Los An-geles Times*," and larger profits, according to Jack Fuller, who was then the president of Tribune Publishing. Fuller pointed out that "by buying the *Times* we had television stations and newspapers in the three largest markets in the country"—Los Angeles, New York, and Chicago—and, he added, "the papers were really just excellent newspapers." Not much was said then about a concern expressed by David Laventhol, who was the president of Times Mirror from 1987 to 1993, that "the people who decide the fate of Los Angeles's news-paper now live in Chicago."

Fuller's first task was to restore credibility to the *Times* after the Staples debacle, and that led him to John Carroll, who at that time was the editor of the *Baltimore Sun.* Fuller had met Carroll when they served on a Pulitzer Prize board and knew that he was seen as someone who improved newspapers and was uncommonly popular with the reporters and editors he worked with.

Carroll was aware that the profit plans of media chains could conflict with the goals of journalists, but he wanted to believe that the Tribune Company saw, as he did, that investing in staff and resources would pay dividends in readership. Carroll thought he understood Fuller. Fuller, after all, had started out as a *Chicago Tribune* copyboy at the age of sixteen. He became a reporter, and eventually took over the editorial page, winning a Pulitzer Prize for editorial writing; he rose to become the paper's editor and then the publisher.

Carroll had a particular interest in investigative reporting. In the 1970s, he had worked for Eugene Roberts, the editor of the *Philadelphia Inquirer*, and had expanded the paper's investigative coverage. A series on detectives who brutalized suspects to win confessions earned a Pulitzer Prize—one of seventeen Pulitzers that the *Inquirer* won under Roberts. In 1979, Carroll became the editor of the *Lexington* (Kentucky) *Herald* (now the *Herald-Leader*). At the *Baltimore Sun*, which Carroll took over in 1991, he undertook such ambitious projects as sending reporters to southern Sudan, to expose the country's slave trade. Michael Pakenham, who had been the *Sun*'s book editor, and had also worked with Carroll at the *Inquirer*, said, "He had a profound sense of the newspaper being a set of integrated parts, but the parts had to be made excellent on their own. He wanted the *Baltimore Sun* to be the best large regional paper in the country." Carroll, though, was not happy with the direction of Times Mirror, the *Sun*'s owner, under Mark Willes, and his situation reminded him of what had happened to Gene Roberts, who quit the *Inquirer* in 1990 after losing too many battles with corporate executives at Knight Ridder. "You really got the impression that you were governed by the fluctuations in the stock price," Roberts told me, recalling that time. By 2000, Carroll was ready for a change, and he expected to become the head of the Nieman Foundation for Journalism, at Harvard. It was at about that point that Fuller called and asked him to come to Los Angeles.

At the *Times*, Carroll's first priority was to hire a managing editor, and he chose someone he had never met: Dean Baquet, the national editor of the *New York Times*. Baquet, who is African

American, was the fourth of five brothers raised in a working-class New Orleans neighborhood. His family lived in the back of a Creole restaurant that his father opened after giving up a job as a mailman. The first time Baquet traveled outside Louisiana was when he went North to attend Columbia University. After his sophomore year, he got a summer internship at the *States-Item*, an afternoon paper in New Orleans—an experience he liked so much that he dropped out of Columbia. He spent seven years in New Orleans and in 1984 was hired by the *Chicago Tribune*, where he and Ann Marie Lipinski shared a Pulitzer Prize for uncovering corruption on the City Council. After six years at the *Tribune*, he was recruited by the *New York Times* as an investigative reporter.

Baquet, who is forty-nine, says that he did not aspire to be an editor, but he was encouraged to make the change by Joseph Lelyveld, the *Times'* executive editor, who had helped bring him to the paper. "I hated it for the first year, and then I started to like it," he says. He started as the deputy Metro editor and was soon promoted to national editor. Newsrooms are notorious for their competition and backbiting, and few editors escape the atmosphere of complaint and resentment. Baquet succeeded. Douglas Franz, a close friend who worked under him, said, "The national desk was situated in the middle of the third-floor newsroom, and I sat a few feet away from it for five years. It was the happiest place in that often dismal building, a desk where editors joked and reporters liked to drop by, rather than slink past. And it was because of Dean." With patience, Baquet might have won the most powerful job in newspapers—the editorship of the *New York Times*.

Baquet recalls that he was torn about accepting the offer from Carroll. His wife, Dylan, did not want to leave New York, and he felt loyal to Lelyveld. "I'm not a careerist, but I did look at what the next job for me would be at the *New York Times*," Baquet told me. "I was too young to be a candidate for anything but assistant managing editor. I just thought, Would my next job at the *New York Times* be as fun as being the managing editor for John?" In addition—although he claims that the subject "never came up"—since Carroll was fifty-seven, Baquet said, "I assumed that if things went well I would succeed him."

Carroll, who has white hair, a square jaw, and a wry expression that rarely changes, is hardly in the charismatic mold of Ben Bradlee. Rather, much like Gene Roberts, he led with an almost gnomic intelligence. James Rainey, a media writer who joined the paper in 1984, says of Carroll, "He got as much done here by silence. At meetings, when he had heard enough he walked out or started typing on his computer." Carroll disliked business-management meetings. If an editor or a reporter needed him, his door was open, but to others he would sometimes say, "Is it a crisis? If not, let's talk next week."

Martin Gottlieb, the associate managing editor of the *New York Times* and Baquet's closest friend in New York, says that Baquet has enormous empathy for people; he thinks that this quality comes from having a close-knit family, and particularly from the pain of watching his oldest brother die as a result of years of heavy drinking and smoking. Baquet attributes it to his early days as a reporter writing about people he knew in New Orleans; a local black political organization was so upset with corruption stories he did that it boycotted his father's restaurant. One exposé led to the arrest of the sister of a close friend. "It's an experience that reporters don't have much anymore, where you cover the town you live in and see the impact of your stories," Baquet said to me. "It's harder to see people as black and white. I don't mean racially. I mean good guys and bad guys." He added, "You learn fairness when you have to face the guys you write about the next day."

Doyle McManus, the Washington bureau chief of the *L.A. Times*, says of Carroll and Baquet, "They were a terrific Mutt-and-Jeff act. They did distinctly different things. John was General Marshall and Dean was General Eisenhower." Baquet "was in my office ten times a day," the national editor, Scott Kraft, said. "John would pay a lot of attention to a few stories, and delegate the rest. Dean likes to be involved in every aspect of the coverage." Kit Rachlis, a *Times* alumnus who is now the editor of the magazine *Los Angeles*, and who admired what Carroll and Baquet were doing, said that Baquet has difficulty making hard decisions about personnel and delivering bad news.

With the support of the *Times'* publisher, John Puerner, who was highly regarded by the Tribune Company, Carroll and Baquet made major changes over the next five years. They replaced ten of the fourteen editors on the paper's masthead. The Orange County bureau, which had employed about two hundred people, now employs fewer than twenty; most of the staff was moved to other sections. (Orange County was scaled back, Baquet says, because "it was marketing; it wasn't journalism.") They expanded the Washington bureau from fifty-five to sixty-one people, which made it second in size only to that of the *New York Times*; and they spent millions of dollars covering Iraq. The paper has twenty-four overseas bureaus—three more than the *Washington Post*. They doubled the number of investigative reporters. Vernon Loeb, a strong investigative reporter at the *Post*, was hired as Metro investigations editor, with a team of ten reporters to supervise.

The paper aggressively pursued investigative stories. Five days before the recall election for California's governor, the *Times* published a story revealing that the Republican candidate, Arnold Schwarzenegger, had sometimes groped women during his acting career. Better to publish now, Carroll reasoned, than "explain lamely to our readers after Election Day why we had withheld the story." Some conservatives saw a liberal bias behind the Schwarzenegger articles and the timing of their publication. More than a thousand readers canceled their subscriptions. A series on the Martin Luther King, Jr. / Drew Medical Center—headlined DEADLY ERRORS AND POLITICS BETRAY A HOSPITAL'S PROMISE—singled out the hospital's leadership, which was African American. The series, which won a Pulitzer Prize, was denounced by black community leaders. The newspaper was willing to commit considerable time and money to a single story, and a November, 2003, series on Wal-Mart's business practices—reported from Asia and Central America, as well as from the United States—remains the definitive newspaper study of the subject; it won another Pulitzer for the *Times*.

For years, under the Chandlers, the *Times* was known as a "cops and courts" paper, although it tried to cover the nation and the world, and often did it well. Carroll and Baquet's obsession with matching America's best newspapers came at the expense of local coverage. The problem was compounded when they hired an editor from *Newsday* to oversee the California section and staffed the local desk with relatively inexperienced reporters, who viewed local news as a path to Washington or overseas assignments. (However, the staff did win a Pulitzer last year for its coverage of the ruinous brush fires that swept through the area.) One veteran reporter, Bill Boyarsky, who had spent his career covering California, accepted early retirement, which cost the *Times* some authority. "We've lost a lot of experience," Leo Wolinsky, the deputy managing editor, who runs the daily page-one meeting, said. Last year, Janet Clayton, a Californian who had been the editorial-page editor, was made assistant managing editor for state and local news. Still, Baquet said, "we haven't mastered making the paper feel like it is edited in Los Angeles."

The geography of Los Angeles has never been ideally suited to newspapers. People do not commute on subways, where the morning paper is a daily companion. The readership area is unusually diffuse. The city's five counties encompass nearly thirty-four thousand square miles—which is about the size of Indiana. The area now has more residents, 17.5 million, than all of Florida. The *Times* prints five zoned editions, but the diversity of the population makes it difficult to create an identity. The most recent census reported that there were over three million more nonwhites than whites living in Southern California; nearly 40 percent of the population is Latino. More than a dozen daily newspapers and numerous weeklies compete for the attention of readers.

Nothing was less locally minded than Carroll's decision, in April, 2004, to hire Michael Kinsley as the editorial and opinion editor, which gave the paper a national voice, approval among the chattering classes on the East Coast, and an innovative editor. But Kinsley spent half his time working from Seattle, where he lives, and so, unlike most editorial-page editors, he was not particularly visible in the community. Kinsley delegated that part of the job to Andrés Martinez, whom he recruited in September from the *New York Times*.

The Tribune Company also wanted to consolidate the Washington bureaus of its newspapers. When Jack Fuller first raised the idea, Doyle McManus recalled, he said that he wanted the bureaus "to work together to find ways to eliminate needless duplication of effort," and to operate under one roof. Fuller assured Tribune Company editors that consolidation would not mean eliminating separate bureaus, as Knight Ridder had done. Still, Fuller's request worried Carroll, who was tired of dealing with Chicago, and he asked Baquet to attend more budget reviews and management meetings. Baquet and an old friend, James O'Shea, the managing editor of the *Chicago Tribune*, came up with a compromise, accepted by Doyle McManus, under which the *Times* would gradually reduce its Washington bureau by six people. Deeper cuts were later made in the Washington bureaus of *Newsday* and the *Baltimore Sun*. But Carroll suspected—rightly, as it turned out—that this was only the start of a bigger campaign to cut jobs and resources. Baquet, who shared Carroll's concerns, thought about leaving the paper in 2003. The *New York Times* had fired Howell Raines as executive editor in June, and Joe Lelyveld had returned on an interim basis. The *Times* was scouting for a successor, and on June 15th the *Times*' publisher, Arthur Sulzberger, Jr., and Lelyveld flew to Los Angeles to take Baquet to dinner. "I made it clear to them that I probably would not take the job if they offered it to me, but they didn't offer it to me," Baquet recalls. The conversation with New York continued, though, and Baquet talked over the prospect with Carroll. Baquet's son was settled in school, his wife's parents had moved to California, and he was devoted to Carroll and the staff they had built. He said that he telephoned Sulzberger a week later and took his name out of consideration. The job eventually went, as many expected, to Bill Keller. There was a sense that Carroll and Baquet were not spending enough time communicating with the Tribune Company. Carroll's strengths—editing stories and recruiting talent—"were also his weaknesses," Leo Wolinsky told me. "He was an old-fashioned editor who did not want to engage with his corporate bosses." Vernon Loeb, who had once worked with Carroll at the *Inquirer*, believes that Carroll inherited Gene Roberts's view that a newspaper is perpetually at war with its corporate parent. Loeb was wary of Chicago, but he felt that the company deserved credit for hiring Carroll and Baquet and for supporting investigative teams, including his own.

In April of 2004, the *Times* received five Pulitzer Prizes, the most ever won by the paper. To the surprise of the reporters and editors, Tribune executives did not praise the *Times* in any sort of public communiqué. "You can't turn on your computer here without getting a missive from Dennis FitzSimons"—the Tribune Company's CEO—"yet there was nothing. Nothing!" Tim Rutten, the associate features editor and a media columnist at the *Times*, told me. And no executives from the Tribune Company attended the awards ceremony, at Columbia University. There was a feeling in the *Times* newsroom that the *Chicago Tribune* was envious, a view that was reinforced after James Warren, the *Tribune's* deputy managing editor, commented to *Crain's Chicago Business*, "What'd they win for? Editorials. Well, I'd say we have a better editorial page, by and large. They won for photography. I think ours is as good as anybody. . . . Front to back, I'd argue that our features still remain stronger day-to-day. . . . And no paper has done better [long-term reporting] projects in recent years than the *Tribune*. That's a fact."

Two months later, Carroll was informed that revenues at the *Times* were stagnant and that the Tribune Company expected him to make large newsroom cuts. According to the newspaper analyst

John Morton, Tribune's other newspapers, before the purchase of Times Mirror, consistently produced profit margins averaging close to 30 percent, while the *Los Angeles Times* was earning considerably less. Margins at the *Times* had increased, but, despite the changes that Carroll and Baquet had made, daily circulation had fallen by 12.8 percent since 2000, to just under a million. Nevertheless, Carroll resisted the demand; he continued to believe that the strategy he and Baquet were following would eventually result in larger profits, and that the cuts could permanently damage the paper. Carroll called FitzSimons and proposed that he and Baquet fly to Chicago over the weekend to discuss the cuts. Instead, that afternoon Fitz-Simons and Fuller took the corporate jet to the Burbank airport, where they met with Carroll and Baquet for more than two hours. The discussion was civil and frank, but FitzSimons kept repeating that revenues were not growing, and Carroll and Baquet realized that they had lost the argument. In the end, they were asked to cut sixty-seven out of about eleven hundred editorial positions. In the prior four years, annual expenses had been reduced by about a hundred and thirty million dollars; further cuts were requested for the 2005 budget. "I don't think Carroll's relationship with the Tribune Company ever recovered," Tim Rutten told me.

A senior editor has described the conflict between Chicago and the *Times* editors as "a wrestling match," attributing it in large part to the fact that executives in Chicago were "a little bit panicked" at the company's relatively low stock price and at weaker circulation and advertising numbers. The paper was constantly being urged to adopt the latest "management fad," this editor said, including schemes to lure young readers with a free youth paper "that people would read on trains—and there are no trains in L.A.!" The "ongoing question" in the newsroom, one reporter said, was "What's Chicago doing to us now?"

Journalists may try to understand the world, but not all of them grasp the business side of their newspapers. On the twenty-third floor of Tribune Tower, on Michigan Avenue, in Chicago, Tribune

Company executives tend to view journalism through the prism of the company's successful publishing business, which in 2004 provided 72 percent of Tribune's $5.7 billion in revenues. "We think everybody in the organization should understand what's happening in the wider world of media," FitzSimons, the CEO, told me recently. "Because if we don't make that attempt, if we aren't relentless about it, how can we expect decisions to be understood? People at the papers need to understand how the business is changing."

Measured by revenue, the Tribune Company is the second-biggest newspaper chain, after Gannett, which in 2004 had $6.6 billion in revenues, from a hundred and one newspapers, including *USA Today*. Knight Ridder, with thirty-one dailies, including the *Philadelphia Inquirer* and the *San Jose Mercury News*, earned about $3 billion. Measured by daily circulation, the Tribune Company ranks third, with about 3.1 million, behind Gannett, with 7.6 million, and Knight Ridder, with 3.8 million. For 2004, according to Morton, Gannett newspapers' operating profit margin was 28 percent, and Knight Ridder's was 19 percent. Operating margins at the Tribune newspapers were down to 18 percent. In recent years, Tribune Company executives have met their earnings goals by relying on "efficiencies"—the euphemism for outsourcing, cuts, and layoffs—and these reductions have impressed Wall Street analysts and annual shareholders' meetings. In a recent report, the Goldman Sachs analyst Peter P. Appert noted that Tribune operating expenses had dropped, even though the costs of newsprint and of employee benefits rose. "A 5 percent staff reduction implemented over the past several quarters was key to this performance," he wrote. "We are particularly impressed with the company's ability to hold newspaper operating margins essentially flat." Despite the Tribune Company's efforts, its stock price fell 18 percent in 2004. (Last week, after a court ruled that the Tribune Company was liable for a billion dollars in tax costs, the stock fell more than 4 percent. The case, which the company is appealing, predates the acquisition of Times Mirror.) Jack Fuller believed that, while Carroll was doing a "brilliant" editorial job in Los Angeles, he wasn't enough of a "team player." Fuller, who had been a rival of FitzSimons for the CEO job, stepped down in December, 2004, in order to return to writing. He was replaced by his deputy, Scott Smith, who is fifty-four. Unlike Fuller, Smith has never been a journalist. He is a Chicago native and has spent most of his career at the Tribune Company. A business-school graduate, he joined the company twenty-five years ago as a financial executive, and rose to become the chief financial officer and then chief corporate strategist. In 1993, he was appointed president and publisher of the *South Florida Sun-Sentinel*, in Fort Lauderdale, and in 1997 he returned to Chicago as president and publisher of the Chicago Tribune Company.

In Los Angeles, Smith is sometimes described as "an empty suit"—a frequent term in newsrooms for a paper's corporate overseers. Leo Wolinsky recalls a meeting soon after he was appointed: "We were talking about good things we were doing and how we were trying to hire the best people. He said, 'I don't think you always have to hire the best people.' I was so stunned I didn't follow up. I may be wrong, but I worried that it meant he did not necessarily mean to hire the best. He wanted us to hire the cheapest." Smith denies saying this. Carroll was there, and although he does not remember Smith's words, he recalls that "several things he said caused concern." He also says, referring to Smith, "Every time I mentioned the idea that the *Los Angeles Times* should be among the four best papers, I had the feeling it made people uncomfortable. Nobody ever said we shouldn't do it. But nobody ever said, Yes, that's a good idea."

Smith is viewed more enthusiastically by Ann Marie Lipinski, who joined the *Chicago Tribune* as an intern in 1978, right after college, and whom he appointed editor in 2001. Lipinski acknowledges the "ongoing conversation" at all newspapers about "how you balance the social mission with the economics," but she says that Smith "talks a lot about the social mission of the paper, and it's music to my ears. I don't know that every editor is as fortunate to have somebody minding the store who actually understands the value of that as deeply as he does." When Lipinski's words were repeated to Smith, he smiled and said the sort of thing that journalists like to hear people say about them. At the *Tribune*, he said, he "learned how a journalist thinks about serving readers every day, great storytelling, and what really matters in terms of our public role as well as our commercial role."

Smith was focused on the diminished circulation of the Tribune papers, in particular the *L.A. Times* and, most worryingly, *Newsday*, where there had been a circulation scandal. Executives presumably intent on meeting the Tribune Company's profit goals had lied about the numbers, inflating advertising rates. This forced the company to set aside $90 million from 2004 earnings to settle claims from advertisers who had overpaid for phantom readers.

Recently, I met with Smith and FitzSimons in a conference room between their offices. FitzSimons, a native New Yorker, started out at Grey Advertising and then became a sales-and-marketing executive for Viacom. He joined the Tribune Company in 1982, in television sales, and rose to run all of broadcasting for the company. He became CEO in 2003 and chairman the following year.

Smith dismissed criticism that the Tribune Company had an unseemly obsession with profits. "We don't think about margins alone," he insisted. "We think about 'Are we growing?' " FitzSimons interrupted to say, "We look at improvements in efficiency. Ideally, you want margins to grow through revenue growth, but we have not had revenue growth at the *L.A. Times.*" He went on, "Seventy percent of our employees are shareholders. Our employees own 11 percent of the company"—and, he suggested, keep their eyes fixed on the stock price. When Tribune bought Times Mirror, in 2000, FitzSimons thought that his company would be cheered as a rescuer. He is still shocked that the *Times* newsroom treats him and the other Tribune executives with such hostility: "Five years later, we have the same questions being asked."

In the first six months of 2005, revenues for the Tribune Company were down 2 percent from the previous year. The *Times* all but froze hiring; the single slot in the paper's Las Vegas bureau has been empty for more than a year. The Tribune Company commissioned a study of staffing patterns at various papers and, according to senior editors, discovered that the *Times* had many more copy editors than the *Tribune*. Carroll told Smith that copy editors were an important part of making a good paper great, but Smith replied that the *Tribune* was sufficiently great with a much smaller staff. Carroll did not tell him what he believed—that the *Tribune* was inferior to the *Times*.

I showed Smith and FitzSimons a clipping in which Carroll was quoted as saying that newspapers set their profit goals too high and that Wall Street was too influential. "That's his opinion!" Fitz-Simons said sharply. "We're looking toward the future and what do we have to do and how do we need to allocate our resources to keep our business healthy, and have the financial wherewithal to continue to do great journalism. Unfortunately, the caricature that develops is frequently 'the greedy corporate suits versus quality journalism.'" Later, I asked Smith how he responds to reporters who ask why a 15 percent profit margin is not enough. He replied, "It's the equivalent of saying, 'I wrote a really good story yesterday, but that's the best I'll ever do.' Our premise is that we can improve." The question is: Improve the paper or the profits?

Not everyone in the *Times* newsroom believed that the first round of cuts damaged the paper. Doug Franz, who followed Baquet to Los Angeles, said, "I know the Tribune Company pretty well, since I worked at the *Chicago Tribune* for eight years, and it's not Knight Ridder or Gannett." Even Carroll says of last year's cuts, "We tried to mask it. We were reasonably successful." For instance, when Carroll cut the staff of the Orange County edition, he was able to use some of the savings to expand the paper elsewhere.

FitzSimons said that journalists make "too many fake arguments" about how newspaper companies are trying "to dumb down," rather than asking how newspapers can attract new readers. "What's the right balance of entertainment and hard news?" he said. "Publishing a paper that just we like maybe isn't enough in this environment. We have to be more open to what consumers want." He showed me a review of several journalism books by Richard A. Posner, a Chicago federal judge, in the *New York Times Book Review*. "This is the point that I felt was interesting," FitzSimons said, pointing to some sentences that he had highlighted: "Journalists express dismay that bottom-line pressures are reducing the quality of news coverage. What this actually means is that when competition is intense, providers of a service are forced to give the consumer what he or she wants, not what they, as proud professionals, think the consumer should want, or, more bluntly, what they want." In a letter to the editor of his own *Book Review*, the paper's executive editor, Bill Keller, asked, "Would he be so cynical about a world he actually knows?" In Tribune Tower, Posner's argument trumped Keller's. Clearly, the news side saw itself at war with people who had minimal interest in ambitious journalism, and the "suits" saw themselves in conflict with sanctimonious and unrealistic idealists.

The Tribune Company's increasing impatience with the *Los Angeles Times* was made clear in March, when the paper's publisher, John Puerner, who had worked for the Tribune Company most of his professional life, announced that he was taking "a self-imposed career break" and would step down. Puerner, who is in his early fifties, was concerned about his wife, who had had a recent health scare, but in Chicago Puerner, who had become close to Carroll, was seen as having "gone native." "I never worked for a better publisher," Carroll said. Asked why Puerner left, Smith looked over at his publicity chief and then said, "John and I came to the conclusion together that he was ready for the next chapter in his life, and the *Times* was ready for the next publisher." When it was announced that Puerner was leaving, Carroll gave him a farewell party at his home. "If John had been there, I likely would have stayed a little longer," Carroll told me. To replace Puerner, Scott Smith appointed

Jeffrey Johnson, a Chicagoan who had joined the Tribune Company in 1984, and who had worked for Puerner at the *Orlando Sentinel* and at the *Times*.

When I asked Carroll to interpret Dennis FitzSimons's argument that newsrooms need "to understand how the business is changing," he said, "I would interpret it as 'We don't understand his problems.' I think actually I do. He is in a position where he has got to hit profit targets regardless of revenues. If the company doesn't do that, there will be consequences from Wall Street and from the board." Carroll does not believe that the battles with Chicago were about miscommunication. "On the surface, it's about cuts. But it's also about aspirations for the paper, and for journalism itself. I think this paper is important beyond Southern California. Among other things, it is test case No. 1 of whether a newspaper chain can produce a first-rate newspaper." Carroll added, "It may be that it is simply structurally impossible."

Tension between L.A. and Chicago reached its peak this past spring, when the Tribune Company told Carroll that it wanted still more staff reductions. "It was becoming an annual thing," Carroll told me. (Over his four years as editor, the newsroom had been reduced, through layoffs, attrition, and buyouts, by nearly two hundred employees.) Some editors feared that the next round of cuts would be as much as 10 percent of the newsroom—about ninety people—although Carroll says that the figure was lower. FitzSimons said, "We don't comment on rumors." The proposed cuts, a senior editor explained, were based on a formula that pegged the newsroom budget to a fixed percentage of revenue; if revenue rose, the cuts went down. In addition, Scott Smith was pressing the *Times* to consolidate its overseas bureaus with those of other Tribune papers.

In late June, rumors circulated that both Carroll and Baquet were going to resign. By then, Carroll had told Baquet and Johnson that he was exhausted by what he saw as the Tribune Company's unquenchable desire to measure success by the accountant's ledger.

Baquet was inclined to leave with Carroll, but Carroll urged him to consider his obligations to the people they both had hired.

On June 30th, Baquet and Johnson met with FitzSimons and Smith in Chicago. By then, the four men knew that Carroll was definitely leaving. "We talked for several hours about the paper," Baquet said. "We debated the size of the paper. We debated why there was a drop in circulation. We talked about what I thought was important. It was the kind of communication you're supposed to have." According to Smith, the discussion was "to make sure that we were in agreement on the important tasks ahead." They were not. FitzSimons and Smith discussed meeting financial targets; Baquet spoke about a newspaper's obligation to cover certain stories no matter what the cost. The discussion ended inconclusively.

When Baquet returned to Los Angeles, he told close associates, "I'm probably going to leave." Over the July 4th weekend, as this possibility seemed more likely, senior editors were called into the office. Johnson told his superiors in Chicago that it would be disastrous for the *Times* if both Baquet and Carroll quit. There were conference calls with Smith; Johnson pleaded with Baquet to stay, assuring him of the Tribune Company's flexibility. "I like Jeff a lot," Baquet said. He trusted Johnson more when he saw how intent the publisher was on keeping him.

The publisher was not eager, however, to keep Michael Kinsley, whose tenure had been controversial from the start. Kinsley had tried to combine ideas from the online world—he was the founding editor of Slate—with the voice of a newspaper, including an experiment to produce "wikitorials," allowing readers to rewrite *Times* editorials online. (The experiment was halted when, instead of posting thoughts, some readers posted pornography.) Soon after Johnson took over, he decided that Kinsley should report to the publisher, not the editor—the arrangement at most newspapers. Kinsley wanted to restructure his agreement so that he could spend even more time in Seattle. "Michael was not used to dealing with someone like Jeff, who is not starry-eyed when dealing with Michael

Kinsley, as most of us were," a friend of Kinsley's told me. "Michael was offended by what he took to be indifference." There was growing strain between the two men, which was personal, and separate from the institutional battle between the newsroom and Chicago.

In mid-September, Johnson decided to sever the *Times'* relationship with Kinsley; he didn't say whether the paper would continue to run the weekly column Kinsley had been writing. "I concluded that it was best to make a clean break," Johnson told me. In the end, Kinsley upstaged Johnson, further infuriating him. He announced that he had been fired and would be an adviser to the *Washington Post*, which would be home to his column, though he hoped that the Los Angeles paper would also carry it. Kinsley's friend and protégé Andrés Martinez, who now has full charge of the editorial page, found all of it painful. When asked whether he would run Kinsley's column, he replied, "It hasn't been decided." Kinsley said, "Your dream editorial-page editor should be part of the community. I thought maybe I'd be a brain asset."

(Editor's Note: Baquet and Johnson both left the Los Angeles Times *at the end of 2006. Tribune publisher David Hiller was named publisher of the* Los Angeles Times. *Tribune managing editor James O'Shea was named editor.)*

ROGER PLOTHOW

Hidden Goldfields: Small-town Papers

❧ ❧

Turmoil plagues America's big-city papers, but there is a quieter place, perhaps—certainly a much smaller place—where the picture is brighter. Roger Plothow, editor and publisher of the Post Register, *locally owned in Idaho Falls, Idaho, closed 2006 with a look at the success of small daily papers.*

To read about it in our own newspapers and industry periodicals, circulation is in freefall, margins are plummeting, newsrooms are being eviscerated, and it's only a matter of time before the daily newspaper is a bittersweet memory.

Of course, the numbers for metropolitan newspapers tell a discouraging story. In some cases, circulation is falling by high single digits per year. I'm no Pollyanna. This performance demands immediate and revolutionary change—change that the metropolitan papers have sneered at for a decade. They have been among the most stubborn resisters of any change in "that's the way we've always done it."

But telling the "metro" story leaves out a major piece of what's happening. While large papers account for a majority of the total circulation in the United States, they account for a fraction of the newspaper titles serving American readers. Said another way, 99 percent of American newspapers have circulations under 250,000, and 86 percent have circulations less than 50,000.

Newspaper circulation follows the old 80/20 rule, on steroids. The top 10 newspapers in the country account for 20 percent of the total circulation. So, in a way, it's understandable why they get all the attention.

But ignoring the other 1,420 daily newspapers means ignoring successful new models for serious journalism that readers are willing to pay for. Wall Street focuses on large, publicly held companies that operate in mostly metropolitan markets, so business writers tend to verify what the stock analysts say. With a little digging, however, a trade journal reporter would learn American journalism is changing from the bottom up.

For example, Inland Press Association conducts a monthly revenue and margin survey of mostly smaller newspapers that tells a pretty upbeat story:

—Profit margins among these newspapers average above 20 percent, and many report margins of more than 30 percent.

—Through October, most are reporting solid revenue increases across all segments, so margins aren't being produced purely through expense cuts.

—Many of these same newspapers are reporting consecutive years of circulation growth.

Beyond the metrics, it's easy to find small daily newspapers doing innovative, cutting-edge work in print and online. We're finding new revenue sources and new ways to attract readers, and we're experimenting with different business models with our long-term future in mind. Because many of us are owned by smaller companies, we are often more agile and able to try (and, when necessary, quickly discard) new things. And perhaps because we're staffed by younger folks, we tend not to be overly invested in defending traditions.

Attend a gathering of the Pacific Northwest Newspaper Association and you'll hear an exchange of ideas rivaling—dare I say, exceeding—those I hear at Nexpo.

212 | – 30 –

Upbeat publishers, editors, and ad directors talking about ways to combat Craigslist and Monster are inspirational. They expect to develop paid online models and to reach young readers. But our industry's trade journals obsess over the metros' devotion to the kind of national and world news readers no longer get from newspapers.

The *Bakersfield Californian*, with a circulation of about 75,000, is one of America's most innovative newspapers. Perhaps it's no coincidence that it's relatively small, serves a comparatively isolated market, and is locally owned. When we redesigned the *Post Register* more than a year ago, we used the *Californian* as one of our models and challenged ourselves to go further still.

The next time you read a grim update of the newspaper industry's inexorable slide into oblivion, check to see if the reporter talked to anyone in red America. Then, perhaps give Inland Press a call to see what its latest report shows.

Odds are that'll tell a whole different story.

DAVID T. Z. MINDICH

How to Tune Back In

How does an industry connect with a generation that is almost completely disconnected from news media at all levels? What does it bode for democracy that so many people are so remarkably ignorant about the basics of government? In Tuned Out: Why Americans Under 40 Don't Follow the News, *David T. Z. Mindich argues that media created this problem—and can fix it, too.*

Leonard Downie, Jr., and Robert Kaiser ended their recent book, *The News About the News* (2002), on a hopeful note. They wrote that despite all the pressures—from the government, the corporate boards, and the tabloids next door—journalism will continue to thrive because of tomorrow's news consumers: "In the end, the most important people shaping tomorrow's news won't be the owners or the journalists, but the readers and viewers. As long as they create a market for good journalism, there will be good journalism. That's the good news." Downie and Kaiser were, of course, correct that consumers can make a difference by choosing quality news. However, the authors' last sentence, "That's the good news," caused me to yell back at the still-open book, "No, that's the bad news!" If researching and writing this book has taught me one thing it is that our democracy is on the brink of a crisis and that the problem will not right itself. Nearing the time when 20- and 30-somethings will be given the tiller of the ship of state, we and they might ask, are they informed enough for the journey? We must do something to address the crisis and we must not let false optimism prevent us from acting swiftly and forcefully.

EXISTING SOLUTIONS

The existing solutions range from unimaginative to useless. For all their business concerns, media organizations have done little beyond identifying the demographic shift away from news. One report by the International Newspaper Marketing Association offers an excellent overview of the consequences to the newspaper industry. But the words "democracy," "voting," and "citizen" never appear; the report looks to the industry itself when it outlines the three possible solutions: "continue the current strategy . . .," "enhance the current efforts . . .," or "treat 'youth' as a current market with unique products and market pitches."

Another report, by the Readership Institute, offers "eight imperatives" to building readership. Many of these are quite impressive, one of which (making the paper easier to read and navigate) I will discuss in my section on improving journalism. But all are too insular, not looking at the society outside the newsroom. For example, the title of Imperative 8 is "Building an Adaptive, Constructive Culture That Is Attuned to Readers and Customers . . ." If the "culture" in the title would refer to the general culture at large, the "imperative" would certainly have a broad impact. Instead, the report suggested a change only in newsroom culture. Newsroom culture is important in itself, but as I have argued, it is insufficient to produce the kind of changes that are needed.

Another typical approach, with all its methodological limitations, is to ask young people who don't read newspapers what they would like to see. One publication, "Recapture Your Youth: How to

Create a Newspaper for Future Generations," reported a range of responses. Young nonreaders claimed that newspapers don't provide political coverage, aren't global enough, disrespect youth, "lack information," and are "irrelevant." To make newspapers more hip, the young nonreaders argued, we must consider running ads about the relevancy of newspapers; these ads should run during soap operas and ESPN shows. Some young people suggested that newspapers on CD-ROM would attract a younger market. The only thing worse than these contradictory theories, purveyed by nonreaders, is that they are taken seriously by desperate news executives. These suggestions fail to understand that fine news organizations already exist; the real challenge is to create a society in which young people feel that reading quality journalism is worthwhile. Newspapers across America are adding Britney Spears and subtracting Tom Daschle; in trying to make newspapers matter to young people, they make them matter to no one.

Take the new Chicago newspapers aimed at young readers. Please! In 2002, the *Chicago Tribune* and the *Chicago Sun-Times* started competing tabloids, *RedEye* and *Red Streak*, respectively, aimed at young adults. On January 3, 2003, the *Chicago Tribune* began the new year with a typically diverse front page. The top story (on the upper right of the page) was about the economy. This was balanced by a picture of Senator John Edwards, who had just announced his candidacy for president. Other stories were about lower fares offered by airlines, Britain's sending troops to Iraq, a charge by the State Department that Boeing had sold sensitive information to the Chinese, J. R. R. Tolkien's 111th birthday, and the Chinese space program.

It would be unfair to compare the diversity of the *Tribune*'s front page with that of *RedEye*. After all, the latter is a tabloid, which naturally stresses fewer stories on its front page. Nor is it unexpected to see that *RedEye*'s lead story (on the airlines) was 11 paragraphs to the *Tribune*'s 20. Or that *RedEye* had only 40 pages, mostly ads, to the *Tribune*'s 108 pages. No, it's the flavor of the paper that is so very different. "Fare Warning" the transformed *Tribune* article, was less about the financial crisis of the airlines and more about what the airlines are doing for *you* in terms of cheap tickets. The second story on *RedEye*'s front page was "New TV Shows Arrive." The third story was about a comic strip. Inside, *RedEye* has much less about politics (although there is a rare primer on the Democrats) and much more about sports, music, movies, food, television, and celebrities. It is not hard to imagine what *RedEye* thinks about its young readers: that they are not citizens but spoiled, selfish, insatiable consumers watching TV, fun entertainment, food, and titillation.

The problem with *RedEye* is that it retained little of the *Tribune*'s most important news. We don't learn about Bush's economic plan. Or Britain's plan to send troops to Iraq. Instead, we get "F.Y.I. Nation" and "F.Y.I. World," two pages offering tidbits about orangutans, a Venezuelan firecracker named after bin Laden, and an Italian murderer who escaped his hospital prison. Completely missing is any depth, process, or analysis of politics. The paper has become Headline News and the headlines are mainly about fluff and consumerism. The paper doesn't serve the primary function of journalism, to make sure we can be good citizens, to make sure we don't get screwed. Rather than offer an antidote to the crisis, *RedEye* perpetuates it.

So what are the solutions? I offer four.

SOLUTION #1: TAKE BACK THE AIRWAVES,
DESKTOPS, AND NEWSPAPER OFFICES

Robert Putnam, whose otherwise brilliant research and ideas have inspired this and other books, had a strikingly implausible idea about how to limit the media's influence on society: Ask the media moguls to help us get Americans to "spend less leisure time sitting passively alone in front of glowing screens." It is difficult to imagine corralling the CEO of Disney, Michael Eisner, into this cause. After all, limiting screen time is precisely antithetical to everything he is working toward with his television network. But if cajoling Eisner would certainly not work, do we have any leverage? It turns out that we have plenty and it comes down to the fact that the airwaves are owned by us and leased to the TV networks. The late 1960s saw a much higher percentage of programming that was devoted to news and public affairs. Why? It is because networks were very concerned that the FCC would reject their license renewals, which actually used to happen from time to time. Since the 1980s, deregulation meant a weakening of the imposed ethical standard on broadcasters. As the Federal Communications Commission was overturning its "public trust" requirement in the 1980s, broadcasters were paring their news divisions and public interest programs.

News for Kids. Because of the growing news options, including 24-hour cable news, most people still could get plenty of news and did not suffer. However a subset of them did suffer—kids. As children's programming used to be held to the same "public trust" standard as adult programming, there was a greater percentage of news and public affairs shows among the programs for kids. My own appetite for news was whetted on Saturday mornings in the early 1970s with CBS's *In the News* program for kids, a show that has been discontinued. The show was brief, sandwiched in between Saturday morning cartoons, but that was its strength. While millions of kids were being entertained, they were being informed about national politics and world events. One of the easiest ways to introduce news into a child's diet is to throw it in with the sugary stuff. We should insist that every network (including the Cartoon Network) carry news as a fixed percentage (let's say 5 percent) of its children's programming. The news would not be like Nickelodeon's *Nick News*—which tends to be lifestyle driven, and apolitical—but geared to the great political issues of the day. Domestically, the children's news would cover decisions by the three branches of government. Internationally, it would provide the latest in geopolitical changes. We may not and should not dictate the exact content of the programming, but we can and should mandate that our own airwaves have some political coverage for kids.

Diversify Broadcast and Newspaper Ownership. During the 1980s and 1990s, the FCC loosened its requirements barring broadcasters from owning multiple stations within a single market. During this time corporations began to gobble up ever-larger shares of markets while arguing that the First Amendment protected them from any regulation whatsoever. In June 2003, the FCC rolled back a series of regulations to make it easier to own media across platforms, greatly accelerating the potential for consolidation. This parallels the ever-increasing corporate influence in the newspaper field. Many media critics, most notably Benjamin Bagdikian, have called for government regulation in these areas to prevent or even roll back consolidation. Bagdikian's view is that corporate centralization of media limits messages, particularly those not friendly to businesses. His solution was to pass laws that make local and national media ownership more diverse. While this book reveals that many young people overstate corporate influence on the media ("they are all bought and paid for"), young people are responding to something real—the corporate and entertainment influences that weaken the purity of the news. We should support legislation that makes it more difficult for major national corporations to edge out smaller local ones, and we must protect against monopolies.

Desktop News, E-mail News. A number of advocates of using the Internet to promote democracy, including Andrew Shapiro, James Fishkin, and Cass Sunstein, have proposed a discussion portal on each home computer, perhaps called PublicNet or Deliberativedemocracy.com. The same could be done for news. We can insist that computer manufacturers and Web navigators include a separate portal for news organizations. In keeping with our tradition of freedom of the press, we would not dictate to the computer manufacturers what news organizations they should choose, but we could and should insist that the news portal be prominent on the desktop and have links to national and local news outlets. Despite the myth that the Internet is driven by private enterprise, its infrastructure was started by and is still supported by the U.S. government, which also is the largest purchaser of hardware and software. Surely the government can insist, like it used to do with television, that computers support the public good. A news portal would make following the news even easier than it is currently. By this same logic, Internet Service Providers (ISPs) might be forced to offer a news option default with its e-mail service. Let's say you sign up for Yahoo e-mail. Unless you choose to avoid it, you would receive a daily news e-mail with top stories and links to the major news outlets. Incidentally, Yahoo and Google each has a great system for disseminating news, devoting a central location to the news of other sources. However, you'll only find Yahoo's or Google's pages if you seek them out. My proposal would put a portal to pages like these on every desktop. This kind of maneuver, creating a default system of news consumption, greatly influenced the New Orleans kids I spoke with.

SOLUTION #2: CHANGE OUR EXPECTATIONS:
COLLEGE ADMISSIONS AND CIVIC KNOWLEDGE

Joel Senesac told me, "People learn what they need to know." In some circles, what we need to know is who plays on the Chicago Cubs. In other circles, it is who plays on the Supreme Court. One of the greatest problems is that there is little perceived need to know about news. In other words, news has less and less currency in conversations. For example, a Brandeis student found that when she tried to talk about news, her friends did the verbal equivalent of grabbing for the remote, changing the topic as fast as they could back to lighter fare. Without a critical mass of young people to talk about news, it will continue to feel like a waste of time for most of them.

How do we change this model? If the examples here are a guide, we can change news habits if we change our expectations. When Andrea Alford walked into her summer internship at Ducks Unlimited, the nonprofit firm, she quickly learned that the coin of the realm among her older office mates was political news in the *Washington Post*. In order for her to feel connected at work, she needed to buy and read the paper. This is in keeping with the work of Bernard Berelson, who wrote that news is often used as fodder for conversation. One of the quickest ways to change news habits is for parents, teachers, and older colleagues to make sure news matters—to us and to young people. And we need to make sure young people know they will be judged on how conversant they are, too.

I have discussed how the entertainment choices of cable television and the Web can weaken one's resolve to keep up with the news. The Web, in particular, is driven by one's own interests, no matter how distinct or arcane they may be. It is difficult to imagine a change in the media environment that would return us to the limits of the past. In the face of the cornucopia of entertainment, the only way to change young people's habits is to alter our expectations in ways that will make a difference. The Web is a poor medium in which to find news by changes, but an excellent one to find it by choice.

Honor Society Requirements. We have learned that part of the rise of volunteerism among high school students may be due to the simple fact that it is a requirement for the National Honor Society. On the one hand, that college entry, and not altruism, may be responsible for some volunteerism is rather depressing. On the other hand, it can give us hope that the decline of news readership may be malleable too. Maybe it tells us that if we change our expectations about news consumption and political involvement—make *that* a requirement for the honor society—then young people's habits in this area will change, too.

C-SAT. In April 2002, I visited a civics class in Colchester High School in Vermont. Many of the students were able to discuss the issues of the day. Some, too, knew about the First Amendment and other matters as a direct result of the class. It left me wondering why civics is not more universally taught. The answer is that civics and current events are valued by neither national standards nor colleges. In this climate, civics and current events are seen as expendable frills.

It is reasonable to encourage colleges to pay more attention to the civic involvement and knowledge of their high school seniors. After all, our country's first president founded a college based on the idea that it would promote democracy. It is also reasonable for our colleges and universities to demand that their students know the issues of the day. Along with the SAT, colleges could ask for a C-SAT, a civics portion of the college aptitude test. In addition to being able to answer static questions about the makeup of our government and reveal some general world knowledge (where is Iraq, for example), incoming freshmen might be asked to identify the Speaker of the House, which of the two Koreas is communist, the nature of the Human Genome Project, which political party controls the U.S. senate, and whether the United States ran a deficit in the last fiscal year. It wouldn't take much effort: ten civics/news questions appended to the standard SAT, coupled with the colleges' commitment to notice them, would completely transform the news habits of young people. The intellectual diversity and political currency that is the staple of any democracy cannot be fully measured by a C-SAT, but it can be promoted by one. We demand a civics test of everyone who wants to become a U.S. citizen; it seems fitting to have high school students take a news/civics test, too.

SOLUTION #3: MAKE POLITICS MEANINGFUL AGAIN

When looking at the problem of young people not following the news, nearly everyone is wrong. The optimists are wrong that young people will eventually pick up the habit. The pessimists are wrong that there is nothing to do about it. And industry believes, wrongly, that the problems and solutions can come from industry alone. They cannot. For example, perhaps the simplest way to making political news matter is to make politics matter.

There was a time when it did. In 1968, for example, the Democratic national convention mattered. As Southern blacks fought to be seated as delegates, many Southern whites resisted this and some even bolted from the party. Outside the convention hall, antiwar protesters clashed with police. Inside, politicians clashed over the platform, embarking on a series of floor fights. CBS's Mike Wallace was on the convention floor, asking an African American delegate from Minnesota about her support of black challenges to the all-white Southern delegations. The two quarreled over labels, with the former saying "Negro" and the latter saying "black." At one point, the white delegation from Georgia tried to steal its banner and leave the hall. In the midst of all this, Dan Rather tried to get an interview with a delegate who was being forcibly removed from the hall. Rather, in turn, was roughed up and punched in the stomach. This all made for great, riveting journalism, making sense of stuff that mattered.

Today, politics still matters, but so much of it is so scripted that its vibrancy is hidden and its meaning is often shrouded by the nonsense of polling. For example, television ads and lawn signs used to say things like "Jones: Democrat for Senator." Today, there is a near-universal view that touting party affiliation is not an effective way to get elected. Rather than party affiliation, you get "Jones: For a Change," or similar pablum (Dave Barry quipped that his own slogan would be, "A Leader Who Will Lead, by Leading.") This practice may have some strategic worth: swing voters, like nonvoters, often shun party labels. In other words, politicians once they are reasonably sure of holding their base, strive for the tiny undecided minority. But although this math might work to win elections, it is a terrible calculus for our democracy. One of the reasons why young people do not see much difference between parties is that they are not told the differences by the candidates. And the decision to use focus groups' views to justify shielding party affiliation is hardly comforting. As E. J. Dionne, Jr., has written about focus groups, "the approach to politics is not even Machiavellian; it is Pavlovian." We need to create a system that will look well beyond election day and build long-term generational affiliations with parties.

FEC Intervention on Ads. To break this Pavlovian approach to getting elected, the Federal Election Commission (FEC) should be instructed by Congress to take specific steps to force the announcement of party affiliation. The FEC should withhold any matching funds from politicians who do not include party affiliation on ads. Individual candidates may not wish to unilaterally announce their affiliation, but if everyone is mandated to do so, it will not hurt either side. Similarly, limiting the soft money PACS that don't use party affiliation, one of the cornerstones of campaign finance reform, would help to make political ads more recognizably partisan.

U.S. Intervention on Debates. The most important element of our presidential elections may be our televised debates. No matter how much politicians offer their canned speeches on the road and their 30-second pabulum over the airwaves, the debates do offer a chance for politicians to have their views held up to scrutiny, live, even if the format is not always conducive to great depth. For 90 minutes, three times each election cycle, the public and the journalists can take a break from horse race reporting, scandals, innuendo, and other superficialities and just listen to ideas. It isn't nearly as useful a window into policy as is the weekly "question time" of the British system, but it is the best window we've got. The problem is that many politicians who are ahead in the polls duck the debates. Congress should pass a law making at least three prime-time debates between major candidates a requirement for federal matching funds. This, along with the intervention on political ads, will go a long way to ensuring that party affiliation and values are on full display each election cycle.*

Open Our Airwaves. The vast majority of industrialized democracies provide free airtime for political advertisements—the United States is a rare exception. Subsidized TV appearances could go a long way in reintroducing political messages into the American dialogue. Unfortunately, the main resistance to this idea comes from the same people who cut checks for broadcast journalists—the television corporate executives. True campaign finance reform would be a good step to breaking the broadcasters' effective veto over free political ads. Another good step would be mobilizing our political will to make it happen. If we join this battle, however, we must remember that broadcast journalists will not be allies, at least not vocal ones.

"Multiply Picnics." After Robert Putnam laid out, for more than 400 pages, the decline of civic society in his seminal book, *Bowling Alone,* he offered numerous solutions. One, echoing Henry Ward Beecher, was "multiply picnics." Part of the solution, I have come to believe, is following Putnam's advice for re-engaging civic life in America. Many journalists and media critics reject the "public journalism" model in which journalists themselves try to reinvigorate public life. However, we are still left with the fact that a vibrant civic life is to journalism as gasoline is to the internal combustion engine. And vice versa.

Nearly a century ago, Walter Lippmann's and John Dewey's views on the press framed what is still an argument in journalism criticism: Lippmann said that correct information is paramount in order to engage an elite minority of decision makers; Dewey said that broader discussion among citizens was more important. They

---

*The coupling of the debates with federal matching funds would not, of course, end the discussion of exactly who gets invited to debates (a common threshold is any candidate who holds 15 percent support in national polling), but it would not necessarily alter the discussion either.

were, of course, both correct—and incorrect. Only a marriage of the two would bring a true dialogue to support democracy and provide a check against governmental authority.

Today, Lippmann's side is holding its own. We have reporters digging for the kind of information Lippmann said we need. When Nixon's men planned and then covered up the Watergate burglary, the press was there. The press was there for Reagan-Bush's Iran-Contra, Clinton's Whitewater, and George W. Bush's extrajudicial arrests of American citizens as suspected terrorists. It is Dewey's side of the equation that needs bolstering. True, an engaged minority is as active as ever, passionately discussing issues and e-mailing journalists, politicians, and activists. But the elite minority is actually closer to Lippmann's model; we need to greatly broaden the discussion. Putnam's book is a good place to start in our attempt to reinvigorate journalism's lifeblood, the public.

SOLUTION #4: CREATE, CONSUME,
AND TEACH QUALITY JOURNALISM

People say that too much time is devoted to the scandals of the day. When O. J. Simpson fled from the police in his white Bronco, when John F. Kennedy, Jr.'s plane crashed, when Princess Diana died, when Michael Jackson was indicted, we cry "sensationalism." But we eat it up, too. The truth of the matter is that this sort of thing sells; each of these stories generated huge readerships and ratings for the journalists who covered them. This book is not going to make people avoid sensational news. However, there are a few things we can do to counteract its influence.

Do Quality Journalism That Is Also Accessible. As we have seen, the rise of narrowcasting (media tailored to specific tastes) provides a series of challenges to journalists. However, it also offers a significant advantage: there will always be at least a niche market for quality journalism. Journalists can (and should) continue to cover O. J. Simpson, Princess Diana, J.F.K., Jr., and Michael Jackson, but they should also remember that, in the words of Kovach and Rosenstiel, "Citizens are not customers." As Kovach and Rosenstiel wrote, "all O. J. all the time—actually leaves most of the audience behind." Some citizens may *like* "all O. J. all the time," but they *need* more than this. They need a great diversity of items, including a substantial amount of political news. There is even evidence that, despite conventional wisdom, quality sells. The Project for Excellence in Journalism, in a study of 146 local TV news programs, graded each show in terms of quality (A, B, C, D, and F) and then evaluated the shows' success, in terms of ratings over a three-year period. Of the newscasts earning a "grade A," 64 percent saw their ratings increase, too. None of the other categories—B, C, D, and F—had a clear majority of stations with a ratings increase.

Too often people in the media seem to think that accessibility means dumbing things down or adding the latest macabre murder or Hollywood hottie. But sometimes responsible journalists don't do enough to make quality journalism accessible to light readers. A thoughtful student once told me that following the news was like trying to keep up with a difficult math class after missing the first half of the semester. It wouldn't kill journalists to provide a few more crib notes. An interesting proposal came from the Readership Institute: put more road signs in the newspaper. Offer more "branded" content, content that readers can quickly recognize to help them navigate around the paper. Offer a "contents" strip running down the left-hand column of the front page. Offer "Follow Up" or "Talking Points" bullets that get tuned out readers up-to-date on stories that they might happen upon for the first time. When reading a story about Kenya, even the best of readers might benefit from a brief sidebar of its history or geography. A profile of a presidential candidate could have a sidebar listing other candidates, or a Web link that lists that information.

Recognize Quality Journalism and Demand It. The only way to get quality journalism is to demand it and pay for it. Max Frankel wrote, "Facts don't inform. Reporters and editors do." Journalists are more than just a window onto the world. They dig, they gather, they uncover, they verify. But they also do far more: they provide an interpretive frame by making sense of the information they get. And the better journalists resist the age-old pressures from government, parties, and marketplace. People who do what I do, media criticism, have gotten very good at explaining to high school and college students how the media can be biased. But too often we do not articulate the benefits and even beauty of a well working and ethical press. We need to help students recognize the value of nonpartisan, ethical, and high-quality news. That way, they will be more likely to pay for it. Reporters and editors, particularly good ones, are expensive. We need to teach young people about the importance of fine journalism and how and where to find it.

The Greatest Democracy for the Greatest Numbers. When Barnes & Noble sells a chai latte, it helps introduce more people to books. But if Barnes & Noble were to throw out all its books to make way for a bigger café, it would lose its raison d'être and serious readers would suffer, too. A business executive might ask the question, "does it increase profits?" But there is also another question to ask: "does chai latte help to produce a net gain in reading?" Barnes & Noble is still a great place for books, but we, as citizens, should insist that it stays that way.

Similarly, journalists need to ask whether adding Britney, and perhaps a few young readers, justifies making democracy poorer by the subtraction of serious news. It may be that ventures such as *Red-Eye* are merely steppingstones to greater news involvement. Or maybe not. Either way, the litmus test should be a utilitarian one: What brings the greatest democracy for the greatest numbers? In other words, if the *New York Times* or the *Wall Street Journal* added 1 percent more entertainment news and doubled its readership, we can applaud that decision as a great success: many more people would be armed with information needed in our democracy. On the other hand, if they added 25 percent more entertainment news (with the same net loss in serious news), for only a marginal gain in readership, democracy would be the poorer for it. If more journalists (especially editors) would ask themselves if changes pass the "greatest democracy" test, many of the new initiatives to attract younger readers would die a quick death.

An example of this is the successful attempt by Fox News to attract viewers with its flash and attitude. But are the viewers becoming better citizens? A recent study suggests that Fox viewers are considerably less informed than consumers of CNN, network television, NPR, PBS, and newspapers. People were asked about three widely held misperceptions of the 2003 Iraq war—that Iraq was directly involved in September 11, that world opinion favored the war, and that weapons of mass destruction had been found. A full 80 percent of Fox viewers believed one or more of these misperceptions, compared to 47 percent and 23 percent of newspaper readers and NPR/PBS listeners and viewers, respectively. These findings need to be clarified: did Fox News viewers start out much less informed than, say, NPR listeners, or did Fox News actually make its viewers less informed? Either way, these findings would suggest that Fox News must immediately rethink the way it conveys news so as to make its viewers smarter citizens, not dumber ones.

Without Compromising Journalism's Prime Objectives, Follow the Ideas, Attitudes, and Topics of Young People. The young people I interviewed, especially the students at Brandeis, described how news doesn't offer the "emotional investment" of the entertainment media. On the other hand, we need journalism that is politically independent. Isn't this a contradiction? The model of political detachment is coupled in networks like CNN with a practiced emotional detachment. But objectivity and political detachment needn't be emotionally detached.

The remarkable success of Fox News, which overtook CNN in 2002 as the nation's most watched all-news network, has been widely misinterpreted by many on the right and the left as an affirmation of that network's conservative values or of its sensationalism. But a more plausible explanation may be that Fox does a great job of showing both the humanness of its reporters and anchors and talk show hosts and that they actually care about the news they're delivering. One could imagine a nonpartisan network with the attitude of Fox. A story about welfare reform, or Americans killed in Iraq, or the "partial birth abortion" debate need not be told in a robotic way; one can be passionate and still remain nonpartisan.

This might be the attraction of something like *The Daily Show*, Jon Stewart's nightly spoof on the news. Like Fox, Stewart has been accused of having a political agenda (in Stewart's case, a left agenda), but the possible leftwing bias is not the secret of Stewart's success—it is that the show is very, very funny and drips with the kind of irony that many young people tell me they appreciate. Another such show is *Real Time with Bill Maher*. In that show, Maher attacks both parties, airs a lot of unconventional pundits, and has an iconoclastic approach that has a much younger vibe than CNN and the networks. Maher's show is not, as far as I can tell, consistently partisan. But it is opinionated, passionate, and entertaining. And its skepticism about power makes it an effective watchdog.

Two other broadcast models are worth mentioning: *Now* with Bill Moyers and *Countdown* with Keith Olbermann. In his show, Moyers takes a decidedly progressive position, which generally jibes with the mainstream and left of the Democratic Party. But while the Moyers model might not work on a major network that seeks political balance, Moyers' empathy for the poor and passion for social justice are not, after all, partisan attributes.

Keith Olbermann opens his show, *Countdown* (MSNBC) with the question, "Which of these stories will you be talking about tomorrow?" This, of course, addresses what young people have told me again and again: that the extent to which news affects conversation is a crucial indicator of news consumption. Olbermann's show is well written and punchy, qualities that seem to have migrated from ESPN's *Sportscenter*, where Olbermann was an anchor in the late 1990s. Any journalism that can increase conversation among young people is worth noting.

Part of this connection may simply be including young people's stories in the news. As Farai Chideya found, a typical television story about education will include shots of young people walking around campus; when the reporter needs to talk to someone, however, he or she will go to the teachers and administrators. "If the news is totally manufactured as a product for older Americans, which is increasingly true, then there's less and less reason for young people to buy into it," Chideya told me. When politicians and the media take the voices of young people seriously, interesting things happen. In 1996, when Clinton answered questions from an MTV audience, he was widely criticized for answering a question about his choice of "boxers or briefs." But along with this politically unimportant question (and response) came a new idea: young people should be included in the discussion. In 2003, when the Democratic presidential candidates debated on MTV, many of the questions were uninspiring. However, many were not. And if young people are included, and not just b-roll, they will begin to make their way back into the process.

One of the interesting aspects of the 2003 MTV debate was that each of the candidates made short videos. Most used fast-cut MTV-style video; most used driving music. Wesley Clark's used humor. Sitting around a table with young people, Clark was depicted on his video as conversant with the issues of the day, including a funny reference to a band: "I am pro-choice, and I am a strong believer in affirmative action . . . it's the right thing to do, it works, it's about the American idea of equal opportunity . . . and I don't care what the other candidates say, I don't think OutKast is really breaking up. Andre 3000 and Big Boi just cut solo records, that's all." Chideya sees this type of engagement as a good step toward getting young people back into public forums.

I agree, but while even facile engagement can be a useful model for journalists who try to connect with young people on a visceral level, it is certainly no substitute for depth and process-related stories. If young people see only superficial references to them and find the majority of the weightier newspaper stories about Social Security, Medicare, and other topics that appeal to older readers, they will be left with the impression that the true political process is outside their realm. And because there are many, many entertainment sources that are far, far more viscerally engaging than news, young people will remain tuned out until they are given a compelling reason that they, *as citizens*, should tune back in.

Solutions might comprise a lot of ideas about journalism, but the problems certainly have more to do with what happens outside the newsroom's walls than inside them. Many reporters reject the advocates of "public journalism" who call for journalists to promote a healthy public life and civic dialogue. But while reporters may conclude that their role should not extend beyond reporting, their bosses—the owners of the print, online, and broadcast news media—have no such luxury. Second only to the goal of quality journalism, making sure young people see themselves as citizens should be the priority of every news executive in the country.

It has been said that nothing focuses one's attention like a hangman's noose. Because they have ceded their own political power, the majority of young Americans who are tuned out pose a huge danger to their own generation; when they are ready to become leaders, they will pose a huge danger to democracy itself. This chilling image focuses me and should focus you, too. The problem is that many do not see the scope of the problem. To use another metaphor, we are like a frog that has been unaware of a slowly heating pot. This book has been an attempt to make the problem, and its consequences, clear and immediate. The last solution I offer is to view this book as an opening salvo in the battle to better inform ourselves. If you share the concerns of this book, I hope you will continue to explore this problem. I also hope you will do something about it.

Amartya Sen found that there has rarely been a famine in a country with a democratic press and free elections. Famines are partly the fault of the environment, but also the product of corruption, poor planning, and often, greedy dictators. These inequities could only be foisted on a people with little power and little knowledge. It is not hyperbole to say that if a citizenry unilaterally abandons political knowledge, it relinquishes power as well. It has been said that America is a system "designed by geniuses so that it could be run by idiots." But this is not entirely true. The Constitution does provide checks against our greatest mistakes of the moment. And elections do provide a quick check against the government's neglect of the people. But nothing in our Constitution protects us against the long-term ravages of neglect *by* the people themselves.

Government supported by an uninformed citizenry is not a democracy; it is a sham. This is our crisis. Let us work deliberately and forcefully to hand the mantle of responsible and informed leadership to the next generations of Americans.

Credits

The editor and the publishers are grateful to the following sources for permission to reprint the selections in this book.

"Money, Technology, Tax Law, and Trouble." From Elizabeth M. Neiva, "Chain Building: The Consolidation of the American Newspaper Industry, 1955–1980," *Business and Economic History*, Vol. 24, No. 1, Fall 1995, copyright © 1995 by the Business History Conference. Reprinted by permission of the Business History Conference.

"What Happened to the Readers?" From David Carr, "The Lonely Newspaper Reader," *New York Times*, January 1, 2007, copyright © 2007 by the New York Times Co. Reprinted with permission.

"Everybody Watches the *New York Times*." From Rachel Smolkin, "Challenging Times," *American Journalism Review*, February/March 2007. Reprinted by permission of the *American Journalism Review*.

"Trapped in Transition." From Joseph Epstein, "Are Newspapers Doomed?", *Commentary*, January 2006. Reprinted by permission, all rights reserved.

"Fighting the Vortex." From "The State of the News Media: An Annual Report on American Journalism," 2006, by the Project for Excellence in American Journalism and Rick Edmonds of The Poynter Institute. Reprinted by permission of the Project for Excellence in American Journalism and Rick Edmonds.

"The Wrong Way to Make Money." From Philip Meyer, *The Vanishing Newspaper: Saving Journalism in the Information Age*, copyright © 2004 by the Curators of the University of Missouri. Reprinted by permission of the University of Missouri Press. Original version appeared in the *American Journalism Review*.

"Tribune Company: Synergy's Broken Promise." From Rachel Smolkin, "Tribune Tribulations," *American Journalism Review*, December 2006/January 2007. Reprinted by permission of the *American Journalism Review*.

"Money! Money! Money! The Profits-versus-Quality War." From Neil Hickey, "Money Lust," *Columbia Journalism Review*, July/August 1998, copyright © 1998 by *Columbia Journalism Review*. Reprinted by permission of the *Columbia Journalism Review*.

"Embracing Extinction: The 1970s and Newspaper Decline." From Jack Shafer, "Chronicle of the Newspaper Death Foretold," *Slate*, November 30, 2006. Reprinted by permission of Slate.com and Washingtonpost. Newsweek Interactive, all rights reserved.

"Glory Days: The Billionaire Solution." From Michael Wolff, "Billionaires and Broadsheets," *Vanity Fair*, February 2007. Reprinted by permission of the author.

"Heartbreak on Wheels: The *Philadelphia Inquirer*." From Michael Shapiro, "Looking for Light," *Columbia Journalism Review*, March/April 2006, copyright © 2006 by *Columbia Journalism Review*. Reprinted by permission of the *Columbia Journalism Review*.

"Still a Powerful Voice." From John Nichols, "Newspapers . . . and After?", *The Nation*, January 29, 2007. Reprinted by permission of *The Nation*.

"Can the *Los Angeles Times* Survive Its Owners?" From Ken Auletta, "Fault Line," *The New Yorker*, October 10, 2005. Reprinted by permission of the author.

"Hidden Goldfields: Small-town Papers." From Roger Plothow, "'Little' Papers Keep Coming Up Big," *Editor & Publisher*, December 7, 2006. Reprinted by permission of the author.

"How to Tune Back In." From David T. Z. Mindich, *Tuned Out: Why Americans Under 40 Don't Follow the News*, copyright © 2005 by Oxford University Press. Reprinted by permission of Oxford University Press, Inc.

Index

A NOTE ON THE EDITOR

Charles M. Madigan was born in Altoona, Pennsylvania, and studied at Pennsylvania State University and at Roosevelt University in Chicago. He worked for the *Altoona Mirror* and the *Harrisburg Patriot*, and then for United Press International as a domestic reporter and foreign correspondent in the Soviet Union. With the *Chicago Tribune* from 1979 to 2007, he served as Washington news editor, national editor, senior correspondent, senior editor, editor of continuous news, and columnist. His reporting on war crimes in Kosovo won an Overseas Press Club award in 2000. Mr. Madigan is now presidential writer in residence at Roosevelt University. He is married with three sons and lives in Evanston, Illinois.